ENERGY AND CLIMATE WARS

Energy and Climate Wars

How naive politicians, green ideologues, and media elites are undermining the truth about energy and climate

PETER C. GLOVER

AND

MICHAEL J. ECONOMIDES

continuum

2010

The Continuum International Publishing Group
80 Maiden Lane, New York, NY 10038
The Tower Building, 11 York Road, London SE1 7NX

www.continuumbooks.com

Library of Congress Cataloging-in-Publication Data
Glover, Peter C.
Energy and climate wars : how naive politicians, green ideologues, and media elites
are undermining the truth about energy and climate / Peter C. Glover and Michael
J. Economides.
      p. cm.
Includes bibliographical references and index.
ISBN-13: 978-1-4411-5307-4 (hardcover : alk. paper)
ISBN-10: 1-4411-5307-1 (hardcover : alk. paper) 1. Energy policy—Environmental
   aspects. 2. Renewable energy sources. 3. Petroleum industry and trade—
   Government policy. 4. Climatic changes—Government policy. I. Economides,
   Michael J. II. Title.
   HD9502.A2G58 2011
   333.79—dc22   2010015177

ISBN: HB: 978–1-4411–5307–4

Typeset by Pindar NZ, Auckland, New Zealand
Printed and bound in the United States of America by Thomson-Shore, Inc

This work is dedicated to
Michael Crichton
(1942–2008)

Michael was a writer and scientist who warned about
the increasing politicization of science, particularly
environmental science, for ideological ends.

Contents

List of Figures

Preface

Very few issues are as hotly debated, and as hopelessly misunderstood, as energy and climate. Most people believe in alleged truths that rest, in fact, upon inaccurate data or mistaken interpretations. Many opinion-makers and most policy-makers are actively propagating the kind of myths that are rightly debunked in this book by Messrs Glover and Economides. You can spot them as they speak about quaint notions such as "energy independence" or "green deal": the more they emphasize such ideas, the more they are unlikely to really understand what they are talking about — unless they are speaking on behalf of some political, ideological, or economic vested interest.

By shedding light on the actual functioning of the energy sector, on the broader debate on climate science, and on the impact of wrong policies, Glover and Economides offer a major contribution to a proper understanding of such complex issues. It is particularly important that American and European readers and voters learn as much as they can from this book: a knowledgeable public opinion is the only vaccine against getting the European disease, for example adopting costly policies for the sake of looking green and politically correct. Europeans are already paying for their mistakes, both in terms of higher energy costs and lost opportunities. Americans and others still have time.

Carlo Stagnaro
Research and Studies Director,
Instituto Bruno Leoni (a free market think-tank),
Torino, Italy

Introduction

When we speak of energy and climate wars we are referring to physical conflict as well as to ideological "wars" which are not any less vicious — as both relate to our use of the world's most precious commodity: energy. What most concerns us is the increasing impact of ideology as it attempts to influence in very radical ways energy and climate policy. This is done often by blurring the distinction between fact and speculation, between truth and propaganda.

We have not written simply for energy "insiders" or those steeped in the climate debate alone. Rather, we have written with the "concerned citizen" in mind; those who have grasped that energy *is* a critical issue for us all; those who recognize that distorting sensationalist headlines have clouded public understanding on energy and climate.

Whether or not the reader ultimately agrees with our views, we guarantee that there will be many surprises in these pages that debunk countless popular myths propagated by a mass media in its "sensationalizing" death throes.

We think it is important to point out that nothing being asserted throughout this book, and particularly Chapter 7, can, intellectually speaking, be construed as "conspiracy theory." What we continue to present here are direct quotes and openly asserted claims to non-democratic political agendas. We have no interest in presenting personal theories as to motivation, conspiratorial or otherwise. Besides which, as we have noted, our opponents are ill-equipped for genuine intellectual debate, rarely relying on facts and reason, preferring instead ideological subterfuge, the intellectually blunt instruments of "consensus" pseudo-science and populist "green" bluster. We see our business as (presenting) facts, (articulated) reason and (derivative) logic, *not* speculation and guesswork.

For us, the greatest threat to mankind does not lie in future energy wars or in the string of apocalyptic eco-scenarios. For us, it lies in the growing need to distinguish between truth and propaganda in the square of public debate. It is up to the reader to judge on which side of the "line" this work falls.

Finally, we would like to give one sincere vote of thanks. It is to our publisher at Continuum, Marie-Claire Antoine, for catching the vision for the work and for her great support and encouragement in its writing.

Peter C. Glover and Michael J. Economides
September, 2010

Part One: Real World

1
Energy and Ideology

The trouble with socialism is that eventually you run out of other people's money.

Margaret Thatcher

Without modern energy Western civilization would grind to a halt, literally. Your refrigerator would no longer keep cheap food chilled for weeks and months; you would need fresh food daily, with all the extra cost and the journeys that entails. Private cars would be obsolete. You would have to read by candlelight. Your home would have to be heated by burning wood or, if you had a local source of hydrocarbon fuels — what we call primary — burning oil, gas or coal. In short, you would be subject to the technology of the mid-nineteenth century.

At this point an extreme idealist may naively insist that life was better in former generations than today. A less extreme idealist may claim that hydrocarbon fuels are no longer necessary and that we could switch, with the right social and political will, to alternative energy sources. The argument runs that, if only we could divest ourselves of our "addiction" to oil, gas, and coal ("fossil" fuels) we could, at a stroke, clean up our environment by making a wholehearted commitment to renewable, clean and "free" energy, wind, wave, hydro, solar, and geothermal power to solve our future energy needs. Only one problem with that: there's more chance of Donald Duck becoming president of the United States.

Just try to make that particular energy switchover and stand back and watch the lights go out all over the world. True, some radicals want it that way. They think it would be "quaint" to return to dark ages lifestyle, the same "quaint," often poverty-stricken, lifestyles to which they would doom other societies who today are desperate to industrialize, as the West has. This is an easy pastime, of course, when you are an armchair eco-liberal enjoying the fruits of a post-industrial society.

The reality of doing that which today's anti-hydrocarbon eco-warriors demand in their relentless, ultimately pointless (as we will show), war on carbon is that the developed nations would simply find themselves among the ranks of those nations whose low energy consumption meant that they never came out of the "dark ages" in the first place. While some environmental activists may perceive the "old ways" as simple, something to hanker after, they conveniently forget the high infant mortality rates, sickness, pollution, and shortness of life that went with that "quaint" lifestyle, a lifestyle that for many even today is an all too unpleasant, even deadly, daily reality.

Ironic, is it not, that in an age when we live longer, healthier, more pollution-free lives than countless previous generations, we should have become even more angst-ridden and obsessive about our health and our environment? Yet such concerns, suffused with an unhealthy self-injected dose of idealism, are not only driving some modern Western governments to make mostly unnecessary and uneconomic social changes, but are also powerfully influencing global and national policies as they affect the world's most important commodity: energy.

The truth is, we owe our longer, greater and healthier life, indeed our economic prosperity in the West generally, to the Industrial Revolution and the economic development that resulted from it. And that prosperity is *a direct consequence of our growing consumption of energy*. Like it or not, the great energy-driven reality of our age is, *whatever idealistic social engineers may desire*, that modern civilization (and those societies currently undergoing their own industrialization) remain wholly dependent upon the per capita consumption of *primary energy* of oil, gas, and coal. What is more, they will continue to do so, as we will see, for decades to come.

So, if you have been led to understand that the oil is about to "run out" or that alternative energies will soon substitute for "dirty" hydro-carbons anytime soon, or if you have imbibed countless other myths about energy and the issues that flow from it, here's your chance to wise up and grasp some basic real world facts. Along the way, you will see that the reason why some science researchers and large parts of the mass media, for varying ideological and personally enriching reasons, are today in the business of speculative, prophetic, end-is-nigh doom-ism; a business that preys on a raft of irrational public fears *of their creation*.

So whether energy is of key interest to you, or whether you are someone whose understanding of energy usually extends to the calorific blurb on the back of your box of cornflakes, this book will help you get a far better handle on the power politics of energy; more specifically, on the social ideology that increasingly influences and impacts them. Even if you think that global and national energy policy is not your bag, you might find that understanding the threat to *your* future energy security and the size of *your* personal energy bill *is*. Especially when you realize that a burgeoning proportion of your income is being siphoned off by government to pay for idealistic fantasies that offer no discernible benefit to the environment, or to you and yours.

At the very least, you will be surprised at how the facts of energy and the key associated issues of peak oil and climate change are far from "as advertised." Along the way, we will see just how many dumb energy policies are being influenced by ludicrous predictions, highly speculative theories and by self-proclaimed Nostradamuses who, surprise, surprise, can make a very tidy living via the headline-grabbing apocalyptic alarmism they generate. It is fair to say that for several decades nothing has "powered" ideologically-driven misinformation more than issues associated with energy.

In this book, we will do our best to avoid technical jargon, though published data and other research is important to clear away the deadwood that currently passes for journalistic reporting on energy and environment. But, before we move on to debunking some of the anti-intellectual, populist assertions about energy etc., we need first to present an absolutely fundamental truth about energy and modern civilization — a truth few modern politicians appear to have grasped.

THE ENERGY CONSUMPTION — WEALTH CREATION LINK

In the modern world there is a direct correlation between the level of energy consumption and national wealth creation.[1] Indeed the relative wealth and poverty of nations is entirely definable by its per capita energy consumption (Figure 1.1).

It is equally axiomatic that demand for energy is connected to wealth; the corollary is also true: *use of energy promotes and generates wealth.* Thus the perennial vilification of the US as the world's largest consumer of energy (25 percent of global use) is wholly misguided, in that it is largely based on the fallacy that US energy demand is only *the result* of its wealth. Rather, energy demand is *the cause* of US wealth, as it is elsewhere. This is vital to understand. Especially in the light of the constant assertions made about the need to cut energy consumption when the right and proper aspiration of any modernizing country and government is to promote and sponsor the wealth, welfare, and prosperity of its constituent peoples. To achieve this, nations will clearly have to *increase* their energy consumption.[2] After all, isn't an

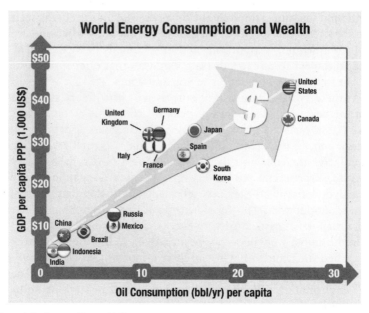

Figure 1.1: *Source: Energy Tribune.*

ever-improving standard of living and greater prosperity the goal to which every caring family and nation aspires?

To the chagrin of environmentalist groups everywhere, however, we still live in an oil-driven (literally in the case of transport) world. Oil and gas (oil around 38 percent, gas around 23 percent — though the gas share is increasing annually) still account today for around 60 percent of the world's energy needs. Add in coal, another 24 percent, and the hydrocarbon energy mix comprises almost 90 percent. Practically all of the rest comes from nuclear and hydroelectric power. And yet massive public subsidies are poured into expensive, highly uneconomic, alternative energy projects and developments, especially wind power. Renewable energy today remains an insignificant factor in the world's energy mix. Put another way, hydrocarbons still rule, OK?

While this market share has remained fairly constant for over 25 years what many fail to grasp is that the market share for hydrocarbons *far from diminishing* is *set to increase further* over the next century with alternative or renewable energies retaining a fairly tiny market share, whatever the political rhetoric. By the year 2030, while the world energy demand will increase by 50 percent over the pre-2008 crisis levels (from about 400 "quads," quadrillion British thermal units [Btu], to over 600) according to all estimates from ExxonMobil to

Petrobras to the International Energy Agency (IEA) and many others, the contribution from fossil fuels to the world economy will continue to retain the same market share. The reason is because, historically, market and economic realities not social engineering, capitalism not socialism, are the "real world" determining factors in national wealth creation. Government or centralizing intervention in the market — note the aftermath of the Russian and Chinese socialist revolutions — has always been disastrous in terms of poverty eradication and wealth creation. Rather, as we have seen, wealth creation depends upon energy consumption and on that score it is the on-going availability of relatively cheap and accessible hydrocarbons that continues to prosper national wealth creation *and* help end social poverty.

The problem for alternative energies is simple. While the capital market will invest in market that offers reasonable profits and returns, alternative energies continue to be highly expensive, offer poor investment-to-energy returns and are thus *only* sustainable through government intervention and enormous taxpayer subsidy — a burden no economy could sustain for long.

OIL AND WESTERN PROSPERITY

For the better part of 40 years, oil has been the great equalizer, in many ways diminishing the huge imbalance between Europeans, their American cousins, and the rest of the world — the latter on the woefully short end of great cultural and economic events such as the Renaissance, the Industrial Revolution, and, certainly, colonialism.

As we have said, what separates rich countries from poor is energy consumption. But even more striking is an oddly inverse relationship: most rich countries are poor in oil, and many poor ones are rich in oil and other primary energy resources.

In the 1960s and 1970s, National Oil Corporations (NOCs) were at the vanguard of the Third World's post-colonial emancipation. Nationalization of formerly foreign-owned oil infrastructures suddenly became a potent political event, rich in symbolism: formerly, multi-national oil companies were the most blatant examples of European and American colonialism and imperialism. But cooperation between the indigenous and the imperialist was unavoidable; if nothing else, the newly minted national companies needed the technology of their recently ejected masters.

It was the Arab oil embargo of 1973 that first utilized oil as a weapon to further national political aims. The embargo ushered in an era of serious conflict and the establishment of the Organization of the

Petroleum Exporting Countries (OPEC) as a hugely powerful cartel. Unprecedented oil price increases led to a sudden shift of wealth that the world had never seen before.

Caracas, Jakarta, Lagos, and assorted Arab sheikdoms were flush with money — often grossly mismanaged — and the ostentatious luxuries and lifestyles the money bought are still the stuff of legend. The ride lasted for about a decade and came to a dead-end with the end of the Cold War. The US President Ronald Reagan, in an attempt to bring the oil-export dependent Soviet Union to its knees, convinced Saudi Arabia to flood the market with oil. Oil prices collapsed and the effects of the "crisis" in almost all oil-producing countries have lasted to this day. The situation certainly brought down the Soviet Union.

A decade later, with OPEC toothless and desperate for technology and cash, many NOCs opened up to the multinationals again, in "joint ventures," alliances, and outright concessions. "Apertura" (opening) became the buzz-word in Venezuela, and served as a fig leaf to cover the reality of the time. Many thought that a new era of cooperation between producers and users had arrived. But the new era of "cooperation" turned out to be something of a desert mirage.

By 2000, the inexorable physics of increasing demand, coupled with a practical lack of exploration and development, resulted in the evaporation of excess production capacity. The event blindsided the developed world because of a sharp but temporary fall in oil prices that followed the 1999 collapse of several Asian financial markets. Oil prices climbed to $30 in January 2000. While some NOCs, such as Petrobras, Malaysia's Petronas, and Indonesia's Pertamina, remained reasonably stable, others went foraging. Populist leaders emerged as energy militants, regaining control of their most valuable asset: Hugo Chávez in Venezuela, Vladimir Putin in Russia, and Evo Morales in Bolivia. NOCs became the vehicle for their political ambitions and provided the treasury to finance them. Previously privatized or opened-up NOCs were taken over in brutish ways, without even the niceties of legalese or lofty pronouncements.

Multinational oil companies are now virtually shut out of big reserves in many NOCs or are reduced to impotent minority players. Oil prices, which shot to almost $150 in July 2008, then collapsed to below $40 after the 2008 economic crisis and then built up again to upwards of $80 lend a lot of bravado and strut. But as usual, the money was not managed or reinvested. Politics and social welfare today still reign supreme. Production is bound to decline, and infrastructure and skills will go by the wayside. Any reduction in oil prices will again bring an unavoidable crash. It's the nature of the beast.

Thus, we see how oil and gas-rich nations can easily remain economic basket cases while a highly dependent energy importing Europe and America, and Western civilization in general, especially in the last century, has been able to develop economic prosperity and thrive. But in these same countries that have benefited so much from energy consumption, the politics of energy has in recent decades become increasingly a tool to be appropriated, most significantly by ideological socialists and the left. And it is easy to see why: energy is power, and in more ways than one.

ENERGY AS A TOOL OF SOCIAL ENGINEERING

It is not just energy *as a commodity* per se that concerns Western political and social groups, especially left-wing elites. Given the steady doom and gloom prophecies of the early peak oil theorists (see Chapter 4) prophesying petro-apocalypse unless modern society is weaned off its oil "addiction," the socialist left has taken up the cause with gusto. Add to that the equally alarmist predictions of planetary disaster if we fail to avert the alleged threat from man-made carbon dioxide (CO_2) emissions, the result of continuing fossil fuel use, and it is no coincidence that it is the socialist not the capitalist free marketer, the left not the right, that has adopted the scaremongering mantras of peak oil and global warm-mongers. Not only to affect global and national energy policies, but in a bid to dictate to us all through increasingly centralized Big Government — the key element enabling socialism (and its parent collectivist system, communism) — *how* we are to live our lives.

While, as authors we come from different parts of the political spectrum, one of us an American democrat and the other an English conservative, both of us share an abhorrence of socialist and left wing, anti-capitalist, liberty-crushing social engineering. Equally, both of us see all too clearly how the energy–climate political nexus is being used unstintingly by the socialist-leaning left as a means to an end: imposing Big Government through centralizing socialist policies that, as they must, inexorably erode personal choice and individual freedom.

What has struck us both in the years of debate over energy and climate issues is how little modern social engineers are disposed to engage with actual facts, articulated reason, and economic reality. A notable theme running through this book is how, time and again, basic facts and reasoned argument cut little ice with the ideologically-driven, intellectually-challenged, socialist or eco-radical. But before going into how this reveals itself explicitly in today's global energy and climate policy "wars," first we must understand the great ideological divide that — at least until President Obama took office — has separated Western civilization into two parts, marking out the worldview of European Socialism from the "American" Capitalism of the US. To understand this is to grasp much about cross Atlantic relations on issues related to energy and climate, and well beyond both.

EUROPE AND AMERICA: THE GREAT IDEOLOGICAL DIVIDE

Less than 20 years after World War II, former Western allies and enemies found themselves on the same side facing a belligerent Russian bear in a world dominated by Cold War. Though theoretically unified in arms and ideals, Europeans and Americans suddenly discovered they saw the world differently. Whether it was war fatigue in Europe, or French and US involvement in Vietnam, France was finding it difficult to disguise its inferiority-cum-superiority complex towards the US. Elements of socialism and other European-invented "-isms," all implying too much government, too much bureaucracy, too little entrepreneurship, too little personal liberty, all in the age of a politically-correct mass media, exacerbated the "great divide" of philosophy and culture that, in truth, has always marked the transatlantic relationship.

The European Union was a French-inspired project aimed at forging established nation states with distinct cultures into a federation with a common identity and voice, under a new super-government. The chief aim was undoubtedly to put an end to the wars that had plagued Europe for centuries. But there was clear secondary focus: to rival America's superpower status in the world. The EU project, not surprisingly, inherited the philosophical and cultural DNA of its Gallic conceivers.

The US is a federation of states collectively imbued "from birth," as its Constitution bears witness, with the Anglo-Saxon/Magna Carta sense of *individual* freedom and personal liberty. Putting it another way, this is the entrepreneurial — read capitalist — spirit writ large, the mantle having passed today from a Britain[3] increasingly in the thrall of the European socialist experiment. Through the last millennium, the distinct worldviews have sat uneasily together, as the warring history of Anglo-French "cultural" relations reveals only too plainly.

It is our contention that this great divide and the simmering resentment of Europe over America's superpower status and global hegemony has two roots. First, it is a status and hegemony Europe covets for itself. Second, Europe's deep-seated fear is that America's success and power in the world is the direct result of America's capitalistic, *non-socialist*, worldview.

The fact is, for all the EU leadership's environmental disagreements with the last Bush administration over the Kyoto Protocol there are some lucid environmental facts about which EU leaders remain in denial. Not least, that the US is certainly one of the cleanest, more environmentally responsible nations in the world. Virtually, no European country can boast cleaner waters, more pristine rural landscapes or air quality. Even Los Angeles, the butt of all environmental jokes in the US, is cleaner than most major cities in the world.

But the environment has been used as a means to politicize economic progress. Environmentalist organizations, many of them the offshoot of anti-establishment, radical movements of the 1960s, may have progressed to wearing a suit and tie but they still show a stark aversion to any development. There is virtually no commercially viable energy project of which the green movement would approve.

Even the most outrageous "green" positions have been legitimized as being "socially responsible." Environmentalism has provided the ideology for people to grab at for meaning in their life. It has become the religion of the "non-religious." As the science writer and novelist Michael Crichton famously put it: "One of the most powerful religions in the Western world is environmentalism. Environmentalism seems to be the religion of choice for urban atheists."[4] Not surprisingly, many of the movement's leaders come from the upper middle class elites including Hollywood stars and wives of celebrities, people that have little or nothing in common with the man in the street, yet in whose name they presume to fight.

The US has been a particular target for environmentalists, not least over its energy policies, for more than four decades. But environmentalism was becoming marginalized till the arrival of the apocalyptic threat alleged to be posed by global warming. Global warming alarmism handed the environmental movement and socialist ideologues, often the same individuals, an unprecedented opportunity, one that demanded a new and unquestioning "consensus" of belief and committed political action. The twin movements recognized this could hand real power and authority to the politicians of the UN and EU. After all, what higher moral action could there be than saving the planet? How can one have enough of a good thing? Save the planet while cutting down in size the most hated, most profligate and, oh so much more successful nation on earth?

The next step was to sponsor a device of trans-national pseudo-governance which underlined who was running the great "end is nigh" show, the world's superpower or the organizations of "consensus" politics. The UN and EU leaders worked hand in hand on the Kyoto project. And it was the EU that, by setting highly ambitious targets of 20 percent cuts in carbon emissions by 2020 from 1992 levels, subsequently proclaimed they held a "world lead" in fighting global warming. Even though CO_2 is NOT a pollutant[5] — it is vital to all vegetation growth — now the EU and supporters of Kyoto could truly turn up the moral heat on the world's greatest "polluter," the US. The US should therefore be the one to make the greatest sacrifices by way of "penance."

It was perhaps the most brilliant politically and ideologically loaded masterstroke in a century. Because the US, one of the least polluting nations in the world, could now, perversely, be accused as one of the largest polluters. And this was directly linked with the use of energy sources, one of the most vital links to a prosperous life. Clearly implied, even if not uttered, is that America's wealth and power has not only been at the expense of the rest of the world, a common refrain of leftist ideologues, but, in addition, it has also put the entire physical world in severe peril.

For the US to sign up to and impose the demands of Kyoto would have been nothing short of economic suicide. The Bush administration and EU leaders both knew it. And if the leftists in Europe thought they might at least have allies in the left-of-center US Democratic Party they were in for a shock. In 1997, with Bill Clinton still in office, the US Senate voted *unanimously* to reject the Kyoto Treaty. The US government, somewhat unreasonably in European eyes, was disinclined to sign its own economic death warrant.

If Europeans believed that the center left of US politics was anything other than much to the right of European socialism, they had a rude awakening. As John Micklewait and Adrian Wooldridge of *The Economist* point out in *The Right Nation: Why America is Different*, "Even with a Democrat in the White House, America would remain a more conservative place than any of its peers in the West."[6] But the moral assault on America's climate credentials wasn't just about carbon emissions; it was always twin-track.

Next to the security of the planet, nothing is as vital to the developed world as energy security. Always high on the environmental hit list is that which powers modern Western lifestyles: hydrocarbons or fossil fuels and the technology which "fails to conserve" the "pristine earth" by digging them up, shipping and burning them. Combining the "end is nigh" message of climate fear with the "oil is about to run out" message of early peak oil theorists has given the enviro-leftist agenda a second line of attack on America and its energy expertise: the renewable energy revolution. Once again, it is the blue and gold EU flag that flies over the revolutionary forces fighting the renewable cause.

Now let's be clear before we go any further. Nobody is against research into new energy technologies, or demurs from the *small-scale, purely supportive* value of renewable energy sources from wind power (it *may* help keep your out-house lit) to solar power (expensive but it might give you hot or tepid bathwater) to geothermal use (maybe, but only in really cold countries). The problem is not the pin-prick, ad hoc uses to which they may be put, but the harnessing of larger projects on a commercially viable basis. On an industrial scale, they amount to nothing more than incredibly uneconomic business propositions that require the constant lifeline of government intervention and tax subsidy. The stark reality is that current technology offers no realistic hope of seeing the current generation of alternative energy sources replacing hydrocarbons for decades to come, *if ever*.

The fact is that the renewable energy revolution is yet another, ideologically-driven, non-starter. Indeed, we would not even be talking about its possibility if it were not for the fact that the tiny impact of renewables on current world energy supplies (meeting about 1–2 percent of world energy demand now *and* by 2050) if governments were not creating "facts on the ground" pouring billions in taxpayer cash into an uneconomic Black Hole producing wildly uneconomic, often meager, return on its massive investment. It is a vital subject we return to in greater detail in Chapter 3.

Only a lack of democratic accountability at the EU[7] has allowed it the clout to sanction vast public expenditure on a renewables industry high on investment, yet appallingly low in energy return. In the US, with Obama's recent public stimulus package and cap and trade policy, the situation there too may be about to change. The reality is that only a centralized socialist system could ever sponsor such a revolution at the political pace currently envisaged. No free society of entrepreneurial capitalists would pursue such a path. Hence America's piecemeal approach to renewable energy projects and the distinct lack of private equity investment in industry, where the federal government is more democratically answerable when it comes to investing public money.

Private equity investors, it seems, have a natural aversion to backing sure-fire industry losers. Lack of US federal investment in renewable energy projects, along with US refusal to sign up to its Kyoto carbon war, has thus handed Europe its twin-track "world lead," which it has relentlessly lauded over the US. Surprising then that it is the US, not Europe, which has achieved the greater results in lowering carbon emissions, and whose private industry is making serious in-roads into energy alternatives that actually work. That has to be a little annoying for the Brussels bureaucracy. Until, that is, Obama's stimulus billions and reversal of his country's policy on Kyoto–Copenhagen accords began changing the US renewables landscape (literally, given time).

A decade on from Kyoto, however, and the science "consensus" is in tatters, with thousands of climate scientists signing up to various non-alarmist declarations and thousands more questioning the UN Intergovernmental Panel on Climate Change (IPCC) climate alarmist position (see chapters 5 and 6). Still political and media elites remain in denial. For them, a loss of consensus undermines their credibility having taken "sides" and attempted to close down the debate. Yet again, a warning from science writer Crichton resonates, "There is no such thing as science consensus. The greatest scientists in the world are great precisely because they broke the consensus."[8] Margaret Thatcher is equally scathing, "Consensus is something in which no one believes but to which no one objects." And, as regards the difficulty in dislodging populist theory with actual facts, Thatcher adds: "Nothing is more obstinate than a fashionable consensus."[9]

The EU's world lead in fighting climate change turns out in practice to be nothing more than the sleight of hand of political rhetoric. The EU's own member states, European industry and a highly corrupt carbon trading scheme have all combined to render Europe's climate targets unachievable and the Kyoto and Copenhagen accords worthless. It was ultimately the "unilateralist" US — and the Bush administration specifically — that called it right when it vetoed what it recognized to be the economy-wrecking, unachievable goals of a deeply flawed Kyoto Protocol. A protocol primarily aimed as much at humiliating and lessening the influence of the US as attaining serious environmental objectives.

The UN–EU inspired bid to clip the wings of the American eagle by harnessing fears over "the greatest threat mankind faces" failed, except perhaps in the popular consciousness and as media myth. Even so, President Obama may yet fulfill European hopes by enrolling the US in the same pointless war on carbon and climate change through his cap and trade policy. More generally, if the Obama administration practices the "consensus" political style he has promised (and the evidence over a year in is that he has not), he should know first of all that it was Euro-style consensus politics that gave the world the wholly unachievable goals of the Kyoto Treaty, which in turn led to the international debacle at the Copenhagen Summit in 2009 (see Chapter 2). A debacle which should reveal to all that, in fact, the war on carbon is over — the alarmists lost (but like the Japanese on a remote Pacific Island who fought on post-WWII, they just don't know it yet). Secondly, consensus politics per se is dominated by a philosophy inherently both alien and ultimately suffocating to the American spirit of liberty and free enterprise. In short, to adopt the consensus politics of trans-nationalism (see Chapter 7) will change America in ways that many Americans did not foresee when they voted for Obama-style "change."

EUROPEAN SOCIALISM VS. AMERICAN CAPITALISM

In a classic display of "throwing the baby with the bathwater," the 2008–09 economic crisis threatens to undo 50 years of progress in the world economic structure. Even more threatening is the specter, constantly barely beneath the surface, of culture-usurping, unrepentant socialist engineers. They think and they gleefully proclaim that the global economic crisis has aided the cause of "European" socialism and dented trust in "American" capitalism. And it did not take long for EU leaders, political and media elites, even the Pope, to queue to read the last rites over the corpse of "American" capitalism.

But what most surprised general observers and anti-capitalist socialists alike was the shocking readiness with which the US Bush administration, allegedly the muscular wing of American conservatism and thus pro-free market capitalism, also opted for a radically *socialist* response. Once the UK socialist leader Gordon Brown took the dubious path of Keynesian monetarism — injecting massive stimuli of public money into the banking and financial sectors — Europe (not surprisingly) and America (surprisingly) followed suit.

Even so, to borrow from Mark Twain, "Reports of the death of capitalism have been greatly exaggerated." Firstly because, as British economist Samuel Brittan pointed out in a speech in 2003, "The Bush administration is much more a pro-business government than it is a genuine supporter of competitive free markets." We would point to former President Bush's refusal to relinquish protectionism for American farmers; but Brittan also noted the "ultra-Keynesian fervour of the Bush Administration"[10] — a distinct preference for government to provide financial impetus and stimulation of the economy. It was hardly a genuinely "conservative" response. Second, at time of writing, all the economic signs are that the various financial stimuli packages — the socialist answer — have not, and are not, delivering the promised results. The banks are not responding to the stimulus by lending, and consequently, businesses have laid off thousands of workers. Quite simply, the queue for public handouts — the mark of a socialist society

— is growing. All the signs are that far from "easing the pain" all the socialist answer is doing is anaesthetizing it, thus greatly extending the period of suffering.

Though it is not our purpose here to discuss these matters in the detail required, no discussion of socialism vs. capitalism could possibly ignore the current economic crisis. But what concerns us more is the focus on how the respective ideologies — and the policies they underpin — have perpetuated the great divide between Europe and America generally, and with energy specifically.

IDEOLOGY VS. COMPETITIVENESS

In 2008, President Obama was given a powerful mandate for "change." One that may mean European-style socialism has a window of opportunity to eclipse American capitalism by default rather than as a superior system. None of which is likely, anytime soon, to reverse the anti-American, anti-capitalist themes of European policies, however. While the EU has used Kyoto and alleged US "obligations" under it — a treaty that was only ever meant to be voluntary — as a stick with which to beat the US, it has also tied environmental themes in with its broader anti-capitalist agenda. And nowhere has this been given greater impetus than in the EU's "unbundling" campaign for industry.

The essence of "unbundling" is the enforced political break up of often successful national global business conglomerates in the name of greater competition, a policy at odds with the spirit of deregulated American capitalism.[11] Enforced unbundling, by definition, remains a hand-tool of centralist control. And in an increasingly global economy, one that can easily pressure successful national industries to relocate beyond home soil, or face takeover from foreign-owned conglomerates domestically under no "unbundling" threat. Chief among the EU's targets have been some of Europe and the world's leading, and to date, most successful energy companies, including oil giants BP, Royal Dutch Shell, Total, and Eni.[12] Together with Europe's equally successful power companies, many have felt the hot breath of EU centralist pressure to divest themselves of major parts of their businesses.

Other European heavy industry too has been targeted by the Eurocracy, especially high energy users, who are also therefore high CO_2 emitters. Such is the relentless pursuit of centralist control in socialist Europe that the EU appears willing even to sacrifice the global competitiveness of its own top companies in pursuit of its market ideology. Even EU leaders have, however, been worried enough by the strength of opposition from European business leaders that protectionism (should unbundling occur) has, once again, reared its ugly head. Protectionism to prevent foreign takeovers of Europe's major industries, along with public subsidy and other publicly funded "perks," have been mooted to persuade heavy industry to stay put. Not surprisingly, the impasse between socialist Eurocrat and Europe's capitalist industrialist, combined with the inevitable impact of the economic crisis, the unbundling program has, for the moment at least, run into the sand. Yet, the serious nature of this on-going political rhetoric vs. energy reality "disconnect" should not be underestimated; a subject we take up in the next chapter.

EU SOCIAL HYPOCRISY

But if the ideological bent of EU philosophy is happy to threaten the global competitiveness of its own "capitalist" success stories, we should not be blinded to the unmitigated pragmatic hypocrisy the EU practices when it suits. The fact is that many governments are finding it difficult to wed preferred new energy policies to aspirational climate-fighting targets. But the EU's own failure to achieve coherent energy and climate policies has not stopped it from persistently berating the US for its failure to ratify Kyoto — even though, in practice, no major economy has carried through on its Kyoto commitments. That's because the EU seems more interested in getting America to repent its "sins" as the world's leading CO_2 "polluter" (though China has lately taken up that mantle) — and bankrupt itself in the process.

The fact is that while the alleged causal link between CO_2 and temperature rises remains mere theory, it has not prevented the EU from designating CO_2 Public Enemy No 1. In this regard, of course, the chief culprit in producing carbon emissions is the burning of fossil fuel; more specifically, coal.

King Coal, however, is currently making a revolutionary comeback[13] with a whole new generation of coal-fired, carbon emitting power plants being built across Europe[14] — and *with* the EU's blessing.[15] The EU will tell us that it will insist on carbon capture or sequestration facilities (adding a billion dollars of extra cost for which *yet more* public funding may be made available) being a precondition for the building of such plants.[16] However, the reality is that carbon sequestration, the storing of CO_2 below ground, is far more difficult and an extraordinarily more expensive, and probably dangerous, process than politicians understand.

As if this energy–climate policy "contradiction" is not enough, in 2008, to fuel the industrial plants, the EU agreed its biggest coal

Figure 1.2 Cover of *The Independent*.

importing deal in a decade[17] — with the US, for its high-grade coal. *The same coal President Obama does not want Americans using for any new coal-fired plants in America; plants he has threatened to bankrupt.* Just socialist inconsistency or rank EU hypocrisy?

The unbundling policy, however, has become a ubiquitous tool that, elsewhere, has developed into an even more overt anti-US edge. In 2008, a complaint was filed with the European Commission claiming Microsoft was breaking EU antitrust laws by bundling its Internet Explorer browser with its own Windows operating system.[18] In January 2009, the Commission ruled against Microsoft.[19] Faced with paying a massive fine for "anti-competitive behavior" Microsoft attempted to strike a compromise deal. It involved what the European weekly *New Europe* called "helping to spread the European spirit, by incorporating the EU flag into the next Windows 7 logo."[20] Not a bad move. Vastly American capitalist enterprise coupled with European socialist free advertising. But here's the far bigger point: *Most* modern electronic gizmos bundle together with their product an array of associated paraphernalia that render it instantly useable for the buyer. That's how good "capitalist" practice works. But the EU chose to pick a high profile fight with the doyen of successful global *American* capitalist enterprise, the Microsoft Corporation, to make its highly illogical ideological point.

But then the American ownership of the Net per se has long been a target for EU ire. While the Net does have a degree of regulation, it still bears the "free enterprise" (and that means free speech) hallmark of its American controllers. Once again, the EU wants far more central control of those twin "hated" elements of capitalism; free enterprise and, above all, free speech. In 2005, European Union regulators formally proposed stripping the US of their control of the Internet.[21] The EU demanded what all socialists want, "intergovernmental control" or centralized control by a group of socialist ideologue control freaks. Control the flow of information and you control the people has always been a socialist maxim. The Internet today is perhaps the only mass medium where genuine debate and free speech is still possible — which is why it flourishes while the government-controlled mass media is dying a slow death. And, once again, it is the Internet-running, liberty-loving Americans who are standing in the EU's way.

The EU, of course, has no legislative mandate for *any* of these anti-capitalist policies. But then that is the point, *it doesn't need it.* Though the EU may have a Parliament, the EU is *not* a democratic institution. This is something we feel many Americans, not to mention Europeans, fail to grasp. Just a handful of EU officials give the EU Commissioners their power. American presidents and administrations along with those of European states can be voted in and out of office. That is democracy. But the 2009 imposed European President and the European Commissioners, the real powerhouse of European politics, those who really set the European political agenda and are striving to become the *de facto* federal government of Europe, are not voted in or out of office by any European electorate. Anywhere else in the world this would practice of rule by non-democratic oligarchy would be called what it is: a dictatorship or tyranny.

As regards the true nature of the European bureaucratic beast, it is well worth recording Margaret Thatcher's finely judged statements about the EU as they impact directly our understanding when we return to consider recent Western energy and climate policies. During her retirement years, Mrs Thatcher wrote: "The most significant shortcoming of the fledgling super-state is that it is not, will not be, indeed, ultimately cannot be, democratic. The Commission and Parliament share the same federalist agenda — and it is not democratic."

Thatcher also notes that EU federalist enthusiasts prefer to use the expression the "United States of Europe" (a title that misleads many

Americans). But as she points out about such a view: "It is flawed, because the United States was based from its inception on a common language, culture and values — Europe has none of these things." In fact, by contrast she notes, "Europe is the result of *plans* . . . a classic utopian project, a monument to the vanity of intellectuals, a programme whose inevitable destiny is failure: only the scale of the final damage is in doubt." Interestingly, she makes a fascinating observation that will resonate loudly with European nationals and Americans concerned with the apparently growing government-usurping power, often ideologically-leaning decisions of the European Courts and a left-leaning US Judiciary. "Whether it is the United States or mainland Europe," says Thatcher, "written constitutions have one great weakness. This is they contain the potential to have judges take decisions which should properly be made by democratically elected politicians."[22] What Mrs Thatcher was alluding to, of course, is that the nature of "rights" in the British and American sense "Magna Carta" sense, is that they are unrestricted *except* where restricted by law; in the French–European socialist "Napoleonic Law" sense, the reverse is true, with rights having to be written down, by definition making man inherently less free in his liberty in the latter system than in the former.

Summing up her abiding hostility towards the anti-democratic nature of the European Union socialist project, Mrs Thatcher has stated, "Socialists don't like ordinary people choosing, for they might not choose socialism." At the same time, she described the USA as, "The greatest force for liberty the world has ever known."[23] We believe Mrs Thatcher's insight has never been more valid than today. And they powerfully echo F.A. Hayek's assertion that, "Although we had been warned by some of the greatest political thinkers of the nineteenth century, by de Tocqueville and Lord Acton, that socialism means slavery, we have steadily moved in the direction of socialism."[24] In the current debate over the socialist direction America is now being taken in by a radical Democratic administration, Americans would be wise to heed their warnings, as that direction can only squeeze capitalist entrepreneurial enterprise, not least in the vital energy sector.

The threat from socialism, an ideologically centralizing belief system, goes way beyond the threat it poses to the politics of energy. As Hayek further pointed out, "When it becomes dominated by a collectivist creed, democracy will inevitably destroy itself."[25] And the problem with idealism, as John Galsworthy observed, is that it "increases in direct proportion to one's distance from the problem." Hence the largely unnoticed, as yet, fiasco of European socialism's publicly-funded, ideologically-driven, rapidly failing renewable energy revolution. A revolution that is already upping stakes and cynically heading for much better government subsidized frontiers.

WHY EUROPE'S RENEWABLES ROAD-SHOW IS ROLLING STATESIDE

Drive out of London west along the M4 motorway and you'll see the shape of things to come: one of the new generations of giant wind turbines. Completed in 2005 and dominating every vista for a hundred miles, the 280 foot mega turbine at Green Park was designed to power up to 500 local businesses and 1000 homes. And so it does. But not by wind power *alone* you understand. The wind only turns the blades for up to 40 percent of the time. For the other 60 percent they have to be powered by electricity — to prevent them rusting and seizing up.

You might think a 40 percent return on the massive investment and on-going maintenance costs associated with such "free" renewable wind power disappointingly low. You'd be right. But here's the thing; the return ratio at Green Park is actually *high* for an industry where the norm is less than 25 percent — this in Europe's windiest land, and in the renewables flagship industry. Worse, during bouts of severe cold, Britain's turbines have been reported as operating at

Figure 1.3: The giant turbine at Green Park, London. *Source: Energy Tribune.*

a mere 5 percent of capacity. The simple fact is that periods of severe cold often coincide with a lack of wind. So at the very time that *most* power is required, wind turbines consistently prove themselves to be at their *least* reliable.

All of which explains why the European wind industry and green energy schemes are struggling to raise finance. Private investors don't want to know. Who but government would throw vast amounts of (someone else's) cash at such a commercially non-viable industry? So even as the green energy tab has been picked up by Europe's long-suffering taxpayers, giving the socialist EU its much-vaunted world lead, it seems the publicly-funded European green energy "road-show" is fast running out of steam — and out of Europe. With funds increasingly hard to come by and with its wheels constantly mired in planning disputes, many of Europe's green energy big-hitters have hitched up their wagons and headed West, to where the next rich vein of easy public subsidy pickings lies untapped: Obama's $80 billion renewable energy stimulus bonanza.

While European Big Oil and power companies nightly parade their green credentials in TV adverts, by day they are ditching their Europe-wide green energy programs. Shell and BP have opted out of the UK renewables market altogether, citing it commercially unviable. Spanish utility company Iberdrola, the big investor in Spain's wind farms and owner of Scottish Power, has slashed its renewables spending by 40 percent. The future of NPower's massive Gwint Y Mor wind farm off the Welsh coast is in doubt. But the biggest blow to the green energy flagship wind industry came when the world's second largest oil company, Royal Shell, pulled out of the London Array, the world's largest offshore wind farm project, in late 2008. The $4.5 billion project due to be built in the Thames estuary would prospectively have powered up to 750,000 homes. While the London Array's other backers, Germany's E.ON and Denmark's DONG Energy, are, at time of writing, in urgent talks for new funds with the European Investment Bank, the project remains shelved. The reality is, however, that Shell's *volte face* turns out to be nothing of the sort. Having made a big show of signing the 2007 pre-Bali conference low carbon communiqué, Shell subsequently quietly sold off its solar business. Environ Energy Global of Singapore bought its photovoltaic operations in India and Sri Lanka. The sale of Shell's solar operations in the Philippines and Indonesia quickly followed along with its solar module production business, with its manufacturing plants in the US, Canada, and Germany.

While Shell vehemently denies it is giving up on green energy — maintaining it will concentrate on biofuel initiatives — both it and other

European Big Oil companies are letting it be known they are "returning to their roots" and concentrating on primary energy initiatives. As the green lobbies duly vented their anger against Shell, it was left to Michael Eckhart, president of the American Council on Renewable Energy to put his finger on the real reason: "Big Oil does not consider renewable energy to be a mainstream industry,"[26] he said. However, during the course of damping down criticism over its London Array pullout, Shell let it be known that it still intended *to pursue* wind power projects in the US. Whether or not Big Oil (and Big Power) considers the green energy business mainstream, its prevailing business philosophy seems less green and more greenback-orientated, especially when massive easy-picking public subsidies are on offer. But the question remains, what is going *so* wrong with Europe's green energy strategy, which should set alarm bells ringing in the US, and beyond?

Well it seems that the days of the great European socialist "blank check" for green energy programs may be over. Having seed-funded the first generation of renewables, especially wind farms, the blatantly poor investment-to-energy return ratio has consistently kept private investors away. What the economic crisis has done is to hasten the day when even ideological-driven European leaders must demand a better return from an industry still commercially unproven. EU strategy has been to throw money into an "unfocused" green energy pot that requires diverse energy protagonists to scrap for every penny. When it comes to funds all manner of energy projects vie for a steadily dwindling pot, as governments are forced to cut back on their financial commitments. Burgeoning planning problems in the face of increasing public (even environmental) opposition has meant that competing for European green energy funding has turned into a business nightmare. Enter Obama's $80 billion "windfall" funds *specifically for renewables projects*. Coupled with a presidential commitment to easing planning regulations, and a whole new, potentially more "lawless," green energy frontier beckons.

While April 2009 saw the UK government throw a further $3 billion[27] — and the EU a further $4 billion — at green energy, once again it amounted to "unfocused" cash, in amounts hardly likely to suggest to Europe's big-boys the need to turn their wagons and head home.

The European renewables players are currently staking out their US ground. Spain's Iberdrola, the world leader in renewable power, is already the second biggest player in US wind generation. Iberdrola has announced it will invest over $2 billion in the US up to 2012. Portugal's EDP Renováveis, already the third largest company in US wind, is set to invest $5 billion in its US holdings. Spain's Gamesa is the third largest, behind General Electric, in turbine manufacture. Denmark's Vestas, the world's largest turbine manufacturer, is becoming a growing force in the US — having closed a key UK turbine manufacture plant in the UK due to a lack of orders brought on by public opposition and planning obstacles. Enel Green Power, a subsidiary of the Italian utility, Enel, is set to invest at least $1.5 billion up to 2013. BP says it remains committed to $8 billion of spending on alternative energy over 10 years including, as a spokesman recently confirmed, its intention to press ahead with 450 megawatts of wind production capacity in the US. The extent of Shell's US wind and renewables capacity is still to unfold. But, as Francesco Starace, president of Enel Green Power told *Business Week*, "The stimulus package is a big incentive to invest."[28]

While European companies will inevitably provide some of the thousands of American green jobs President Obama's stimulus wants to create, he should appreciate that the American renewables industry will be operating at a severe advantage. European companies are often subsidiaries of much bigger parent companies and as such have greater financial clout, not to mention expertise, than their smaller, inexperienced, US counterparts. That competitive edge is likely to ensure that much of Obama's taxpayer energy stimulus package will flow directly from the US taxpayer to European companies. Historically, America has made a better job of "revolution" than has mainland Europe. But in the coming US renewables revolution, all the signs are that it will be labeled "made in Europe" and, ultimately, mirror all the same mistakes Europe has made.

On his next trip to Britain, President Obama could do worse when he lands at London's Heathrow than take a short trip along the M4 to see Green Park's mega-turbine; the "shape of thing to come." He and his policy team could also do worse than perform a simple math exercise in energy investment-to-returns; then scale-up the results to reveal the shape of renewable energy costs for Americans. It might help explain why the pioneers of the first wind revolution are so readily ditching Europe's renewables revolution, and cynically heading to the new frontier "out West." At least, for as long as the rich vein of taxpayer subsidy holds out, that is.

OBAMA'S ENERGY RADICALISM

Only a few years ago radical environmentalists would have been more circumspect in their energy pronouncements than members of the Obama administration, many of whom seem to want to govern by slogan and sound bite rather than reality.

On 17 April 2009, the Environmental Protection Agency (EPA) declared finally what many had hoped and others dreaded: that there is "overwhelming and compelling evidence" that "greenhouse gases in the atmosphere endanger the public health of current and future generations."[29] In spite of a growing chorus of skeptical scientists on the causes of global climate change and even more objections on the expected effects, the EPA went on to adopt the most strident and alarmist presumed catastrophes from climate change such as rising sea levels, more wildfires, more hurricanes and degraded air quality.

While international pressure was often cited for the Obama government actions it was clearly ironic that *Pravda*, the former official instrument of the Soviet Communist Party, implored the US to stop its "carbon communism."

The EPA of course did not offer solutions to the 87 percent problem, i.e. where the US energy that currently derives from hydrocarbons would come from. It deferred to Congress to do so. Surely Congress would find the right solution from a position of knowledge as demonstrated by the honorable Nancy Pelosi who on NBC's Meet the Press said "I believe in natural gas as a clean, cheap alternative to fossil fuels," and lest one thought she misspoke, she went on to say in the same interview that natural gas "is cheap, abundant and clean compared to fossil fuels."[30] Apparently, the Speaker missed the high school class that taught how the dinosaur-era foliage turned into oil, coal *and* natural gas.

Secretary of Energy Steven Chu, in a 4 April 2009 *Newsweek* guest editorial, also proved that — his Nobel Prize notwithstanding — common sense and rudimentary knowledge are lacking. First he did not offer one sentence on securing the US 87 percent of energy supply other than "advanced biofuels." This . . . *from the Energy Secretary?*

The point is that biofuels, as practiced thus far, give a negative energy balance; that is, they require more energy to produce than their consumption provides. And even ignoring this science, if we were to use all of the corn grown in the US to produce motor vehicle fuel, without regard to what that would do to food prices, it would still be less than 20 percent of US gasoline demand, and a lot of the world would go hungry.

Chu also went on to say "we must move beyond oil because the science on global warming is clear and compelling: greenhouse-gas emissions, primarily from fossil fuels, have started to change our climate. We have a responsibility to future generations to reduce those emissions to spare our planet the worst of the possible effects." His main solution? Conservation as "the most direct way to reduce our dependency on foreign oil is to simply use less of it."[31]

"Let's just become less" seems to be the Obama administration's mantra and it has many adherents all over the world, especially when it refers to the US. This in spite of the fact that beyond ideological feel-good there is no evidence historical or otherwise that conservation can reduce energy consumption. In fact the opposite is true. Energy conservation and efficiency in one sector has led to increase in total energy demand, finding new uses of energy such as the Internet and next-day package delivery.

There is some merit to another suggestion by Chu: electrical cars, but he destroys the notion when he writes "generating that electricity from clean, renewable sources like solar and wind power."

Not to be outdone in slogan-style exaggeration, Secretary of the Interior Ken Salazar, on 6 April 2009, in Atlantic City to discuss America's offshore energy resources, in what the *Wall Street Journal* characterized, "raised eyebrows when he said offshore wind farms could replace 3,000 coal-fired plants."[32] The US currently has only 600. He also claimed that offshore Atlantic could deliver wind electricity equal to 1,000 gigawatts. That's the entire electricity generation capacity of the US.

One has to wonder at the ideological motivations behind the "gusher of lies" that amount to psychobabble when what we ought to expect is intellectual coherence in formulating energy policy. Why is it that potential changes, which would take many decades to accomplish, are presented as imminent solutions? Why such a total "disconnect" between fantasy and reality?

Notes

1 M.J. Economides and R. Oligney, *The Color of Oil* (Round Oak Publishing), p. 10.

2 Neither will conserving energy or using energy more efficiently lead to cutting rising consumption as nations pursue industrialization, as we will see as we review the effect of the "Jevons Paradox" in Chapter 10.

3 It would be more accurate to say the "English" spirit, as the Celtic fringe of Britain (Scotland, Wales and Northern Ireland) is far more receptive to the socialist-European system than is England, as the 2005 election result bears eloquent testimony (when Euro-skeptic England — the majority population — voted Conservative, yet Britain as a whole, once again, put the socialist Labour Party into power).

4 Michael Crichton, speech "Environmentalism as Religion" Commonwealth Club, San Francisco, CA, September 14, 2003.

5   Testimony of Dr Patrick Michaels, Professor of Environmental Sciences, University of Virginia to the Subcommittee on National Economic Growth, Natural Resources and Regulatory Affairs, US House of Representatives, October 6, 1999.

6   John Micklethwait and Adrian Wooldridge, *The Right Nation: Why America is Different* (Penguin), p. 357.

7   The EU has never produced an authorized set of accounts signed off by independent auditors since its inception. Worse, when the EU finally hired its own highly qualified chief accountant to sort out its financial affairs it ignominiously "constructively sacked" her when she attempted to report widespread fraud and corruption at the EU. For more on this fascinating story read: Marta Andreasen's *Brussels Laid Bare* (St Edwards Press).

8   Michael Crichton, speech "Aliens Cause Global Warming," California Institute of Technology, Pasadena, CA, January, 2003.

9   From a 1981 speech. Here is the fuller context: "For me, pragmatism is not enough. Nor is that fashionable word 'consensus' . . . To me consensus seems to be the process of abandoning all beliefs, principles, values and policies in search of something in which no one believes, but to which no one objects — the process of avoiding the very issues that have to be solved, merely because you cannot get agreement on the way ahead. What great cause would have been fought and won under the banner 'I stand for consensus'?"

10 UK economist Samuel Brittan, speech "The USA and Europe: Two, three or more economic cultures?" Gulbenkian Foundation Conference, Lisbon, October 21, 2003.

11 And, perversely, Russian and Chinese socialism too, both of which hold their enormous national energy companies in the highest esteem.

12 "EU To Propose Energy Overhaul," *Wall Street Journal*, September 17, 2007.

13 "The Return of King Coal," *Investor's Chronicle*, August 28, 2008.

14 "Europe Turns Back to Coal, Raising Climate Fears," *The New York Times*, April 23, 2008.

15 "Coal Subsidies Maintained Until 2010," *Euractiv*, June 29, 2007.

16 "EU Spending Spree Brings Carbon Capture Back to Reality," *The Guardian*, January 29, 2009.

17 "Europe To Import US Coal," *Energy Tribune*, January 7, 2008.

18 "Microsoft EU Legal Troubles Continue," *Euractiv*, May 14, 2008.

19 "EU Takes Legal Action Against Microsoft," eFluxMedia, January 19, 2009.

20 "Microsoft to Put EU Flag on Upcoming Windows 7," *New Europe*, January 29, 2009.

21 "EU and US Clash Over Control of Net," *International Herald Tribune*, September 30, 2005.

22 Margaret Thatcher, *Statecraft: Strategies for a Changing World* (Harper Collins), pp. 275, 342 and 358. Italics in original.

23 Margaret Thatcher, from a speech in 1989, quoted in S. Blake and A. John, *The World According to Margaret Thatcher* (Michael O'Mara Books), p. 144.

24 F.A. Hayek, *The Road to Serfdom* (Routledge Classics), p. 13.

25 Ibid. p. 73.

26 "Oil Companies Loathe to Follow Obama's Green Lead," *New York Times*, April 7, 2009.

27 And set up a new government-funded investment bank controlling £2 billion as announced in Alistair Darling's March 2010 Budget plans.

28 "European Green Energy Chases U.S. Stimulus Cash," *Bloomberg Business Week*, April 22, 2009.

29 "Flying Pigs and Other Media Myths," Michael J. Economides, *Oil Online*, June 30, 2009.

30 Nancy Pelosi speaking on NBC TV's "Meet the Press," Sunday April 19, 2009.

31 US Energy Secretary Steven Chu, Guest Editorial, *Newsweek*, April 4, 2009.

32 "Breezy Talk: Interior Secretary Ken Salazar's Offshore Wind Dreams," *Wall Street Journal Blogs*, April 7, 2009.

2

The Energy Disconnect

Rogues are preferable to imbeciles because they sometimes take a rest.

Alexandre Dumas

The quote above should not imply that we view all politicians as rogues or imbeciles. But you could be forgiven for thinking that some leading politicians today may be one or other, given the chasm between their energy rhetoric and aspirations and a realistic understanding of the energy realities. The prospect of quite a few Western politicians taking a rest from setting unrealistic energy goals and targets anytime soon appears unlikely. And nowhere is this intellectual energy "disconnect" more perceived than in the mantra-like claims that the "oil is running out" (see Chapter 4), that we should aim for (unachievable) "energy independence," and that our future energy goals need to be hitched to the war on carbon and climate change — via the substitution of hydrocarbon resources with alternative energies.

The basic interpretation why many politicians of both the left and the right have jumped on the global climate change band wagon and, especially, on efforts to do something about, arguably, a futile effort, is that it leads to the greatest form of revenue ever handed to them. It is a tax that can be levied on goods and services across industry and society both overtly and covertly with the very important distinction that it is not so called. And anyway, who could argue with it anyway if the saving of the planet is at stake?

But politicians are also playing to a gullible gallery that they helped create. They are looking for cheap votes. They know that, as politicians, they are in it for the short haul. Thus, it ought to fall to the journalist to question the policies and statements of politicians and the alleged expertise on which they claim to base their policies. But much of the mainstream media (MSM) has long since given up its historic and impartial role of asking hard questions in lieu of the latest political and scientific pronouncements. CNN, BBC, CBS, NBC, New York Times, The Guardian and countless American and European media have long since abrogated their Fourth Estate responsibilities, choosing instead to becoming cheerleaders for the latest scaremongering, left wing cause. Skepticism, once an important element of journalistic integrity, has today largely been replaced by wholesale acceptance of even the most outrageous and patently false pronouncements.

For all that the media and politicians clash in other areas, when it comes to issues with a powerful left-leaning ideological bent, especially in the energy-climate debate, an unhealthy "social" pact has been forged which has led to a stifling of genuine public square debate. It is a serious problem in itself, and a subject which we will look at more closely in Chapter 6. For now, however, we will focus on how the public have been, and are being, misled by the on-going "disconnect" between the political rhetoric vs. the real world energy facts. It is a disconnect that consistently reveals our politicians saying one thing then, time and again, being forced to *do* something else entirely when confronted by the realities.

THE DISCONNECT

One day the UK Energy Secretary, Ed Milliband, sets out his proposed expansion of the UK's wind power led alternative energy revolution; the next, Vestas, the UK's largest wind turbine manufacturer, closes for business, citing "low demand" and public opposition to onshore wind farms.[1]

Just bad luck, or bad PR? Neither, in fact. It's just another example of the on-going "disconnect" over energy between those suffering from WTS (Wishful Thinker Syndrome) and the hydrocarbon-fuelled energy verities. Driven by panic-inducing UN IPCC theory over the alleged threat from man-made CO_2 — after a decade where the scientific data shows a downward trend in global mean temperatures — and supplemented with irrational fears over early peak oil theories, Western politicians and others remain consistently inured to the economic energy "facts of life."

A COMPENDIUM OF PROPHETIC FAILURE

In 2006, Germany's Angela Merkel was hailed as the "Green Chancellor" for promising to rid her country of coal and nuclear power, in its bid to give a clean energy and climate change "world lead." Three years on and Merkel's government was actively supporting the construction of a new generation of 26 coal-fired power plants as well as keeping Germany's nuclear power stations open. In addition, she was arguing for special protection for German heavy industry via free cap and trade permits. A powerful German industry, the need to remain competitive, and a desire to work with the lights on, all combined to help Ms Merkel "reconnect."

In 2008, Italy, to everyone's surprise, reversed its decades long "no nuclear power stations here" policy, in the face of its urgent national power needs. And Italy's PM Silvio Berlusconi, along with leaders from Austria, Poland, and a bandwagon of other countries, also demanded special protection for their heavy industry if the time came for handing out free cap and trade permits for their high-energy-using industries if binding emissions legislation were imposed at a European level. Across in the UK, the government has been wriggling out of its Kyoto "clean energy" commitments for years as the country inches towards building an urgently needed new generation of *coal-fired* power plants. To help critics swallow the bitter pill of yet more coal use, the UK government plans to subsidize — that word again — "clean coal" technologies through CCS (Carbon Capture Sequestration).

But adding $1 billion to the cost of each plant for a hugely speculative unproven technology has already created a politically paralyzing impasse in pursuit of a coherent UK energy strategy. The specter of the UK facing "South African-style power cuts" and being plunged into "third world darkness" looms ever closer.[2] Notwithstanding the UK's grand wind power plan, in December 2008 the British Wind Energy Association (BWEA) was forced to scale down its overblown calculation of harmful CO_2 emissions from 860 to 430 grams for every kilowatt hour of electricity produced.[3]

With more coal use in prospect and less help from wind sources the UK thus has no chance of getting near its Kyoto CO_2 commitments. In fact, with less than 2400 wind turbines in operation across Britain currently, the UK would still require a further 100,000 turbines to meet its targets. Plenty of scope for massive wind turbine growth, we might think. So why the Vestas wind turbine manufacturer pull-out, mentioned earlier?

Not that Eurocrats are easily deflated by the failure of wind power facts on the ground. Speaking at a key European wind power conference in March 2009, EU Energy Commissioner Andris Piebalgs, claimed, "Wind energy can replace a large proportion of the polluting and finite fuels we currently rely on. It makes good sense to invest in indigenous sources of power which hedge against unpredictable fossil fuel prices and in which Europe has a real competitive advantage." Piebalgs adds pompously, "Wind energy is Europe's contribution to peace, progress and prosperity."

Mr Piebalgs' claims epitomize the energy disconnect. As Michael J. Trebilcock has shown, wind power is, in terms of industrial scale economics (whether we can afford it), a complete disaster,[4] with the much-vaunted "Danish green miracle"[5] turning out to be an another media myth in a industry that would blow out tomorrow without government intervention and subsidy. And all this hype is about an energy source that can, in the next few decades, provide a miniscule contribution to the world's power supply.

For all the political bluster, the best energy estimates suggest that by the year 2030 energy demand will rise by a further 50 percent[6] and that oil, gas and coal will *still* fulfill 87 percent of the world's energy needs, according to the IEA. As we have seen, Shell has already dumped its alternative energy program (except for biofuels)[7] in part of a broader trend of European alternative energy companies heading to the US[8] drawn by the rich pickings of President Obama's stimulus billions. In 2009, Germany's REpower US subsidiary relocated its US HQ to Denver, Colorado to take full advantage of the "supportive business climate"[9] along with (surprise, surprise) Vestas (remember them?), late of the UK?

The Obama White House has been recycling all the same European political energy rhetoric so familiar to Europeans. Yet, the US has its own instructive case study. One day billionaire T. Boone Pickens had a Grand Wind Plan for Texas, with further plans to forest the nation with turbines "from Canada to Mexico." The next, T Boone, in the

Filling Green Holes

Obama's energy plans use the power of government to create an **enormous green hole in energy supplies** (through taxation, regulation, lack of access etc.), then it uses the power of government to **pay people to fill these green holes** with less affordable, less practical, but more fashionable alternatives.

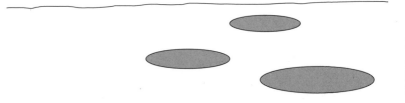

Figure 2.1: *Source: Energy Tribune*

face of the down-to-earth economics, was forced to drop his wind plan in favor of . . . you've guessed it, *a hydrocarbon* (natural gas) solution instead.[10] Even billionaires, it seems, can bridge the politics of energy "disconnect" when their personal billions are at stake.

Meanwhile, the political energy disconnect has fuelled an almost ethereal, religious vision among those who seek to appease the earth and climate gods. In 2003, Al Gore predicted we had just 96 months (ten years) before fossil-fuel assisted climate Armageddon kicked in. At the time of writing, that's just three years away. In 2006, Steven Guilbeault of Greenpeace warned us, "Time is running out to deal with climate change. Ten years ago, we thought we had a lot of time." Yet, back in 1997, Greenpeace's Chris Rose was claiming, "Time is running out for the climate." The UK's Prince of Wales ruminates that, "Capitalism and consumerism have brought the world to the brink of economic and environmental collapse." The Prince adds, "The age of convenience is over."[11] In the light of the Prince's comments, a highly pertinent observation was offered by international columnist Mark Steyn: "The Prince then got in his limo and was driven to his other palace."[12]

Meanwhile, NASA's James Hansen continues to lead the war against the green's *bête-noir* of fossil fuels: coal, at the very time Europe and the UK, indeed much of the world, is turning to the black stuff as the fuel for a new generation of power stations. For millions in China, India and elsewhere cheap coal is *the* answer ending their poverty. Poverty-ending it may be, but Hansen remains unmoved, instead obsessing over his private vision that coal use *could* effect "progressive, unstoppable global sea level rise, shifting of climatic zones with extermination of many animal and plant species, reduction of fresh water supplies for hundreds of millions of people, and a more intense hydrologic cycle with stronger droughts and forest fires, but also heavier rains and floods, and stronger storms driven by latent heat, tornadoes and thunderstorms." and "lock us into future climate disasters."[13] France *could* become the most popular nation on earth, but it's not likely.

For men like Hansen, *the reality* that coal power *is* a key energy resource in the war on global poverty means little if it clashes with his climate-appeasing, prophetic insights. We will look more closely at the claims of James Hansen later. But given the eco-alarmist capacity generally for chronic failed prophetic utterance, at this stage, we merely offer the sage advice of one Lao Tzu, a sixth-century BC Chinese poet: "Those who have knowledge don't predict. Those who predict don't have knowledge."[14] Could Lao Tzu have been a (failed) sixth-century weather forecaster?

OLD FOSSILS AND COPENHAGEN

In August 2009, ahead of the "world saving" Copenhagen Summit event in December of that year, UN Secretary-General Ban Ki Moon ramped up the politico–energy disconnect further. He claimed:

> *We have just four months. Four months to secure the future of our planet. If we fail to act, climate change will intensify droughts, floods and other natural disasters. Water shortages will affect hundreds of millions of people. Malnutrition will engulf large parts of the developing world. Tensions will worsen. Social unrest even violence could follow.*[15]

As we now know, the December 2009 summit ended in total failure, so, presumably, we must now be doomed to suffer the ills of Ban Ki-Moon's prediction? The problem at Copenhagen was straightforward enough, when all is said and done, national leaders will, ultimately, refuse to impoverish their economies and industries, even to save the planet. Hence, the failure of Copenhagen to advance any meaningful agreements on binding carbon emission laws that would further facilitate greater impetus towards alternative "clean" energies. The still "disconnected" flower power generation and its idealistic offspring now in high office would do well to grasp that the energy future is not green as they understand it; rather, it is hydrocarbon (black, grey etc.) — and will continue to be for, at the very least, another century.[16]

EUROPE'S INVESTMENT BACKLASH

They live in the lap of taxpayer-funded luxury, driven around in gas-guzzling limousines enjoying "personal allowances" that a rock star would covet. And all within a thoroughly "legit" organization that, since its inception, has successfully evaded the public scrutiny and democratic accountability that legally audited accounts provide. It's a thriving culture of which Mafia bosses would be deeply proud, much less EU Commissioners.

It can't be easy to be an EU Commissioner. Deeply committed to the ideology inherent in the European social model, they are compelled to believe in a mythology that insists capitalism is the enemy. The story is compelling: Big Business is less efficient and less corrupt than Big Government. And oh yes, with the UN having "settled" the scientific issue, carbon fundamentalism must become a governing principles in the David vs. Goliath fight against climate change.

Except, it seems, for one teensy irritation: heavy, energy-using industries, responsible for Europe's prosperity, aren't playing ball. By 2008, the EU bureaucracy and European heavy industry were locking horns over the prospective imposition of sweeping climate laws by the following spring, in particular, tough new legislation aimed at cutting CO_2 emissions by 20 percent (from 1992 levels) by 2020. The bureaucrats intend to achieve this by rolling in energy and other heavy industries into the European Trading Scheme (ETS) and forcing them to have to buy greenhouse gas emission permits from 2013. But energy and other firms, anticipating giant income drops, decided to "vote with their feet" and have, over recent years, dropped a litany of investment projects worth billions of dollars, with reports that some firms are contemplating leaving Europe altogether.

"A lot of investment projects have been cancelled in the last couple of months," Johannes Teyssen, CEO of German utility E.ON, told a press conference in February 2009. Presenting a new World Energy Council report "Europe's Vulnerability to Energy Crises,"[17] Teyssen added, "You can't count fast enough how many of them get cancelled now. Every week a project is cancelled." Teyssen said he knew of at least four power station projects in Germany alone cancelled since the beginning of 2008, with the potential cost of CO_2 permits cited as a major reason. And Teyssen warned the EU that, "Full auctioning (of CO_2 permits) could lead to more vulnerability." Under current EU proposals energy companies will have to pay for their pollution quotas from 2013 with other energy-heavy user industries gradually phased in to the program thereafter.

Der Spiegel reported in February 2008 that while energy profits generally were up, "Germany's energy sector is in turmoil."[18] Germany's nuclear power plants are due to be taken offline entirely by 2020 with others moth-balled. To replace them, a raft of 26 or so new coal-fired plants are due to be built over the next decade. However, the imposition of binding carbon targets and extra cost of CCS storage presents a serious threat to their financial viability. In January 2008, Hans-Peter Villis, chief executive of German utility EnBw said that Germany risks power shortages unless it builds more power stations, and may be forced to re-think its nuclear exit plan. And the cloud forming over new plans for coal-fired power stations is being felt beyond Germany. The UK, Italy, Spain, and the Netherlands are among the countries where coal is also re-emerging as the fuel of choice for power plants. Coal is the one hydrocarbon fuel Europe possesses, and in abundance. Ironically, it is the EU's self-imposed target of 20 percent of its power from alternative energy sources by 2020 that will require many new power stations to be built — as back-up facilities, because of the lack of reliability of newly established renewable energy sources.

Meanwhile, in a bid to meet ambitious EU renewable targets, companies have already begun rolling out expensive carbon cutting plans. In 2008, Germany's RWE announced a $44.5 billion renewable investment plan to cut its carbon emission by 60 million tons per year by 2015. It is a move analysts at Citigroup said could only limit future shareholder returns diverting money into green technology instead of dividends. And just to add to industry woes the EU has been additionally considering rolling carbon capture and storage (CCS) into the trading scheme equation. Considered a crucial technology for the prevention of CO_2 emissions, it will, once again, greatly add to the cost of electricity production. Yet, EU Energy Commissioner Andris Piebalgs informed a group of 14 major energy executives that until 2013 at least "there is no money" in EU budgets to support CCS projects. Given the expense of potential CCS technology, neither public nor private sector funding is likely to be forthcoming on a commercial scale either. According to figures presented at the European Business Summit in Brussels, Europe's overall investments and venture capital flow into clean energies has been in decline since the 1980s, amounting currently to just one-third of the US investments in the sector.

France-based Alstom SA, Europe's largest coal-fired plant maker, has stated that the current carbon strategy lacks funding of $18 billion. In 2008, the EU called on its 27 member states to subsidize the necessary CSS projects. While "clean coal" technology breakthroughs may make CO_2 capture more possible, it seems that it will fall on national governments and the energy companies themselves to stump up payment, which will inevitably be passed on to customers.

As if all this is not enough, the EU continued throughout 2008 to pursue the break-up of energy majors through its unbundling policy, to allow new competition into the market. However, eight countries, headed by Germany and France, aimed to sink the proposal via court action. Yet another summit meeting to resolve the impasse at the end of February 2009 failed to achieve its goal. Major EU member states are clearly determined to defend against the break-up of their national champions. Weakened energy majors would of course not only leave disparate elements open to foreign takeover, but reduce their capacity to amass the financial muscle necessary to meet the very climate obligations the EU seeks to impose.

Resistance to binding emission laws has been building from all quarters. In November 2007, the International Air Transport Association (IATA) warned that 170 countries opposed the EU's carbon proposals, as they would impose billions in extra costs on an industry that makes a global profit of just $5.6 billion. In January 2008, the Confederation of European Paper Industries warned that including them in the ETS reforms would wipe out paper industry profits entirely. Peugeot cars next chimed in adding that any CO_2 legislation must be tailored to industry cycles as cars for the market in 2012 were already in development. The European Trade Confederation also fears that a serious loss of jobs, including 50,000 in the steel industry, are highly likely as key industries consider moving to "lower cost areas." Business Europe Secretary General Philippe de Buck has written to the Commission president pointing out that the auctioning of a permits system will harm "the competitiveness of Europe."

Even so, in the face of such mounting opposition, European President Jose Manuel Barroso felt able to announce "historic" plans to make Europe "the first economy for the low-carbon age" declaring the cost "manageable." Having announced the EU's "world lead" in fighting climate change in 2007, it seems Mr Barroso has been determined not to lose face. But, if data from the US Energy Information Administration (EIA, published 1 March 2008) is right, the EU is already set to do so. CO_2 emissions in the USA fell by 1.8 percent in 2006, compared to a 0.3 percent rise in emissions in the EU. In fact, between 2000 and 2006 the US maintained an annual rate of increase in CO_2 emissions of just one-third of 1 percent compared to the EU's more than 1 percent over the period. For all the berating of US climate policy, it is the US reliance on technological advances that continues to eclipse the EU's climate rhetoric.

To cap it all, according to figures published in early March 2008 by the Hadley Center for Climate Prediction, world average temperatures over the twelve months of 2007 *cooled* — a trend that has continued to late in 2009 — entirely wiping out the warming trend over the previous century. But, in the carbon fundamentalist scheme of things, *how is this possible*? Global CO_2 emissions should still be *climbing*. The bottom line? Evidence for a menacingly high price tag for unproven carbon fundamentalist beliefs may yet prevent Eurocrat carbon fundamentalism morphing into draconian climate laws. So will facts being "durable things" trump Eurocrat carbon fundamentalism? Energy and heavy industry leaders, and *non*-believers everywhere, could only hope so.

EUROPE'S KYOTO "BAILOUT"

It has to be the irony of ironies. Just as Obama's New Green Deal was set to seal the US finally buying *into* the Kyoto/European model of planet-saving after the president took office in January 2009, EU nation states steadily embarked on a European bail*out* from their Kyoto-sponsored commitments.

As the full horror of the cost of cap and trade binding targets sank in, the leaders of EU states lined up, CO_2 sick notes in hand, to "renegotiate" their carbon "obligations." Of course, green ideologues everywhere are blaming the loss of political will of former carbon crusading leaders on the credit crunch. But the fact is, before the ink was dry on the Kyoto Protocol — as a few of us were saying way back then — it was the George W. Bush administration *not* the EU which was grasping the full industry-busting economic ramifications of Kyoto.[19]

Europe's industrialists had been warning vociferously enough. But it was only when the credit crunch turned up the hearing aids for ideologically poor of hearing Eurocrats in 2008 that the latter were forced to listen. Suddenly, Germany's so-called Green Chancellor, anti-CO_2 crusader Angela Merkel began turning shades of red, as political "back-pedalling" became the latest EU renewable. With the potential of a legally binding agreement on CO_2 cuts looming at an EU climate summit in late 2008, the list of carbon rebels had grown to include some of the EU's big hitters. By October 2008, Germany and Italy were now in cahoots.

By 2008, Italy was estimating the cost of complying with its imposed target would be 25 billion euros ($32 billion) a year. A research report concluded that Germany could lose around 300,000 jobs by 2020.[20] In fact, German industrialists, by late 2008, were urging a moratorium on the climate package and have since been lobbying hard for the Chancellor to cut the political climate rhetoric before German industry takes up permanent residence beyond its own borders. Essentially, Germany's public support for the Italian position — Germany and Italy being Europe's leading manufacturers — was already making a 27-state approved EU climate package look a political impossibility.

Poland and at least eight other eastern European countries with coal-dependent power stations have long lobbied against a non-voluntary CO_2 cutting European Trading Scheme (ETS) regime. Even some last-minute carrot dangling by France in 2008, offering the prospect of millions of euros of free carbon emission allowances (halving their emission allowance quota until 2016), failed to head off the fears of the eastern European nations. France and Austria too asked the EU to ease its climate ambitions of 20 percent reduction in CO_2 emissions from 1990 levels and 20 percent of power from renewable sources both by 2020.

The EU and the UN each see themselves as a federal-style "government-in-waiting." Thus both were desperate to cobble together some kind of world-changing agreement at the Copenhagen climate summit in December 2009. Both saw a Copenhagen-sponsored global energy-climate consensus as pivotal to their planet-saving proposals. With a European legally-binding agreement — the first of its kind globally — and with an Obama White House prospectively on board and ready to sign the US up to a "Kyoto II," EU and UN world stock would never have been higher. To that end, in desperation just prior to the summit, the UN's IPCC chair, Rajendra Pachauri, called on the EU to "show the way" to the rest of the world. If the EU could not, Pachauri believed, "all attempts to manage the problem of climate change will collapse."[23] As we now know, "collapse" is precisely what happened.

The fact is, if no global agreement was possible at Copenhagen, largely because nations like China, India, and Brazil were simply not prepared to forego hydrocarbon-fuelled industrialization, it will not be possible anywhere. Equally, the developed nations are hardly likely to sign up to economic suicide by footing the enormous bill demanded by the industrializing nations as a penalty for their previous fossil-fuel, carbon emitting ways.

But the fact is that *any* deal on binding emission cuts directly threatens the renaissance of a key energy resource for the West: coal. The UK needs urgently to build six new coal-fired power stations. America has masses of the stuff — much of it high quality. And while the Brussels agenda may prefer that Russia, Poland, the UK, the Czechs etc. all leave their coal in the ground, the need for European energy diversity and the EU's push for more (CO_2-neutral) nuclear power is working against it. Europe needs to get real. If it leaves its coal in the ground, it would have to rely even more on natural gas. Russian natural gas, mostly. What then of the EU's other high priority, divergence away from Russian energy dependence?

And the bottom line, globally? China is bringing online one coal-fired power plant a week. India is fast-industrializing using coal-fired power. Both render carbon cutting agreements worldwide meaningless. Over 40 coal-fired plants are in planning across Europe over the next five years with 26 planned for Germany alone.[24] The World Bank has been investing enormously in coal projects around the world in recent years. Clean or otherwise, King Coal is set to continue punching massive holes in global carbon emission targets. In a market where carbon prices have already collapsed, just imagine the scale of the carbon taxes for which these burgeoning state industries would be liable if a Kyoto model was *ever* adopted.

For the Kyoto Protocol and any of its successors to succeed, carbon emission targets must be binding. However, if it cannot even be achieved in an ideologically-committed socialist Europe, *then where*? No wonder the EU and UN fear they are witnessing their anti-carbon strategies going up in smoke. And what does that say about the chances for President Obama's cap and trade campaign under the New Green Deal? A deal that includes the grandiose scheme to create millions of green collar jobs? Even on that score, once again, the "lead" given by Europe turns out to be anything but "as advertised."

GREEN JOBS: FAST-TRACKING ECONOMIC SUICIDE

Creating *ex nihilo* — literally, out of nothing — used to be a theological concept, God's prerogative. Today, it seems President Obama and certain Western politicians claim to possess the ability to perform it. Against all the laws of economics and the marketplace, President Obama and others believe they can create millions of "green" real jobs *ex nihilo*, literally, out of thin air, via cap and trade legislation.

If Obama and company would remove their politically green-tinted glasses for just a moment and take a long hard look at the experience of the "Old World" they profess to cite as "proven," they would discover that their glasses on green job creation have been rose-tinted all along. The basic assumption is that technology per se *generates* jobs. Mostly, it does not.

Rather, it is technology that *enables* jobs — real and genuinely sustainable jobs — based on how useful the technology is to the marketplace.

Figure 2.2: *Source: Energy Tribune*

To generate real *industrial* jobs, however, you need a basic commodity to trade, such as oil, gas or coal. Yet "green" politicians and eco-lobbyists expect to create a revolution in green jobs based on . . . renewable energy sources. The trouble is that alternative energy technologies currently don't work. That is to say, they remain appallingly inefficient, offering a very poor energy return on investment. Cut off the flow of massive public subsidies and the alternative energy industrial revolution would grind to a halt — as the European experience bears out.

What the EU-style experience actually shows is that for every green job created per installed MW power, a real job is *destroyed* elsewhere in the economy. Not to mention, it aids the reduction of competitiveness, investment in expansion and, ultimately, promotes the relocation of major companies to countries without draconian carbon regimes that drive otherwise unnecessary energy price hikes.

It's a shame that the members of the US Congress who voted for the Cap and Trade Climate Bill did not bother to check up on the economic realities that are causing European states to back away from their expensive alternative energy commitments and the "green job" creation schemes associated with them. Specifically, how the EU version of cap and trade is actually replete with substance-emptying "get-out" clauses.

Germany's Angela Merkel has already insisted on major exemptions for German heavy industry had binding emissions targets been agreed at Copenhagen in 2009. Hardly, the domestic agenda of a "Green Chancellor" who is a true believer in the low-carbon "green jobs" economy.

Italy also rocked the EU climate boat by insisting on exemptions for

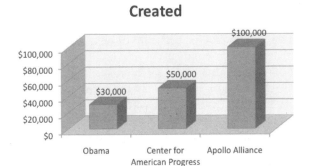

Figure 2.3: Green job chart.

its own energy-intensive industries in late 2008.[25] Most significantly, it was an exemption that required the EU to renegotiate Europe's entire climate policy after the UN summit in December 2009 — effectively, giving Italy a veto. A veto it would have used if, as they did, China and India and others had not demanded their own exemptions sinking the summit's chief objective. In June 2009, deputy head of Poland's Solidarity trade union, Jaroslaw Grzesik, estimated that the EU's climate policy would cost 800,000 European jobs. The think-tank Open Europe has already estimated that the same policies would cost the UK $9 billion a year, leaving an extra 1 million in fuel poverty by 2020.[26]

These are the real world economics for "countries like Spain, Germany and Japan" that Barack Obama insisted in January 2009 were "surging ahead of us" in the low carbon-green jobs revolution. Cited as a role model, Spain is the only country to have produced an in-depth analysis of the impact of renewables on the jobs market. Now, if you are squeamish about having economic theories about green job creation blown away, move on to Chapter 3.

SPAIN'S RED-FACED GREENS

The *Study of the Effects on Employment of Public Aid to Renewable Energy Sources*[27] was published by the team at the Universidad Rey Juan Carlos in March 2009. Though it grabbed a few headlines in the spring, it was largely ignored by the mainstream press; yet it is the most intensive review of the impact of a state-aided green job creation policy available.

Here are just a few of its key statements suggesting why the state should stay the heck out of manipulating the job creation market:

- "Despite its hyper-aggressive (expensive and extensive) 'green jobs' policies . . . **Spain has created a surprisingly low number of jobs.**"
- "Since 2000 **Spain has spent €571,138 ($800K) to create each 'green job,'** including subsidies of more than €1million ($1.4million) per wind industry job."
- "The programs creating those jobs also resulted in the destruction of nearly 110,500 jobs elsewhere in the economy or **2.2 jobs destroyed for every 'green job' created.**"
- "**Each 'green' megawatt installed destroys 5.28 jobs on average** elsewhere in the economy: 8.99 by photovoltaics (solar), 4.27 by wind energy, 5.05 by mini-hydro" [our emphasis].

The report also notes that according to Spain's energy regulator, "The price of a comprehensive electricity rate (paid by the end consumer) in Spain would have to be increased 31 percent to repay the historic debt generated by the subsidies to renewables."

The report cites key examples of "massive unemployment, loss of capital, dismantlement of productive facilities and perpetuation of inefficient ones"[28] the direct result of, "the arbitrary, state-established price systems inherent in 'green energy' schemes." The report also cites specific examples of domestic companies choosing not to expand specifically because of the carbon regime, and other companies indicating they would move abroad if binding carbon schemes forced up energy prices making them less competitive.

At each stage the study highlights clear and compelling statistics in support of its findings and expansively reveals its rationale for coming to the conclusions it does. In doing so it carries a stark warning for any state desiring to pursue the same economy-busting, job-destroying path. It concludes, "Policymakers must recognize that because of government action, other jobs are not created." And, most significantly for international consumption, "These costs do not appear to be unique to Spain's approach but instead are largely inherent in schemes to promote renewable energy sources."

President Obama maintains his planned 5 million new jobs will cost the taxpayer $30,000 per job. Bad enough, we might think. But The Center for American Progress, whose CEO headed up Obama's transition team, calculates it would take government spending of $100 billion to create 2 million green jobs.[29] That's a bill for the US taxpayer of $50,000 per every "green job" created. The Apollo Alliance, whose founder served on Obama's campaign team, calculated it would take $500 billion to create 5 million jobs. That's a mere $100,000 per green job created.[30] Commenting on these figures, the Institute for Energy Research (IER) demonstrates how the market itself is far better at creating real jobs, including using Google as an example. The IPR says, "Without imposing on the American taxpayer, they [Google] made a superior product for consumers creating 20,000 new jobs. As a result humanity reaps the benefit . . . and, as an added bonus, Google pays millions in taxes each year."

Real and sustainable industrial jobs are market-led, technology-aided, *not* state-subsidized and technology-inefficient. Real jobs are not created *ex nihilo*. The Obama administration, like the EU leadership, is not a team of miracle-workers. They cannot buck the trend of how the market works. Worrying about others "surging ahead" hardly matters once the realization that it is the fast-track to economic suicide becomes clear.

The plain truth is, "green jobs" are just not good for the economy, stupid.

THE CHINA FACTOR AT COPENHAGEN

The elephant in the room full of sclerotic European politicians and ideologues from the US Obama administration is that there is no chance that China would ever have played along with any mandatory Copenhagen accord.

China's top climate representative walked out of a meeting in Bangkok in October 2009, two months before the Copenhagen Summit, over the Kyoto Protocol, finding little to agree with the Western countries, especially the Europeans who have much less to lose. Almost whimsically, the Chinese are all too agreeable to be Gored by Al (even without bothering to perform any independent scientific research of their own), and are ready to go along with slogans that the internal combustion engine and carbon emissions are the "biggest threat to humankind," as long as whatever needs to be done is done by the "rich countries." Clearly, if China does not play along the entire planet-saving movement is doomed.

But China, the world's manufacturing behemoth, and an ever careful up and coming revived superpower, does not want to take any chances. The threat of carbon tariffs proposed by countries such as France, Germany, and the United States worries the Chinese enough that two major reports, one by the NDRC, the country's highest authority, were released in late 2009 on how to cope with the situation. Both reports suggested that China may start collecting carbon taxes in the next five years. While on the surface such tax may appear ludicrous, increasing the cost of energy and products in China itself, it is actually a masterstroke.

The logic, as outlined in the Chinese reports, is compelling. Since the 2008–09 global financial downturn, trading frictions have been surfacing. Climate change related initiatives and carbon tariffs by Western countries are nothing more than trading protection schemes, using the pretext of climate change to put pressure on China, especially under the new economic situation. The clincher for the Chinese is this: carbon tariffs not only violate the World Trade Organization (WTO) free trading and most-favored-nation status principles, they also violate the Kyoto Protocol and the tenet of "different responsibility." This kind of trading protection will have a fatal effect on the economic future of developing countries, prominent among which is China.

Because carbon tariffs from the developed countries are to push the developing countries towards "promising" carbon emission reduction, saying "no" to the pressure of carbon tariffs is not a safe option. A proper measure has to be adopted, such as collecting carbon tax by China before a carbon tariff is charged in a foreign country. The reports conclude that if China sets a national policy to collect carbon tax, it will be considered as a "promise" for carbon reduction by the international community.

After applying a carbon tax, carbon tariffs on the same product by Western countries would amount to double taxation, expressly not allowed by the WTO. Without carbon tax in China, carbon tariffs might be permitted by the WTO. This will put pressure on the US to reconsider carbon tariff legislation. For the Chinese, passing these costs to foreign consumers and finding new tax revenues can look very good domestically by reducing other taxes.

The reports actually suggest starting with energy tax collection immediately, gradually transforming the energy tax to carbon tax in four to five years time. The actual action should be consistent with the international climate change legislations, such as the expiration of the Kyoto Protocol in 2012.

The message from China is clear. The country is not eager to jump on climate-related initiatives but it will not allow other countries to collect carbon tariffs on products made in China. Taxes can be collected and kept in-house, as an energy tax or a carbon tax or whatever name one likes to call it.

Actually, China has been trying hard to reduce real pollution and emissions along with it — thousands of small and old inefficient coal-fired power plants have been shut down and more will be eliminated in the coming years. Equipment was installed on 60 percent of the coal-fired power plants to scrub sulfur and to remove particulates, and more improvements are underway. Zero emission nuclear power capacity has been planned to increase ten-fold over the next 10 years and a lot of money has been invested on wind power.

But China's GDP (gross domestic product) per capita is still one of the lowest in the world, only $3,300 in 2008, about one-fifteenth of the US. For even a semblance of catch up moves, China needs a lot of energy, especially cheap and abundant local coal. The country will simply not sacrifice its economic development for a Western "climate change" which, if real and anthropogenic, is not a concern for the Chinese, it being a Western creation. Pushing China towards a massive emission reduction will simply force China to play the name game, changing "energy tax" to "carbon tax," which, ultimately, would be paid by Western consumers.

But if the political rhetoric and strategies of Western leaders increasingly reflects the green-tinged, vote-grabbing, short-termist, political "disconnect" helping to overshadow the energy realities, Western energy policy *per se* is today largely being driven and influenced not by hard facts, but by beliefs in two "juggernaut" *theories*: peak oil and climate change. It is these theories that are responsible for the current skewing of international, trans-national and national core energy policies. Primarily, it is these theories that are propelling Western governments *away* from cheap energy policies (policies that especially penalize the poorest in society), towards economy-sapping green taxes (that fail entirely to impact the environment or conserve energy) all in pursuit of an illusory holy grail: the great *ideological* "switchover" from hydrocarbon-based to alternative energy-based economies.

But *why* is the great energy "switchover" proving such an economic disaster? Just why is the alternative energy renewables revolution seemingly permanently dependent on the life-supporting "oxygen" of government handouts?

Notes

1 "Miliband Promises More Green Jobs But Vestas Wind Turbine Plant Is Closing," *The Times*, July 9, 2009.
2 "Britain's Energy Crisis," *The Economist*, August 9, 2009.
3 "Promoters Overstated The Environmental Benefit of Windfarms," *Daily Telegraph*, December 20, 2008.
4 "Windpower Is a Complete Disaster," op-ed comment by Michael J. Trebilcock, *National Post*, April 8, 2009.
5 "The Myth of the Danish Green Energy 'Miracle,'" comment by Michael J. Trebilcock, *National Post*, May 11, 2009.
6 US Energy Information Administration study reported at: www.msnbc. msn.com/id/25368258
7 "Shell Goes Cold on Wind, Solar, Hydrogen Energy," *Reuters*, March 17, 2009.
8 "Why Europe's Renewables Roadshow is Rolling Stateside," Peter C. Glover, *American Chronicle*, May 1, 2009.
9 "Wind Energy Company REPower Moves to Denver," *Portland Business Journal*, August 15, 2009.
10 "Pickens Continues Drive For New Energy Resources," Associated Press, July 14, 2009.
11 "Just 96 Months to Save The World, says Prince Charles," *The Independent*, July 9, 2009.

12 "Gaia's Right: Environmentalism Seeks to Return Us to the Age of the Kings," *National Review Online*, July 11, 2009.

13 Open Letter to British Prime Minister Gordon Brown, dated December 19, 2007 and copied to Queen Elizabeth II and members of British scientific community.

14 Lao Tzu Quotes, Altius Directory at http://www.altiusdirectory.com/Society/lao-tzu-quotes.php

15 UN Secretary General Ban Ki-Moon, Remarks to the Global Environment Forum, UN News Centre at http://www.un.org/apps/news/infocus/sgspeeches/search_full.asp?statID=557

16 "World Dependent on Fossil Fuels for a Century," Reuters, July 15, 2009.

17 "Europe's Vulnerability to Energy Crisis," study published by the World Energy Council on February 6, 2008.

18 "Energy Giants Groan as Tough Future Looms," *Der Spiegel*, February 1, 2008.

19 While Kyoto laid down no penalties for failure to meet national commitments, Copenhagen 2009 was supposed to remedy the lack of teeth of Kyoto.

20 "Merkel To Defend German Jobs Against Climate Deal," AFP, December 8, 2008.

21 House of Lord's Hansard debates, extract at http://www.parliament.the-stationery-office.com/pa/ld200708/ldhansrd/text/81117-0006.htm

22 Climate Law "Could Cost Billions," BBC News online reporting the UK Government's Impact Assessment o the profposed new Climate Bill, November 25, 2008.

23 "Africa Meeting Key Step in Climate Talks," UN climate chief, AFP, August 20, 2008.

24 "German Greens Fight Coal-fired Power Station Plan," *The Independent*, March 23, 2007.

25 "Italy Defies EU Summit Deal on Climate," *Euractiv*, December 9, 2008.

26 "EU Climate Package to Cost UK £9 billion per annum," press release issued by the independent think-tank Open Europe, October 9, 2008.

27 http://www.juandemariana.org/pdf/090327-employment-public-aid-renewable.pdf

28 The report cites "massive unemployment" as especially hitting the energy-intensive industries, those including iron and steel, basic chemicals, plastics, transformation of base metals, and cement.

29 *Green Recovery*, a report by the American Center for Progress, published September 2008.

30 "Does Green Energy Add Five Million Jobs?" *Wall Street Journal*, November 7, 2008.

3

Renewable Energy: The Doomed Revolution

Success is going from failure to failure without losing enthusiasm.

Winston Churchill

We live in a postmodern world, so we are told. In the former world of the modern enlightenment, hard empirical facts, *reasoned* faith and speculative theory all vied for intellectual dominance in the public mind. To understand the postmodern mind, however, it is important to grasp its one key doctrinal *absolutism* — an irony totally lost on the postmodernist mind — that truth, *all* truth, is relative. Thus, the postmodern mind is not concerned with the certainties of absolute or empirical truth. Facts and reasoned logic derived from facts are all relative. No wonder hard data, facts and reasoned thinking are having such a hard time of it in the mainstream of public square debate.

In the postmodern world, authority, doctrines, laws, rules, judgment, and dogma are "intolerant," so they are out. Nature — in this case human nature — abhorring a vacuum has to fill the intellectual void with something, however. So we have seen the rise of the age of speculative theory presented *as if it were* fact. In such a climate idealistic romanticism marginalizes empirical, perhaps more complex, truth, preferring to deem whatever the transient "consensus" may be as "current truth." How else could science research and the mass media regularly collude on the latest "threat to humankind" in the form of a whole litany of viruses, threats and other scaremongering that ultimately come to naught — and keep getting away with it? Mark Twain famously commented on this early trend away from empirical evidence, observing: "There is something fascinating about science. One gets such wholesale returns of conjecture out of such a trifling investment of fact." One does indeed.

Thus it becomes easy to see, in the prevailing atmosphere of anti-intellectual, fact-averse public square debate, how "experts" become celebrity headline grabbers — and magnets for government research cash. The more chilling their pronouncement the more regularly the mass media — it's great for ratings — is likely to book them. In the era of the 30-second TV sound bite, how a new generation of prophets of doom, those who have exchanged the "white collars" of yesterday's religious prophets for the "white coats" of a pseudo-scientific persona.

Fascinating as all this may be, you ask, *what has any of this to do with the theories associated with renewable energy?* Good question. *Everything*, we answer. Once upon a time it would have been possible to dislodge the false notions of popular science or a fashionable consensus lodged in the public consciousness. Not in the postmodern age. Facts having become "optional" romantic notions, have a habit today of propelling a widespread false belief in the view that renewable energy is a serious contender in the future energy mix. The age of renewable energy, so many today insist, can, indeed *must*, revolutionize and supersede the fossil-burning, hydrocarbon age. For them, it is simply a question of political will or, literally, "mind over matter." But what may have become a no brainer for some, is set to be confounded by the facts surrounding matter itself, which for the reason of simple math is just not playing ball with today's idealistic mindset.

As most energy insiders already know, renewable energy, while it *does* have a minor, supportive role to play in the overall energy scheme of things, is negligible. And yet, it is the erroneous *blind* faith — very different from *reasoned* faith — in the viability of renewable energy as a future energy "solution" that is currently driving massive public investment in alternative energy projects. To borrow a catchword of our times, that is "*un*sustainable" in the longer term. Before turning to *why* this is the case, we would ask our readers to bear in mind all that has been said here about the anti-intellectual postmodern mindset as it is equally pertinent to other notions of popular science, especially alarmist predictions associated with the twin issues currently panicking us in the direction of the global "quick-fix" renewables revolution. They are: **peak oil** (the theory that the oil will quickly run out) and **global warming/climate change alarmism** (the theory that CO_2 from fossil fuel burning is catastrophically warming up the earth).

We will come to these two in Chapters 4–6. But first, we must deal with the hard facts, which identify the path to a more realistic energy strategy than that touted by "green" politicians and eco-activists; those who, too often, are setting national energy agendas.

THE ALICE IN WONDERLAND WORLD OF THE GREENS

"Curiouser and curiouser," said Alice. Not an unnatural response to the wholesale departure from common sense she experienced at the Mad

Hatter's Tea Party. And we have precisely the same head-scratching response to the refusal of green ideologues to grasp the energy realities of our age, especially as they affect the role for what we refer to as "renewable"[1] energy sources.

If any particular group could be said to be emblematic for those setting the agenda for Greenism in our age, it is Greenpeace. In 2007, Greenpeace produced a film called "The Convenient Solution," which put forward the case for renewable energy's "urgent" solution. Introducing the film on their website, Greenpeace say, "We all know that, to stop climate change, we need to stop burning fossil fuels." Within minutes of the film getting under way then, we are informed of the "unnecessary dependence on fossil fuels." The Greenpeace Gospel claims "we all know" that mankind's use of fossil fuels emits carbon dioxide, a greenhouse gas that *significantly contributes to anthropogenic global warming.*

As "entirely missing the mark" statements go, this one is up there with the publication of Mark Twain's premature obituary. The hundreds of scientists and informed climate observers who signed the Manhattan Declaration[2] (both authors of this book are signatories) clearly don't "already know." Neither do a raft of the world's leading climatologists and scientists who have made their views publicly known in Japan,[3] the UK,[4] Australia,[5] Russia,[6] New Zealand,[7] Denmark,[8] Poland,[9] the United States,[10] and hundreds[11] of other prominent scientists,[12] not to mention that more Americans now believe that planetary trends rather than human activity are responsible for any degree of warming there has been[13] while over half the British population (and growing) now

Figure 3.1: *Source: Energy Tribune*

doesn't accept that climate change is man-made.[14] Indeed of the famous 2,000+ who proclaimed to "know" on behalf of the UN's IPCC, and set the global agenda on climate, it seems a mere 20 percent (around 400) worked in *any* climate science capacity.[15] None of which should come as a surprise when even the UN's own objective climate data reveals that the latest cycle of global warming ended in 1998.[16] So when Greenpeace states: "We all know . . ." what they actually mean is all committed Green ideologues "know."

It is this apocalyptic sense of impending doom created by Greens that, together with a mainstream media with a shameful penchant for scaremongering, has set in motion the panicky international energy-climate renewable energy juggernaut. The EU has today set itself the target of producing 20 percent of its energy from renewable sources by 2020. President Obama has promised to double US renewable energy production within three years, up from under 10 percent at present and up a further 25 percent by 2025. Obama's ultimate goal is to set a course for an 80 percent reduction in fossil fuel use by 2050. The high priest of green alarmism, Al "Planet" Gore, goes way further, demanding the US target 100 percent from renewable energy sources *within a decade.*[17] Basic physics and facts don't figure highly when you are a snubbed "next-president-of-these-United-States," it seems.

As we have already noted, by 2030, while world energy demand is likely to increase by 50 percent, all serious projections agree that oil, gas, and coal — hydrocarbons — will account for around 87 percent of world energy production. That's at least the same and even an *increase* from the situation currently. Somebody's math somewhere is clearly wildly awry. So let's look at some brief basic facts about renewable sources, before we address wind power, the key renewable, in greater detail.

WIND POWER

Wind power is the flagship green energy industry if renewables are to become a serious player in the global energy mix. Indeed, so central is wind power to the success[18] of the entire renewable energy program that we devote a whole section to its viability later in this chapter. A typical and, deliberate at times confusion by wind promoters, organizations and even government officials, is the fact that they do not distinguish between installed capacity and actual power output into the system. Neither do the government or the industry give us "like for like" costs when speaking about the cost of wind power. These are obvious and serious discrepancies, and it frequently blurs reality with fantasy and sloganeering.

SOLAR POWER

Solar power requires high subsidies because the best solar cells have to be grown from silicon crystals, an extremely slow and costly process. While new solar technologies are addressed, solar power is unlikely to become a commercially feasible source of energy anytime soon. But while reliable solar energy in less sunnier climes is a key drawback, even sunny countries like Spain[19] are finding the high rate of heavy subsidies difficult to sustain.

In the US, far less than 0.1 percent of the 7 percent of energy currently produced from renewable sources is achieved from solar sources. Both the wind and solar industries continue to demand more of the public pie. Yet, as a *Wall Street Journal* editorial commenting on the EIA's standardized figures has pointed out, "Wind and solar have been on the subsidy take for years, and they still account for less than 1 percent of total net electricity generation."[20]

What is clear is that solar energy needs a major new technological breakthrough. But while a breakthrough may reduce costs, there are two other unassailable facts: solar works where there is sun, but even then it is a very diffuse energy source (the sun, the source of the energy, itself being 93 million miles away). Thus, it requires large and expensive facilities to produce any energy of relevant capacity on an industrial scale, even in the sunniest climes. And even then it needs back-up facilities — and additional cost. In short, without government intervention, it is well beyond market viability.

WATER (HYDRO, TIDAL) AND GEOTHERMAL

Some Greens already hate hydroelectric because of the widespread effect it has on the environment. They would, if they knew the facts, hate the notion of geothermal too, in view of the type of facilities that it would need to produce feasible, commercial, energy capacity. Equally, hydroelectric and geothermal facilities are very site specific. One cannot generate new mountains laden with running water nor can a geothermal anomaly with prolific hot water or steam reservoirs on tap be made to order.

There is nothing wrong with either hydroelectric or geothermal[21] per se, but they happen where they happen and cannot be manufactured anywhere else. Indeed, more hydroelectric dams are being dismantled today — including 200 across the US alone in the last decade — than are built, due to their massive environmental impact. Equally, as we shall see, the need for vast amounts of water becomes a problem in itself. Tidal energy has been just talk for at least 40 years, an academic exercise with little relation to implementation reality.

BIOFUEL/BIOMASS

Biofuel is perhaps the biggest energy scam, ever. People hate to hear statistics like this, but biofuels present what energy insiders call a *negative net energy balance*. That means they require more energy to produce than is contained in the final product. But even ignoring this science, if we were to use all of the corn grown in the US to produce motor vehicle fuel, without regard to what that would do to food prices, it would still be less than 20 percent of the gasoline demand — and a lot of the world would go hungry.

The EIA study mentioned above (see "Solar power") reported that ethanol and biofuels received a whopping subsidy of $5.72 per 1 million British Thermal Units (MMBTU) compared to just 3 cents per MMBTU for natural gas and petroleum products.[22] In short, biofuels from primary biomass make no economic sense.

NUCLEAR

Environmentalists can't decide whether nuclear power should be classed as a renewable energy source. On the whole, most green ideologues have been anti-nuclear from the beginning. But, by opposing its proliferation they end up shooting themselves in their own carbon-reducing footprint, given it is largely carbon emission-free. Nuclear has been particularly targeted by the environmental movement in its history of anti-energy campaigning. That's a shame, as the EIA reveals nuclear power, as we shall shortly see, receives 15 times less in subsidies than wind.[23]

So what can we conclude? We know from our history that an irrational fear of "climate apocalypse" and the arbitrary actions of the "weather gods" has driven nature-worshipping green ideologues' fears in every generation. Being inherently anti-capitalist in our day, they care little whether their demands threaten to bankrupt modern economies, or deny poorer nations the same hydrocarbon-powered path out of poverty taken by the industrialized developed nations. For many green ideologues, preposterous self-righteous claims are morally self-evident. Real World facts and reason are (postmodern) irrelevancies. So the push for unrealistic alternative sources of energy is all-consuming. "The adventures first," said the Gryphon to Alice, "explanations take such a long time."

So let us turn to the principle alternative energy source, wind power; upon which the success of the renewables revolution largely depends — with special reference to the European countries including Britain, Denmark, and Germany; those nations who claim a global lead in wind technology and, thus, in exporting the technology, and its underlying philosophy.

WIND POWER: THE FLAGSHIP RENEWABLE

If you have a hankering to see England's green and pleasant land or Britain's rugged coastline, you shouldn't wait too long. That is, before it disappears under the swirling of thousands of massive 400 foot tall wind turbines that the British government would like to erect. In 2007, former UK Industry Secretary John Hutton shocked UK energy insiders in the UK by proposing an unprecedented 25 gigawatts (GW) of offshore wind power capacity, adding to the 8 GW already in development. A grand plan aimed at powering *all* of Britain's 25 million homes as early as 2020.[24]

But even the British government cannot hide the fact that the cost of its proposals are huge, attracting no private equity of significance thus leaving the taxpayer to foot the entire bill. The full scale of Britain's commitment to wind power can be grasped if one considers that the 8 GW of wind power capacity already under construction will, by itself, give Britain a world lead in installed wind power.

WHY BRITAIN?

Currently, just 2 percent of the UK's power comes from renewable energy sources, with wind providing less than half on gigawatt (GW). (**Note:** Both here and elsewhere in this book the reader should be aware of the game played by renewables advocates between installed power capacity vs. actual contribution to the power grid. For wind, the latter may be as little as 5 percent and rarely above 25 percent.) So the former Industry Secretary's grand plan would mean an astonishing leap for the British wind power industry.

Of the 8 GW capacity currently planned, the London Array, with 271 wind turbines to be built in the Thames estuary, would be the world's largest plant providing one GW capacity on its own. The plan was to have the London Array operational by 2014 and powering around 750,000 homes. That was until Shell pulled the plug on its participation in 2009 when it dumped the bulk of its renewable energy program (recognizing there's no profit in it) and leaving the project looking for a big chunk of new investment.[25] If it ever gets built, the London Array would be upstaged by an even bigger project currently under consideration: the $6 billion Atlantic Array — a proposal to build 350 turbines off England's south-west coast.

John Hutton's plan would literally change the face of Britain. He told the BBC's "Politics Show" that it would mean around 7,000 turbines or *one every half-mile around the entire coast of Britain.*[26] His justification: "There is no way of making the shift to low-carbon technology without there being change and for that change to be visible and evident to people." And there it is, right there. The key to understanding wind and water renewables projects is the need for truly vast amounts of wind and water, land and sea, for industrial scale use.

WHO PAYS?

While the renewables-at-any-cost lobbies applauded Hutton's announcement, the more realistic wind energy groups were more circumspect. Welcoming the commitment to the goal of greater wind power sufficiency, even Gordon Edge, the British Wind Energy Association (BWEA) Director of Economics and Markets, described the government's plan as "pie in the sky."[27] Edge's view was that the plan suffered from one major flaw: private capital investment will not be forthcoming. Dan Lewis, of the Economic Research Council, added his opinion that the British government was "deluding itself on a grand scale. There will be no race by investors to build offshore wind farms."[28] These commentators recognized that, to date, the taxpayer has picked up the entire wind power tab — and would continue to do so.

THE REAL COST OF WIND POWER

Despite public subsidies to the UK wind industry of over $500 million the government has so far only seen that such a massive investment provided less than half of one percent of the UK's electricity needs. In August 2007, the BBC's Radio 4 *Costing the Earth* program had already whistle-blown on figures that revealed how government financial incentives were encouraging wind industry firms to cash in on massive government subsidies while building many land-based wind farms on non-viable sites.[29] Even in Europe's windiest country, it seems, the winds are just "too variable," with most turbines consistently under-performing and, at times, failing entirely.

Michael Jefferson, Policies Chairman of the World Renewable Energy Network and former Chief Economist with Shell, told BBC Radio 4's "*Costing the Earth*" that too many wind farms were being sited across the UK in areas without enough wind. Jefferson went further, stating he believed the renewables industry, encouraged by high public subsidies, were inclined to exaggerate both wind speeds and the amount of wind energy a farm can supply.

Figure 3.2: *Source: Energy Tribune.*

One of the main reasons for plants being built in the "wrong places" is the high cost of transporting the energy produced to the UK's national grid from more remote windier sites. The average load factor necessary to make a wind farm viable is a minimum of 30 percent. Many wind farms in the UK currently operate at less than 20 percent. Engineering consultant Jim Oswald told the BBC that many turbines underperformed because wind speeds in the UK were just "too variable." While wind power is currently the fastest growing renewable energy sector in the UK, it still only meets less than 0.5 percent of the nation's electricity needs. As the UK has a key natural advantage denied to other nations — the windiest in Europe — it should sound a warning note for green ideologues outside the UK, with far less advantageous geography.

Just days earlier, the British government was embarrassed when a leaked briefing paper to ministers was exposed in *The Guardian* newspaper.[30] The paper warned that Britain had no chance of getting anywhere near its EU energy target of 20 percent based on the faith (and cash) it was investing in the renewables industry. In the document, officials from the UK's Department of Trade and Industry urged ministers to work with the EU to obtain better "statistical interpretations of the target." The paper also acknowledged that the UK "has achieved little so far on renewable" and that even reaching a target of 9 percent of its energy, up from the 2 percent at a cost to the economy of £4 billion (almost $6 billion) annually, would be "challenging." Most damaging of all however, the document warned that renewables are a more expensive way of reducing carbon emissions than the European Emissions Trading Scheme (ETS). Given the disastrous year suffered by the ETS just prior to the breaking story, that was some admission.

Having analyzed figures submitted to the UK electricity watchdog, Ofgem on every farm's load factor, Engineering Consultant Jim Oswald explained to the BBC, "It's the power swings that worry us. Over a

20-hour period you can go from almost 100 percent wind output to 20 percent." Oswald believes that an over-reliance on wind power will result both in major power failures across the UK and an increase in electricity bills of up to 50 percent. But while nothing comes close to the capriciousness of nature itself, the wind industry has been less than "windy" on the severe technical difficulties.

GERMANY AND DENMARK: TILTING AT WINDMILLS?

In August 2007, Germany's *Der Spiegel* reported the rising incidence of "mishaps, breakdowns and accidents" associated with ever-larger turbines.[31] When one rotor blade broke away in Oldenburg, Northern Germany, leading to an examination of six others, the results proved so alarming that the authorities immediately ordered the other four to be shut down. The *Der Spiegel* article noted that manufacturer's promises that turbines would last for 20 years had proven "hollow." German manufacturers simply cannot build turbines fast enough to meet current demand. By late 2007, the German wind power industry had expanded by 40 percent, according to the German Wind Energy Association, providing work for 74,000 people. But the "success" of the industry is not allowing time for proper stress testing procedures.

Industry insider Jerome à Paris, writing on the *Oil Drum: Europe* website admitted in December 2007 that the industry was suffering from "unresolved technical difficulties with some turbine models that have been withdrawn from the market."[32] Given that turbines are the *backbone* of the wind industry, this has provided a further deterrent to investors — but not to governments, which have no compunction about wasting other people's money.

Equally, Denmark's status as global wind power pioneers via the oft-repeated claim that the country "generates 20 percent of its electricity demand from wind sources," proves, on an investigation of the actual facts, to be overblown. For a start (and importantly), 20 percent of Denmark's electricity is *not* supplied *continuously* from wind power.[33] And such is the variability of supply that it relies heavily on the proximity of near neighbors Norway and Sweden to take Denmark's regular excess capacity. Electricity, of course, cannot be stored. In 2003 its export figure for wind power electricity production was 84 percent, as Denmark found itself simply unable to absorb its own highly variable wind output capacity domestically. In light of this, and the scale of public subsidy in Denmark in 2006–07, the Danish government was under increasingly severe scrutiny from its own media, claiming wind power subsidy and industry were "out of control."

And, if increased wind power would at least mean some reduction in hydrocarbon use and thus a massive drop in carbon emissions, reality, in Denmark, again raised its ugly head. Wind power's inherently poor investment-energy return requires even further investment in high maintenance gas turbine back-up facilities to cope with wind's unreliability. Of course, gas use means *more* carbon emissions. Yet Greens continually cite Denmark as the key example of how wind power plays a central role in reducing carbon emissions. As the *Copenhagen Post*[34] has revealed, the Danish government has come under serious fire over its inflated claims for cuts in CO_2 emissions. It seems that less than a quarter of the Danish government's 66 million tons of carbon cuts (down from 71 million tons in 2007) were actually achieved domestically. It turns out that the government had included cuts achieved *overseas* through various climate projects in which Danish organizations were involved and through Denmark's participation in the European Trading Scheme, in its figures. The reality is quite different. In fact, Denmark has one of Europe's *highest* rates of per capita CO_2 emissions, and has been consistently cited by the European Environment Agency for having "not lived up to the Kyoto criteria."

According to *Wind Energy: The Case of Denmark*, a critical report published by the Danish Centre for Political Studies in 2009, Denmark only keeps its electricity supplies balanced by having the geographical benefits afforded by the close proximity of particular neighbors who, effectively, act as "electricity storage batteries."[35] At the same time Denmark has had to export up to half of the electricity production it was unable to use. In conclusion, the report cites the Danish wind experience as of "limited transferability" elsewhere. Denmark is not alone in inflating the wind power figures, however.

In December 2008, the UK wind farm industry too was forced to halve its own overblown claims for the benefits of wind power in reducing carbon emissions.[36] What the new figures meant in practical terms is that the UK's 2,400 onshore and offshore turbines would need, in reality, a further 100,000 turbines to be built to enable it to meet its Kyoto commitments by 2020. In short, the mass media's constant invoking of the Danish and British wind "experience" simply reflects how ill-informed many politicians and journalists are on the subject.

BIG BUSINESS AND THE DOT-COM BUBBLE FACTOR

Back in Britain, the high maintenance costs associated with the same problems Germany and Denmark have lately reported — problems that can only be exacerbated in even larger offshore plants — are yet to be reaped. Quite simply, the inability to store highly variable power output while sustaining a consistency of supply to the UK national grid (or to any grid system) presents major problems. On top of the enormous technical problems with turbines and maintenance, it becomes increasingly easy to understand why it takes the political will of government to plug the private investment funding gap.

A US report in 2008 about Silicon Valley's investments in clean energy technologies, Vinod Khosla, founder of Khosla Ventures (representing dozens of US clean energy companies) says he worries about over-investing by firms that don't understand the energy markets. "I worry about a repeat of the dot-com bubble," says Khosla, "Unfortunately we don't seem able to avoid these things."[37] He's not alone. In an astute article at *Energy Pulse.com* (June 2007) Consulting Engineer Brian Leyland warned that the entire alternative energy renewables investments boom may well turn into just another "dotcom bubble."[38] Leyland also notes that the boom in renewable energy is driven by "a belief that we must reduce emissions of manmade CO_2," that in turn "led to direct and indirect subsidies for otherwise non-economic renewables. These subsidies and tax breaks caused the boom. Without them, it wouldn't have happened."

In spring 2008, faced with a vastly expensive "Manhattan Project" for green energy proposals in America, the US EIA sought to standardize the cost of public subsidy per megawatt hour. It found that coal was subsidized at 44 cents, natural gas at 25 cents and nuclear power at $1.59. Wind power came in at $23.37 per energy unit. As high as it is for wind, subsidy for solar, however, is even higher at $24.34 per megawatt hour. It is easy to see why private sector investment steers well clear.

Why does wind power require CO_2 emitting gas turbine back-ups?

WIND POWER EXPOSED

Such facts as those above are not what President Obama's energy and climate strategists want to hear. So too it is anathema to Al Gore and other assorted luminaries touting renewable energy sources as the way to go if we are to get away from the "tyranny" of fossil fuels, and to mitigate global warming. As if these realities were not enough, remember oilman T. Bone Pickens' plan for wind farms across North America that was supposed to bring about a replacement for natural gas use for power generation and lead the US toward energy independence? Eventually, Pickens was forced to ditch the plan when the economics hit home. Instead Pickens came up with a much more realistic plan based on . . . a (hydrogen) natural gas alternative.

But for wishful thinkers however, wind remains the cornerstone of almost all environmentalist and social engineering proclamations. Europe, getting a head start, has had to cope with the reality borne by experience however, and Europe's early pioneers, Denmark, Germany and Spain, have all been forced to scale back their claims — and their subsidies.

As a result in the summer of 2009, the UK, under pressure to meet an ambitious EU climate target of 20 percent CO_2 cuts by 2020, finally assumed the mantle of world leader in wind power production. It did so as a direct consequence of the UK government's Renewables Obligations Certificate, a financial incentive scheme for power companies to build wind farms. Thus the UK's wind operation provides the ideal case study — one that points to some key conclusions.

As we have seen, the UK has all the natural advantages. It is the windiest country in Europe. It has one of the continent's longest coastlines for the more highly productive (and less obtrusive) offshore farms. It has a long-established national power grid. In short, if wind power is less than successful in the UK, its success is not guaranteed anywhere.

To begin with, wind infrastructure has come at a steep price. In fiscal year 2007–08, UK electricity customers were forced to pay a total of over \$1.4 billion to the owners of wind turbines. That figure is due to rise to over \$6 billion *a year* by 2020 given the government's unprecedented plan to build a nationwide infrastructure of over 25 GW capacity, in a bid to shift away from fossil fuel use.[39]

Ofgem, which regulates the UK's electricity and gas markets, has already expressed its concern at the burgeoning tab being picked up by the British taxpayer which, they claim, is "grossly distorting the market" while hiding the real cost of wind power. In 2008 alone, UK domestic energy prices for electricity and gas rose twice as fast as the European Union average according to figures released in November by the Organisation for Economic Co-operation and Development (OECD). While 15 percent energy price rises were experienced across the EU, in the UK, gas and electricity prices rose by a staggering 29.7 percent. Ofgem believes wind subsidy has been a prime factor and questions the logic when, for all the public investment, wind produces a mere 1.3 percent of the UK's energy needs.

In May 2008, a report from the Cambridge Energy Research Associates (CERA) warned that an over-reliance on offshore wind farms to meet European renewable energy targets would further create

supply problems for Britain and drive up investor costs.[40] But worse
was to come.

BRITAIN'S NEW DARK AGE: A PREVIEW FOR THE REST

Even so, British wind and renewable technology, and thus the philosophy of its "success," is constantly touted in the US and beyond. But
we wonder if the current upsurge of international interest in the British
experience might not be assuaged somewhat by the knowledge that
the British energy-climate policy which has chosen to invest heavily in
renewable energy at the expense of replacing its ageing nuclear power
facilities, is in crisis and threatening to plunge the UK into a new dark
ages, by 2014 — *within just four years.*

We have already documented the economic-non-viability geographical unacceptability of renewables, especially of wind power. But the
final "nail in the coffin" for all hopes of industrial or commercial scale
renewable energy viability comes from physics, the simple math.

In his brilliant essay "Understanding E=mc²"[41] William Tucker
helpfully applies the understanding of energy = mass to the issue of
renewables. Above all he demonstrates *why* renewables, and wind and
water specifically, are *mathematically* unable to produce the industrial
scale energy power *essential* to keeping the lights on in an industrialized
society.

Tucker explains, "Wind and water are matter in motion that we
harness to produce energy." In a nutshell, what Tucker shows is that
the density of mass in both wind and water, being critically far less
dense than oil, coal and gas, is simply unable to produce anything

This just doesn't make it

Figure 3.3: *Illustration by Mohammed Sami for* Energy Tribune.

approaching a reasonable "renewable" energy output. Tucker calculates, for instance, that a land mass of about 375 square miles with around 660 widely spaced giant windmills would be necessary to get a power return of just 1000 MW, the average production capacity (or candle) of one large scale hydrocarbon-powered facility. With offshore wind turbines associated problems of distance, leakage and maintenance costs must all be significantly scaled up. A traditional power plant requires about one square mile of land to do the same job. Put bluntly, Tucker shows that industrial scale renewable energy is, realistically and mathematically, an economic, geographical and social non-starter.

But while in the UK itself a rash of studies have been sounding alarm bells over the government's current energy direction, one key report has sounded serious alarm bells, that should echo well beyond UK shores.

DOES IT REALLY TAKE AN EINSTEIN?

In October 2009, the UK energy regulator, Ofgem (The Office of Gas and Electricity Markets), warned that Britain was facing 1970s style power blackouts within just four years — a much shorter timescale than previously thought. Project Discovery[42] cited the British government's failure to renovate its "crumbling power infrastructure" due to compliance with new EU "pollution rules," that will force the closure of a quarter of the country's power stations by 2015. In a typically British understatement, Alistair Buchanan, Ofgem's chief executive, warned, "There could be a potential shortfall in the period 2013–18 . . . Life might be pretty cold." Buchanan's assessment is that only an "involuntary curtailment of demand" — power cuts — can conserve household supplies, unless the government acts urgently to upgrade its nuclear plants. Jeremy Nicholson, of the Energy Intensive Users Group, representing some of Britain's biggest manufacturers, warned that power cuts that hit UK business first would present a "material threat to heavy industry." Nicholson also warned that once the crisis hit, the 60 percent hike in British energy bills currently being acknowledged by the government will, more realistically, hit the 120 percent mark.[43]

Bottom line? If Einstein's $E=mc^2$ as it applies to current "renewable energy" projects doesn't cut the intellectual ice for prospective investors and foreign governments alike try this:

UK energy-climate policy, circa 2010 = a blueprint for black-outs, circa 2014.

Maybe so, but isn't one of the main reasons we *must* urgently pursue these alternative energy sources because the oil (and gas) — the fuel(s) that principally drives our industrialized societies — is about to run out?

Notes

1 When we invoke the term "renewable" in relation to energy, it has for many come to imply an energy-power source that produces power that can be equated, relatively, to the energy-power ratio of hydrocarbon energy-power production *and* at a economically viable cost. But that is the whole point, *on both counts*, the current generation of "renewables" produces a lamentably low and unreliable production of power *and* at an extremely high cost. In the sense of energy-power source equivalence then, the term "renewable energy" may be misleading many.

2 The Manhattan Declaration is sponsored by the International Climate Science Coalition and can be viewed at: www.internationalclimate scienceinternational.org

3 Three senior Japanese scientists engaged in climate-related research, reported in "Japanese Scientists Cool on Theories," *The Australian*, March 14, 2009.

4 Dr Vicky Pope, heading a group of scientists working on climate from the UK's top climate research facility, the Hadley Centre Meteorological Office, launched a blistering attack on scientists and journalists who exaggerate the effects of global warming, as reported in "Apocalyptic Climate Predictions Mislead the Public, say Experts," *The Guardian*, February 11, 2009.

5 Dr David Evans's work as consultant to the Australian Greenhouse Office 1999–2005, led him to change his position as a CO_2 alarmist to become an opponent of climate alarmism. See Dr Evans's article "No Smoking Hot Spot," *The Australian*, July 18, 2008.

6 Dr Oleg Sorokhtin, of the Russian Academy of Sciences Institute in Ocean Studies and Dr Vladimir Arutyunov of the Russian Academy of Sciences Institute in Chemical Physics were among other senior Russian scientists who attacked the notion of a science consensus as well as that of anthropogenic global warming, reported in India's national newspaper, *The Hindu*, July 10, 2008.

7 Leading New Zealand climate scientist Professor Christopher de Freitas giving evidence debunking climate alarmist theories during an Environment Court appeal hearing for a proposed new wind farm project was reported in "Professor denies Greenhouse Effect," *Otago Daily Times*, January 30, 2009.

8   A study by geophysicists Mads Faurschou Knudsen and Peter Riisager of the Geological Survey of Denmark and Greenland (GEUS) challenged the theory of man-made global warming as reported in, "The Earth's Magnetic Field Impacts Climate: Danish Study," *Space Daily.com*, January 12, 2009.

9   The Polish Science Academy Geological Science Committee published its position paper questioning the alleged man-made threat of global warming in February 2009. An English version can be read at Dr Benny Peiser's CCNET site at: www.staff.livjm.ac.uk/spsbpeis/PAS.htm

10   The Physics and Society Forum of the American Physical Society reversed its former stance on climate change, stating that many of its members do not believe in "human-induced global warming" and calling for more public debate, reported in "Myth of Consensus explodes: APS Opens Global warming Debate," *Daily Tech.com*, July 16, 2008.

11   "Over 700 International Scientists Dissent Over Claims of Man-made Global Warming Claims," a US Senate Committee Minority Report that debunked claims to a climate science "consensus," published December 11, 2008.

12   Inevitably, especially with the one or two pan-international reports, there is a degree of overlapping of endorsees.

13   Rasmussen Report "Energy Update," published November 13, 2009.

14   "More Than Half of the UK Population Doesn't Accept Climate Change is Man-Made," a research poll by Populus reported by the *Daily Mail*, November 14, 2009.

15   "Schlesinger Acknowledges that 80% of IPCC Members Have No 'Dealing with Climate,'" excerpts from the William Schlesinger-John Christy Global Warming debate with links to actual video, posted by Dr Roy Cordato at The Locker Room, John Locke Foundation, February 11, 2009.

16   "Will The UN Chill Out On Climate Change?," World Climate Report, December 2, 2008, at: www.worldclimatereport.com

17   "Gore Urges US to Try For 100% Renewable Energy Within a Decade," *The Guardian*, November 10, 2008.

18   The greatest investment is being made into wind power because of its greater accessibility and, potentially, its greater flexibility. Infrastructure is also a lot less expensive than its next rival, solar.

19   "Is The Sun Setting On Solar Power in Spain?" *Scientific American, October 20, 2008*, at: www.scientificamerican.com

20   "Wind ($23.37) v. Gas (25 cents)," *Wall Street Journal Opinion Journal*, May 12, 2008.

21   Iceland and Sweden have both been among the front-runners in geothermal utilization. But Iceland's economy collapsed in the 2008 economic crisis and Sweden's investment has been, again, site specific, and small-scale (i.e. not on an industrial scale).

22 Ibid.

23 Ibid.

24 "Britain's Wind Power Revolution," *The Independent*, December 9, 2007.

25 "Shell Pulls Out of Big Wind Farm," *BBC News Online*, May 1, 2008.

26 "Wind Energy To Power UK By 2020," *The Guardian*, December, 10, 2007.

27 "Government's Offshore Wind Power Target Branded 'Pie in the Sky,'" *The Guardian*, December 11, 2007.

28 Ibid.

29 You can listen to the BBC's "Costing the Earth" radio report "Wind Rush," August 30, 2007, at: www.bbc.co.uk/radio4/science/costing theearth_20070830.shtml

30 "Revealed: Cover-up Plan on Energy Target," *The Guardian*, August 13, 2007.

31 "Wuthering Heights: The Dangers of Wind Power," *Der Spiegel*, August 20, 2007.

32 "Offshore Wind," *The Oil Drum: Europe*, December 10, 2007.

33 Michael Trebilcock's, "The Myth of the Danish Green Miracle," *Financial Post* (Canada), May 11, 2009.

34 "Government Criticised for Finding Emissions Cuts Abroad," *Copenhagen Post*, March 30, 2009.

35 "Wind Energy: The Case of Denmark," a study published by Denmark's CEPOS (Center for Politiske Studier) think-tank, September 2009.

36 "Promoters Overstated the Environmental Benefit of Wind Farms," *Daily Telegraph*, December 20, 2008.

37 "$1 Billion Invested BY Valley VC Firms," *The Mercury News* (San Jose), January 18, 2008.

38 Brian Leyland, "Is Renewable Energy a Safe, Long-term Investment — or Will It Soon Crash?," *Energy Pulse.com*, June 13, 2007.

39 "£1 Billion Wind Farm Subsidies Pump Up Power Firm Profits," *Daily Mail*, February 5, 2008.

40 "Offshore: It's Not a Breeze," CERA report, May 2008.

41 William Tucker, "Understanding E=mc²" (adapted from his book "Terrestrial Energy: How Nuclear Power Will Lead the Green Revolution and End America's Energy Odyssey," Bartleby Books), *Energy Tribune.com*

42 Project Discovery, available via Ofgem online at: www.ofgem.gov.uk/ Markets/WhlMkts/Discovery/Pages/ProjectDiscovery.aspx

43 "Power Cuts Forecast to Hit UK in Four Years," *The Times*, October 10, 2009.

Part Two: Fantasy World

4

Petro-Apocalypse Now?
The Myth of Early Peak Oil

Oil is found in the minds of men.

Wallace Pratt, the great petroleum geologist

In 1798, economist Thomas Malthus caused widespread alarm with his prediction that population growth would soon outstrip the food supply. The fear of the realization of Malthus' prophecy gripped the popular consciousness for two centuries. But the Malthusian economic model proved far too "static" ignoring vital factors. Plainly, Malthus was wildly wrong — as Malthusian's are to this day. Yet, Malthusians are unrepentant.

Four decades ago the Club of Rome[1] was established with a mission "to act as a global catalyst for change through the identification and analysis of the crucial problems facing humanity and the communication of such problems to the most important public and private decision makers as well as to the general public." Commissioned by the Club of Rome, *The Limits of Growth* was published in 1972, selling over 30 million copies, almost all in Western Europe and the US. The book was the first ever formalized self-flagellation of the West. It has been the precursor to almost all subsequent environmentalist movements and ushered in the era of "sustainable development," a phrase destined to become the watchword as the only virtuous lifestyle primarily because "the rest of the world can't have a Western style of life."

In many ways, *The Limits of Growth* established the guilt-ridden liberal mantra that our exploitative-to-the-rest-of-the-world lifestyles have to change. Some, such as Amory Lovins, Matt Simmons and an array of western politicians, claim that far from life being diminished economically, if weaned from certain natural resources, the world will prosper from new technologies and new types of resources. The problem with the Club of Rome (a subject to which we will return in Chapter 7) is that it predicted that almost all resources would be exhausted not far into the future. That 1972 prediction was due to be fulfilled well before the end of the first decade in the twenty-first century. Clearly it was a totally wrong prediction, not least as it was based far more on ideological and thinly-disguised moralistic motivations rather than sound economics, or even the physics of production. Fatally flawed as the prophecies of the *The Limits of Growth* were, there are still many activists today who believe that that type of irrational thinking is both morally and intellectually correct.

It is our contention that precisely the same mistake is being made today concerning one of the major global scares of our age: fears that oil production — and mainly the oil that fuels modern industrialized societies especially transport — will no longer be sufficient to meet demand, as it will soon run out.

Peak oil alarmists maintain that oil production has pretty much reached its production peak. Supply is, or will soon be, in decline and, unless we change our fossil fuel burning "sinful" ways, hydrocarbons will be spent entirely within decades. In essence, unless we *immediately* turn to alternative energy sources, our current oil dependency is set to cause us to face an energy crisis of epic proportions. But energy crises, as we shall see throughout this book, come in a variety of forms and are caused far more by "above the ground" political, social and geo-graphical circumstances, than by the depletion of core resources. The latter, including oil, are likely to dominate for decades if not centuries, helping to usher a far smoother and saner transition to other sources and a constantly changing energy mix; one that is propelled by real market forces and not ill-conceived government fiat.

A frequent and understandable confusion for the public, but not forgivable for the authors of the oil-running-out apocalypse, is the difference between resource, in other words the oil and gas "in place," and "reserves." How can the US, for example, have 20 billion barrels of oil reserves in 1940, produce more than 200 billion in the 70 years since then, and still have today 20 billion barrels of reserves? The definition of reserves means they are economically recoverable with today's techniques at today's prices. This adds to the requirement of definitive geological discovery which in itself has changed over the years. Earlier, it was required that oil and gas volumes were specifically reached by drilled wells and tested with elaborate and rigorous tech-niques. Today, seismic measurements are gradually adding, and in some cases subtracting, reserves by providing more accurate descriptions of sub-surface geological structures. Throughout the world, reservoirs that were unthinkable to access and produce only a few years ago are added to reserves.

In confronting the peak oil issue, there is one indisputable fact that should tell the reader much: *no peak oil alarmist prediction has to date proven remotely accurate.* You might think that a 100 percent failure rate would lead peak oil alarmists to show a little more humility. Not a bit. A steady flow of scaremongering "end-of-oil" scenario literature continues to pour forth, feeding the media's penchant for chilling, if nonsensical, oil scare stories. Books that bookstores would be well advised to remove from "current affairs" or "popular science" sections to "science fiction" shelving are always around. But peak oil theorists believe that one day — oil being a finite resource — they have to be right. One day, maybe, but not, as we are about to see, not one day anytime soon.

That's not all. Link the fear over oil running dry to the other global mega-fear of our age: that man-made carbon dioxide (CO_2) emissions are primarily responsible for warming the planet, and the stage is doubly set to charge the eco-activist to sign up to become an anti-hydrocarbon evangelist, with one fear "fueling" another. As in every generation, the end is nigh, and alarmists are only too willing to take their message to the streets. They may have traded the medium, taking up PowerPoint presentations alongside book and Hollywood mega-deals, but the message and strategy are unchanged: to scare the pants off people.

The trouble is that peak oil alarmists appear to have learned little from defective Malthusianism thinking. Just like Malthus, they forget that necessity is the mother of invention and leave vital and unpredictable factors, such as the ingenuity of man, out of their computation model predictions. In consequence, like false prophets in every age, though their analyses ultimately prove vacuous, they skirt criticism by claiming that *only* their prophetic timing was out. What they cannot see is that with scientific speculation, as with comedy, timing *is everything.* But for peak oil alarmists, keeping the dating of their dodgy predictions "fluid" is a way of life.

A SHORT HISTORY OF PEAK OIL THEORY

"I take this opportunity to express my opinion in the strongest terms, that the amazing exhibition of oil which has characterized the last twenty, and will probably characterize the next twenty, years is not only geologically but historically, a temporary and vanishing phenomenon — one which young men will live to see come to its natural end." A quote from the latest peak oil alarmist literature? In fact, they are the words of a US state geologist J.P. Lesley — spoken in 1886. Peak oil errors go back even further than that.

Figure 4.1: The peak oil myth. *Source Energy Tribune*

In 1859, right after the now-famous Colonel Drake drilled the first oil well in Titusville, Pennsylvania, shortages of the illuminant camphene caused by the US Civil War made the price of oil shoot up to $15 per barrel (more than $1,000 in today's world). By the autumn of 1861, following a reckless race for production and the 3,000-barrel-per-day Empire Well, the price had plunged to 10 cents a barrel, $7 in today's money. Four years later, newspapers in the Eastern US were printing stories about running out of oil. However, such peak oil fears were generated against a background that technology back then only allowed access to oil that was easily available. The wrong predictions were founded then, as now, on a failure to grasp twin basic factors that don't fit neatly into any static Malthusian-type economic model: human ingenuity and adaptability. First, discoveries of new and enormous, *less accessible* reserves of oil still lay ahead. Second, human ingenuity has always devised new technologies to help not only new discoveries, but extractions from situations that, just a few years ago, would have been considered economically non-viable.

In 1914, the US Bureau of Mines predicted the world would run out of oil within ten years. In 1920, the US Geological Survey (USGC) claimed that the world only had 60 billion barrels of oil left. By the 1950s geologists were warning that only 600 billion barrels of oil were left. Since then, the USGC has variously estimated that world reserves were down to 1,500 billion barrels of oil (1970), 2,400 billion barrels (1994) and 3,000 billion barrels (2000).[2] The 2000 figure is 50 times larger than the 1920 figure, this after 80 years of ever-increasing production.

In each generation, Peak Oil theory has dictated an end to oil production about 20 or so years hence. That is, until new technological advances deal the prediction a death blow when formerly unsuitable resources suddenly became "viable." David Strahan's book, *The Last Oil Shock: A Survival Guide to the Imminent Extinction of Petroleum Man*, published in 2007, typifies the angst-ridden alarmism of the twenty-first century theorist. Here's the hyped PR pitch delivered on Amazon's synopsis:

> *This may be the most important book you or anyone else will read in the next fifty years.* Assuming humanity survives that long. *Draining the lifeblood of industrial civilization, the* terminal decline *of oil and gas production will* spark a crisis far more dangerous than international terrorism, *and* just as urgent as climate change. *World leaders know it, so why aren't they telling? The last oil shock is the secret behind the crises in Iraq and Iran, the reason your gas bill is going through the roof, the basis of a secret deal cooked up in Texas between George Bush and Tony Blair, the cause of an imminent and unprecedented economic collapse, and the reason you may soon be kissing your car keys and boarding pass goodbye. David Strahan explains how we reached this critical state, how the silence of governments, oil companies and environmentalists conspires to keep the public in the dark, what it means for energy policy, and what you can do to protect yourself and your family from the ravages of the last oil shock* [emphasis added].[3]

Get that? Peak oil and rising prices are all part of a conspiracy cooked up by Tony Blair and George Bush when they were in office — and all unearthed by Mr Strahan. Personally, we look forward to seeing how this particular oil conspiracy plays out in the conveyor belt of anti-capitalist, anti-Big Oil Hollywood blockbusters starring George Clooney (*Syriana*) or Ralph Fiennes (*The Constant Gardener*).

Remember the 1973 oil crisis? When the queues at the gas pumps went on for miles? Far from being a genuine shortage of available oil the incident stands as a classic example of how modern energy crises are almost entirely the result of "above ground" political manipulation. In this case, Organization of the Petroleum Exporting Countries (OPEC) turning off the supply in response to the US decision to re-supply the Israeli Army during the Yom Kippur War.

BACK IN THE REAL WORLD

In *The Color of Oil*, Michael Economides and his co-author predicted that the world would not run out of oil for **at least** the next three centuries.[4] For natural gas, which is rapidly becoming the fuel of choice, the scenario is even more optimistic. Even without taking into account the enormous volume of gas hydrates, the world's natural gas supply will last for at least several centuries more.

Predictions of the future supply of petroleum have typically been far less veracious than predictions of demand. Flawed predictions have caused public bewilderment, distrust and, more importantly, government inaction or poorly conceived reactions. A constant theme from the infancy of the industry at the turn of the nineteenth century has been the depletion of reserves. This worried governments in the 1930s and 1940s. It also became the main focus of public discourse following the energy crisis of 1973. Yet, it is amusing to read both optimistic and pessimistic predictions of the future of oil from people who have no clue about the basic fundamentals of the industry: how oil is found? How it is produced? And how much of it is recovered over the life of an oilfield?

Since 2000, over a dozen authors have produced books warning of impending peak oil disaster, some linked to the extraordinary increase in oil prices to almost $150 a barrel in 2008. Once again, much of the rhetoric is wishful thinking from two types of individuals. Those who are politically or ideologically tainted: environmentalists and anti-capitalists, who for often irrational reasons, *want* the world to run out of oil — and those who are terrified of foreign energy dependency.

For a more complete energy picture, we must first understand something about the geopolitics of energy, which is how the "above ground factors" affect production and supply.

OPEC AND THE GEOPOLITICS OF OIL

The Middle East members of OPEC, especially Saudi Arabia, supply much of the world's traded oil. OPEC is not what it used to be. It no longer has the power it once wielded to manipulate the market. The organization's *excess* capacity has dropped from a demonstrable surplus of over 10 million barrels per day, more than a decade ago, to virtually nothing in almost all countries other than Saudi Arabia, which may have 2 million barrels per day of excess supply. This represents OPEC's current production capacity "behind the valve," or the oil they can turn on and off at will.

This type of statement confuses most people. How can supply be so short when we claim that all that oil is still available in the ground? The answer to this conundrum goes to the heart of the physics and technology of producing oil, even when one knows that it is there, not just theoretically, but with certainty in several geological basins of the world.

It takes huge reinvestment to maintain production capacity and massive exploration, drilling and production budgets to sustain and replace lost and declining production. Venezuela, for instance, reinvests less than half of what the country needs to sustain constant oil production. The Hugo Chávez government has long been mismanaging a stagnant oil industry. This was one of the reasons for the conflict in Venezuela (the US's largest oil supplier) between the government and the technocrats of its national oil company, PDVSA. In early 2010, Venezuela was producing less oil than it produced during the first nationalizations in the 1970s, although the country's known reservoirs can demonstrably produce at least twice as much and perhaps three times. The situation in Venezuela and the Chávez type of politics does not bode well for future oil supplies, though $100 a barrel does wonders for that government's populism.

Optimism about the transition from oil to natural gas as the premier fuel for the world economy stems from the fact that there is an abundant supply of natural gas around the world, and it has also a far more diverse supply. There are three dozen countries that are legitimate potential suppliers of world-class volumes of natural gas. This will further de-emphasize OPEC. For the US and Europe, it will considerably reduce major geopolitical vulnerabilities, directly related to the Middle East, where one finds five of the six countries in the world with over 75 billion barrels of oil reserves.

Eventually, decades from now, there will be a substantial push towards the electrification of transportation and an integration of energy resources. One of the often ignored, but vital issues is that the world uses virtually no oil for power generation and uses practically nothing but oil for transportation. Constant invocations of energy conservation are thus tantamount to barking up the wrong tree. For example, lowering thermostats in the winter or elevating them in the summer would result in practically no reduction in the use of oil.

The simple fact is that much of the current petroleum situation, including prices, is related to geopolitical issues rather than to the physics of production and reserves, not least because of the rise of a new "axis of energy militants." This small but strategically important group of energy producers has only one desire: to increase already high oil prices — and make as much cash as possible by tightening global supplies, creating instability in the energy markets. Thus energy crises are rooted in politically-motivated production cuts, not shortage of reserves.

Conventional logic used to say that oil-producing countries do not want to cause a world economic recession. The danger posed by the axis of energy militants — Venezuela, Iran and, increasingly over the last several years, Russia under President and then Prime Minister Vladimir Putin — is that they could not care less. These militants hardly have real functioning economies whose workings would be adversely affected by a recession. For these militants, if America and the West get their economic come-uppance, so much the better.

Ever since the 1973 Arab oil embargo a few countries and societies, "abysmal failures to absorb modernity," have become emboldened and outright arrogant with oil money. Their governments' corruption is covered up by welfare giveaways; their societies' ineptitude and poverty are presented to the populace, and often to outsiders, as strength.

Militancy always accompanies surging oil revenues. Venezuela is run by a Fidel Castro wannabe. Hugo Chávez, whose frequent pronouncements are often bracketed between the whimsical and the insane, is a man of empty populism, clearly propped up by oil money and appealing to an unfortunate Latin American predilection: the anachronistic male equivalent of Eva Peron. But the fact is, Venezuela is one of world's largest petroleum suppliers. It was Chávez who inadvertently linked his country, Iran, and Russia in back-to-back visits. From Iran he flew to Russia, which he publicly urged to keep a militant profile on oil production. We will return to Chávez and the importance of Venezuelan oil in Chapter 8.

Under Putin, Russia, which gets more than half of its revenues from oil, has moved towards a clear path of what amounts to re-Sovietization and energy-imperialism, and has deteriorated into the same dysfunctional and corrupt economy that has become a tradition in petroleum-rich countries.

Russia is an important reason why the peak oil advocates are "all wet." The end of the Soviet empire opened the doors for a breed of new Russian capitalists, and the industry responded with an unprecedented surge in oil production. This new class of Russian entrepreneurs took advantage of the residual potential left over from a bloated and inefficient Russian industry. At that point, oil wells throughout Russia were significantly under-producing compared to their potential. Headcount in the industry was out of control, functioning as a welfare employment agency. Operating costs were exorbitant. Technology, a hallmark of

Soviet "scientific socialism," was completely absent, and most operating practices were either grossly outdated or obsolete.

Russia's oil production increase couldn't have come at a better time for the country and the world. Oil prices increased dramatically after their slump in 1999, following the "Asian flu." Worldwide economic recovery meant that the developing world, led by China, was demanding more and more crude oil while the traditional petroleum-producing countries were finding it increasingly difficult to maintain production levels.

During that time, Russia added incremental oil output, equivalent to Norway's entire output, and added more than one "Oman-equivalent" in each year for those years. Russia's increase in oil production represented almost half of the entire world's growth in that period. The movement was led by YUKOS, with Sibneft joining the party a bit later. It was a heady time; the country quickly became a competitive arena, with each Russian company trying to outperform the others. International stock analysts and reporters stoked the fires of competition. The former communist country began to resemble the Wild West of nineteenth-century America: a free for all in production of the world's most vital commodities.

YUKOS' performance during the period was amazing, doubling from 800,000 to 1,600,000 barrels per day. More remarkably, this happened while the company's headcount was dropping from 22,000 to 14,000 personnel and the number of active wells was plunging from nearly 14,000 to just over 7,000. This was possible because the average rate per well increased four-fold to 260 barrels of oil per day. New well drilling was slashed to just 300 wells per year, the reserves-to-production ratio was halved to 20, and proven reserves grew by 31 percent — or 3.5 billion barrels — to 14.9 billion barrels.[5] Alas, the Russian oil production miracle was not to continue for both political reasons and the re-Sovietization enacted by the Vladimir Putin government. What all this shows, however, is that current production levels are not necessarily *any* indication of current reserves, or of prospective future enhanced capacity.

And then there is Iran. Iran has not wavered in using oil for what it perceives as its national emancipation and international posture under very diverse governing regimes. This was true in the 1950s under Mohammad Mossadegh, eventually overthrown by the CIA, and it was true when the Shah ruled Iran. It's true now, too, under the Islamic Republic. Iran today holds the second-largest oil and gas reserves in the world. The scope for even greater production and exploration is immense.

Equally, we are seeing the emergence of massive growth potential in the post-Saddam era in Iraq. At the time of writing, the Iraqi government is in the process of signing a whole raft of deals with foreign oil companies presaging massive growth production, as well as the exploration of highly promising new fields. Whether we view the current democratic realities in Iraq, especially in the Kurdish north, as an intended or unintended consequence of regime change, Iraq is undoubtedly set to greatly enhance its status as a world-class producer of oil and gas.

The fact remains that the world's main supply of oil today, and for the foreseeable future, is dominated by the Middle East. Saudi Arabia is in a class by itself as the world's largest exporter of oil, with a capacity, with significant investment, to increase supply far beyond past levels. The supply of oil is being used by the Saudi and OPEC as a serious political weapon keeping prices high, fuelling further the illusion that it is *also* in short supply. Thus, it becomes easy to see how a highly politicized environmental movement has used the theories of peak oil to bolster their claims about the evils of fossil fuels, and the urgent need to divert enormous investment into unproven alternative energy sources.

Unfortunately, for peak oil alarmists, regular new discoveries, greatly expanded production from existing fields, a whole new conventional oil frontier and even greater prospects of extracting oil from unconventional resources, are making a nonsense of their predictions. Moreover, much of the new oil is likely to come from far more politically stable parts of the world.

THERE WILL BE OIL!

The widely asserted tipping point for peak oil suggests that when 50 percent of the world's ultimately recoverable oil has been consumed — with global oil consumption still rising — industrialized societies will face a major crisis over declining reserves. It was M. King Hubbert, a Shell geologist, who in 1956 famously developed the bell curve graph which describes the inevitable process of exhausting extractable oil resources.[6]

Hubbert accurately predicted that US oil production would peak between 1965 and 1970. It actually did in 1971. It is the timing of arrival of the tipping point that consumes the interest of early peak oilers. Like Hubbert himself however, most of those concerned about early reserve depletion fail to factor in how new advances in technology enhance the ability to recover what were previously considered unrecoverable resources. Furthermore, while there is nothing wrong with Hubbert's theory, the actual application implies that all oil resources are known and, in fact, connected with production. Hubbert could not therefore factor in the Alaskan North Slope oil production, since it did not start until 1976 and, by the mid-1980s, when it peaked, total US production came close to surpassing the 1971 peak.

Then there is the impact of natural gas on oil consumption levels, and the potentially massive impact of oil extraction from unconventional sources. But first, let's look at some ballpark figures to help give us context.

While estimates vary, approximately 6–8 trillion barrels of oil from conventional resources, with the same or more from unconventional (tar sands, shale oil etc.) resources are believed to be "in-place" and, as yet, untapped. Since the first wells were drilled in the mid-1800s, the world has consumed just one trillion out of this total. Given that around the same amount of unconventional oil, 6–8 trillion barrels, is estimated to be "in-place," that offers a grand total of around 12–16 trillion barrels of oil as yet untapped. Not all in-place oil is, of course, recoverable.

Historically, the petroleum industry has been able to recover just one in three barrels of conventional resources with the recovery rate dropping significantly for unconventional resources. But as energy analyst and former Aramco chief reservoir engineer Nansen G. Saleri points out, "This benchmark is poised to change upward. Modern science and unfolding technologies will, in all likelihood, double recovery efficiencies." Saleri estimates that even a 10 percent increase in extraction efficiency will unlock 1.2–1.6 trillion barrels of extra resources — or an additional 50-year global supply at current consumption levels.[7]

Wolfgang Schollnberger, retired technology VP for BP, writing in *Oil Gas European Magazine* in January 2006 said that while global hydrocarbon reserves were 4.5 trillion barrels of oil equivalent, after as much as 6 trillion barrels equivalent of oil and gas are produced in the twenty-first century, "there will be enough hydrocarbons left so that somebody might estimate on Jan. 1, 2101 the then remaining reserves plus resources to be . . . 4.7 trillion barrels of oil equivalent . . ."[8]

In 2009 world oil consumption hit 31 billion barrels per year, or around 85 million barrels a day; figures which will continue to rise in the next few years. However, new technology is already having a key impact on oil recovery rates. And while peak oil alarmists regularly claim the oil reserves of the current key players, especially Saudi Arabia, are over-estimates, it is especially in this arena that we are already seeing the impact of new technology. The reality is that new technology is raising the recovery rate for two largest Saudi oilfields (Abqaiq and Ghawar) from 1 out of 3 to 2 out of 3 barrels. This has further boosted expectations over Saudi oil assets, assets that account for one quarter of the world's proven reserves. The raising of expectation and the increasing recovery rate in Saudi Arabia can be extrapolated to struggling fields all around the globe, including major fields in Russia, Venezuela, and Iran.

Greater recovery efficiency is also likely to mean we must review again the prospects for emerging oil-rich nations like Iraq. It is estimated that by 2040 Iraq's oil production and reserves could rival those of Saudi Arabia today.[9] Russia, as we have seen, remains in a class of its own when it comes to energy resources. As regards its oil reserves, estimates vary wildly. BP estimates Russia holds 72 billion barrels; the ten top Russian oil companies, 82 billion; the US Geological Survey (USGS) estimates 112 billion barrels. Other estimates are still higher, with some suggesting Russia holds as many as 200 billion barrels. So why the wildly varying estimates? Well one reason some claim lower Russian reserves is that production problems often obfuscate the issue. For instance, in 2007 Russian officials expressed concern that oil production had only risen by 2 percent. In 2008, production levels dropped again as they had a few years before. This led some analysts and speculative peak alarmists to see it as evidence of reserve decline. In reality, none of these "above the ground" production issues had anything to do with the level of known reserves or other potential in-place resources. More than that, analysts were failing to take into account Russia's potential deepwater oil (and gas) bonanza via their claims over vast areas of Arctic waters, a vital subject to which we will return.

In other words, there is much more to come from the usual energy-rich sources, not least via the ever-growing revised recovery rates, as well as prospective new finds. Before we move on to review prospects in deepwater and unconventional resources, let us not disparage — as peak oil alarmists (aware their reputations are on the line) often rush to do — either the latest discoveries or what they may mean.

NEW DISCOVERIES

For peak oil alarmists, 2009 was a bad year. Over 225 discoveries had been reported across five continents. In the first half of 2009 alone, new finds added up to 10 billion barrels of new oil reserves.[10] According to IHS CERA, at that pace of discovery 2009 would register the highest level since 2000. In September 2009, BP made a giant deepwater find in the Gulf of Mexico — an estimated 3 billion barrels — that may turn out to be the largest ever in the region.[11] The prospects for further finds remain exciting. Equally significant, the Gulf of Mexico find also belies peak oil assertions that there are no major new players left.

Yet, after every announcement however, peak oil theorists were quick to inform the media that none of these new discoveries was as big as those in former decades. True enough, but such finds have a nasty habit of adding up — and becoming more significant than originally thought. Reserve estimates have a habit of rising over the life of a field. All of which bears out what many in the industry have long been saying: *that there is much more oil in the ground*, even if it is becoming harder to extract.

In his book, *The Battle for Barrels: Peak Oil Myths & World Oil Futures*, energy analyst Duncan Clarke quotes: "Leonardo Maugeri of Eni, a world-class company, estimates that there are now some 2 trillion barrels of recoverable reserves not yet classified as proven that will, in time, become commercially exploitable as technology and subsoil improves and higher prices improve margins. This is a significant volume."[12]

THE GREAT DEEPWATER "BLACK GOLD" RUSH

In August 2007 the Russians pulled a headline-grabbing, flag-planting stunt two miles beneath the Arctic ice cap. In a scene redolent of the Cold War, Vladimir Putin's government was sanctioning a subsea land grab. Within days Canada, the US, Denmark, and Norway were publicly asserting their own rights to map and claim — and militarize — huge areas of the Arctic. Then, in October 2007, in an entirely unexpected move, the British government confirmed that it was planning to assert its sovereign rights over one million square kilometers (386,000 square miles) of seabed off Antarctica.[13] The response again was predictable. Chile, Argentina, Australia, and New Zealand quickly declared their intention to stake their own claims.[14] The Russians were not looking to boost their vodka martini ice reserves, nor were the British seeking practice grounds for their water polo team. The fact is the world's latest black "gold" rush is on — and Russia fired the start gun.

Speaking at the Deep Offshore Technology Conference in Norway in October 2007, John Westwood, president of Douglas-Westwood market strategists, confirmed what many already knew about new oil: "The serious prospects are in deepwater." Westwood predicted that subsea spending will reach $41 billion between 2007 and 2011; a 25 percent growth in what is already the world's fastest growing industry. He also warned that on these "new frontiers" we should expect a "great deepwater land grab."[15]

WHAT LIES BENEATH?

According to the USGS published at the end of 2007, the Arctic may contain as much as 412 billion barrels of oil equivalent (BOE). The USGS estimates that the area north of the Arctic Circle alone may have reserves of 1.7 trillion cubic feet of natural gas and 90 billion barrels of oil or around 22 percent of the world's undiscovered energy resources. It also estimates that just one offshore basin east of Greenland could contain over 110 billion of barrels of oil — about 42 percent of Saudi Arabia's current proven reserves.[16]

The Battle for the New Frontier, published by the Oxford Institute for Energy Studies in the summer of 2007, claims "Russia's extractable offshore hydrocarbon resources are approximately 100 billion tonnes, 80 percent of which are located in the Arctic," about 600 billion boe. To put it all in perspective, as the Oxford Institute confirms, "If Moscow is successful in its bid for more Arctic territories, its hydrocarbon share could increase by at least 10 billion tonnes (73 billion boe)."[17] The USGS believes that 25 percent of the world's undiscovered reserves of oil and gas — far *more* than known Saudi reserves — lie beneath Arctic waters. And that's a *conservative* estimate. The Oxford Institute report concludes that whatever the Arctic's true potential "Russia will play a dominant role in Arctic gas, accounting for three-quarters of peak production."

There is no question that oil and gas will continue to fuel the world's economies for decades yet and that the serious new prospects for conventional hydrocarbons lie in deepwater. As if Russia does not already control much of the world's hydrocarbon reserves, offshore expert John Westwood, predicts that when the "dust settles" over new deepwater discoveries, "Russia will control 60 percent of the acreage."[18] And Russia is just one of a growing list of governments that have applications outstanding under the 1982 UN Law of the Sea Convention. Every one of them is laying claim to vast tracts of potentially oil- and gas-rich offshore and subsea regions.

But it is not just deepwater under and around the poles that offers new energy riches. As we have seen, the Gulf of Mexico has lately begun yielding up its energy riches. In April 2009, a joint report by the USGS and the US Interior Department stated that as much as 115 billion barrels of "technically recoverable" oil may well lie offshore inside US federal waters.[19] In addition, the same report concluded that as much as 565 trillion cubic feet of natural gas may also be contained in the Outer Continental Shelf off the US.

But while it clearly has formidable oil resources, under President

Barack Obama the US has been performing a self-castration in its energy prowess and posture. Brazil, on the other hand, under Luiz Inacio Lula da Silva, a firebrand socialist and not a particular friend of the US, has been poised to develop into an energy superpower, all thanks to its formidable offshore oil resources. From the late 1990s, Brazil, which has emerged not only as the location of some of the largest offshore oil and gas fields ever discovered, but, through its excellent oil company, Petrobras, a publicly traded company, is a world leader in what is arguably equal to space-age technology, drilling and producing in deepwater. In contrast to what many Americans and Europeans think of their oil companies, Brazilians think of Petrobras as a national treasure.

Brazil, a nation of 180 million people, has been riding on its oil resources to become one of the economic superpowers in the not too distant future. After reaching self-sufficiency in oil in 2008, it's ambition is to become a leading exporter of oil. Lula da Silva has already made overtures to the obvious — China — heading a large delegation to Beijing in mid-May 2009, showcasing oil, and walking away with a $10 billion oil export deal. This is just the beginning.

Ironically, US politicians have expressed interest to imitate Brazil for all the wrong reasons. A few years ago, former President Bill Clinton asked, "Why can't we be like Brazil?" But he was admiring Brazil's ethanol production as part of their motor fuel mix. That was done before the discrediting of biofuels and, even for that issue, Brazil does it better, using the far less destructive sugarcane as a base, rather than corn. Brazil also shows their relative emphasis: their budget for oil and gas development is more than 30 times their budget for biofuels.

The far more important energy news is that Brazil has discovered massive oil and gas reserves in the offshore Campos Basin (where 82 percent of their current oil and gas comes from), Espirito Santo Basin, and, thanks to new technological advances, in the pre-salt formations of the Santos Basin.[20] Of the oil fields discovered in the last 30 years, only Kazakhstan's Kashagan is bigger than Brazil's Tupi field, discovered in 2006 below 7,200 feet of water. The field contains at least 8 billion barrels of oil, and could contain as much as 30 billion.[21] In 2008 the Jupiter field was discovered, which is at least comparable to the Tupi field. Others are on the way.

The discovery of these fields is in itself quite a technological accomplishment, capping a more than 30 year evolution of deeper and deeper water drilling. In 2009 Brazil had already accounted for 22 percent of world deepwater oil production. It will continue to grow.

Petrobras has been operating as many sophisticated deepwater offshore floating production systems as the next three, Shell, Norway's Norsk Hydro, and ExxonMobil, combined. The brashest message by Petrobras was delivered by its CEO José Sérgio Gabrielli de Azevedo in a mid-2009 trip to China, stating that the company's oil production, at 2.76 million barrels per day in 2009 will climb to 3.66 million by 2013 and will double by 2020 to 5.7 million barrels per day.[22] It will make Petrobras the largest oil producing publicly traded oil company, a third larger than ExxonMobil.

An interesting example for the egalitarian potential involvement in offshore oil discoveries was offered by a much smaller company, Spain's Repsol. In just 2008, the company was involved in three of the world's biggest oil and gas discoveries. Among them was the Guara field in Brazil's Santos Basin. Another was the biggest-ever natural gas find in shallow waters in the Gulf of Venezuela. A third was the first deep-water oil discovery off Sierra Leone, West Africa. While the amounts involved for oil might appear relatively small in the overall scheme of things — the equivalent of around 2 billion barrels of oil and gas at Guara, Brazil, and around 1.4 billion barrels equivalent off the Gulf of Venezuela, for instance — it is highly revealing that far more oil and gas "lies beneath."[23] Equally, the massive natural gas finds are indicative of something else that affects the peak oil scenarios: prospects for future natural gas discoveries eclipse even those for oil.

THE NEW NATURAL GAS PARADIGM

In November 2009, our colleague Robert Bryce highlighted a key finding in the latest IEA report on world energy reserves that the media largely ignored. The IEA's executive summary concluded that, "The long-term global recoverable gas resource base is estimated at more than 850 trillion cubic meters." As Bryce points out, "That translates to just over 30,000 trillion cubic feet of gas. That's more than double the 2008 estimate put forward by the IEA."

Bryce adds, "At current levels of gas production, the available gas resources could last for 280 years." While reminding us that "resources are not reserves," even so, what it bears out is how natural gas is set to become the world's most vital hydrocarbon. In doing so, of course, it is bound to further reduce, by virtue of increasing wider application, take the heat off oil demand and supply. As Bryce says, "What makes the new gas paradigm so intriguing is that no one saw it coming."[24] Least of all, it seems, alarmist peak oil theorists.

It is essential to note that even the almost stunning new IEA estimate of natural gas resources does not include natural gas hydrates for which estimates, even conservative ones, dwarf all hydrocarbon volumes by orders of magnitude. The technology to actually produce natural gas hydrates is not yet available and it has not yet been necessary to develop it.

While world energy demand will increase by 50 percent over the next 20 years, oil and gas is slated to increase from 61 percent to about 67 percent. In spite of all the rhetoric on alternative energy resources, sunshine may be free, but solar energy is very expensive. Natural gas will command a market share that is practically unthinkable today. And, as if this review of future conventional oil (and the impact of burgeoning natural gas discoveries will have) is not *de*-alarmist enough, it may prove a drop in the ocean compared to the riches on offer from unconventional sources.

UNCONVENTIONAL SOURCES OF OIL

Unconventional oil is the production or extraction of petroleum from mineral sources using techniques other than the traditional oil well method. Unconventional sources include oil shales, oil or tar sands, coal-based liquid supplies, biomass-based liquid supplies and liquids arising from chemical processing of natural gas, referred to as gas-to-liquids (GTL). We will concentrate here on the most important and promising, oil in shales and in heavy (very viscous) oil sands.

Historically, conventional extraction has been preferred as unconventional extraction has been economically unviable because the production rate from wells in these fields is very low. But higher energy prices, new technologies, and the increasing difficulties, both physical and political, associated with hard to reach conventional oil have combined to make unconventional a far more viable proposition. This is good news for us all as appropriate shales and tar sands contain — wait for it — *nine times more oil than the world has thus far consumed.*

There are around 600 known oil shale/sand deposits around the world. Together they are estimated to hold between 2.8 and 3.3 trillion barrels of oil. One of the world's largest deposits, however, is found in the Green River Formation in the US. The Green River alone, which covers parts of Colorado, Utah and Wyoming, is estimated to contain a staggering 1.2–1.8 *trillion* barrels of oil — over half of the world's entire oil shale resource[25] and, again, more oil than the world has used since drilling first began. While not all resources are recoverable, even a moderate estimate of 800 billion barrels would be three times greater than Saudi Arabia's proven oil reserves.

One estimate suggests that with current US demand at around

20 million barrels of oil per day, if the Green River Formation were geared to producing just a quarter of US demand the play would last around 400 years.[26] And the even better news for Americans is that more than 70 percent of the Formation lies on land already controlled by the federal government. But while the black gold of the Green River Formation dominates the oil shale landscape, even it, on the North American continent, is not the whole "good news" story.

According to *Growth in the Canadian Oil Sands: Finding a New Balance*, a report published in May 2009 by IHS CERA, technological advances in extraction from Canadian oil sands have made Canada the world's second largest holder of recoverable oil reserves, after Saudi Arabia. The Canadian oil sands have long been recognized as an immense resource containing between 170–200 billion barrels. With production doubling from 600,000 barrels a day in 2000 to 1.3 million barrels a day in 2009, Canada has already become the number one foreign supplier of oil to the US. In CERA's top 15 countries with the greatest potential to increase oil production over the next decade, Canada now stands in fourth place. In one of three scenarios posited by the CERA report, Canadian oil sands production could reach 6.3 million barrels per day by 2035 with Canada accounting for 37 percent of US oil imports, up from 19 percent in 2008.[27] And that is not all.

Across the US territories of North Dakota and Montana and the Canadian territories of Saskatchewan and Manitoba lies the Bakken Formation. First discovered in 1951, by 1995 the USGS estimated recoverable oil reserves at around 151 million barrels of oil. In 2008, the USGS upped its estimate to between 3 and 4.3 billion barrels of "technically recoverable" oil in the North Dakota and Montana sections — 25 times more than the 1995 estimate. According to the USGS, however, there may be in excess of 500 billion barrels of oil in the Bakken Formation, with a figure of 413 billion barrels being most likely. Compare that to the 125 billion barrels at the massive El Ghawar field in Saudi Arabia. As geologist J.W. Price comments, "This knowledge that 413 billion barrels of in-place oil exists in the Bakken source system rocks presents the oil industry with an unparalleled exploration opportunity."[28]

Not least because while all of the shale and tar sand oil formations present technological challenges — and we acknowledge that they do — they also present an unparalleled opportunity. It would enable the US to finally reduce its foreign oil dependency, and the influence of despotic modern "oil barons" like Venezuela's Hugo Chávez. Even more spectacularly, as an *Energy News* editorial pointed out in February 2008, "The US imported about 14 billion barrels of oil in 2007, which means US consumers sent about $340 billion dollars overseas building palaces in Dubai and propping up unfriendly regimes around the world. If 200 billion barrels of oil at $90 a barrel are recovered in the high plains the added wealth to the US economy would be $18 trillion."[29]

We are neither isolationists nor naive in the energy trade and business. The reasons that the US and the developed world have been importing so much oil from the current list of petroleum exporting countries is because, in spite of the unsavory nature of many, they have still provided the cheapest and most readily available sources of oil. But as it usually happens in this business the cost, both real and indirect of present oil sources, makes the development and application of new technologies attractive and compelling.

What we have sought to show here is that while we may have used around 1 trillion barrels of the world's oil, *it is a small fraction of the estimated 12–16 trillion that remains.* As much as it has got harder to extract conventional oil, man's ingenuity through technological advances and higher energy prices have colluded to make the economically unviable, viable; and the unrecoverable, recoverable. With declining populations in Japan and many European countries, with more cars using diesel and such, some analysts are already talking about peak demand *rather* than peak production. However, with growing demand from China, India, Brazil, and other industrializing countries, it is hard to see global demand declining in the near future.

During the 1990s, the consensus among peak oil theorists was that

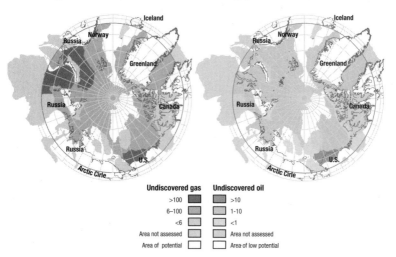

Figure 4.2: Polar regions and their energy riches. *Source Energy Tribune.*

half of the world's 2 trillion barrels of recoverable oil had already been consumed; therefore oil supply must have peaked, or be peaking. We now know that those estimates and that consensus were wildly inaccurate. Today's estimates of what is "recoverable" and what is "out there" have increased dramatically. As analyst Michael Lynch points out post the 1990s, "Since then, most analysts have produced estimates of around 3.5 trillion barrels of recoverable petroleum with somewhere like around a 35 percent recovery rate, implying approximately 10 trillion barrels of oil in place."[30] Lynch considers, and we agree, that 10 trillion is actually a highly conservative estimate given that the figure only relates to conventional oil, when there is easily just as much unconventional oil around. Add to all this the impact of burgeoning natural gas resources on oil consumption and key analysts are now contemplating a future where oil consumption may *never* peak at all.

In *The Future of Global Oil Supply: Understanding the Building Blocks*, IHS CERA expects global oil productive capacity to grow through 2030 with no evidence of peak throughout that time. The report expects capacity to reach as much as 115 million barrels per day, up from the current level of 92 barrels per day. After that, rather than a peak followed by a steep or long decline, the CERA report envisages a decades-long "undulating plateau" of supply and demand fluctuations. IHS CERA senior director, Peter Jackson, has said, "Supply evolution through 2030 is not a question of resource availability. The crucial issue lies not below ground. It is the aboveground factors that will dictate the ultimate shape of the supply curve."[31] We believe CERA's is a fair and accurate assessment of the geopolitical realities surrounding oil production — geopolitical realities that too many peak oil theorists fail to factor into their predictions.

Peter W. Huber and Mark Mills, in probably the definitive book on this subject, put it this way: "Energy-capturing technologies are improving across the board, and faster today than ever before. The logic of the fuel-retrieving machines has advanced much faster than the fuels have retreated — we keep getting closer to the receding horizon. Environmental concerns are a separate matter, important in their own right. But the issue of exhaustion is resolved. Energy supplies are — for all practical purposes — infinite."[32]

What we have written about oil, and the evolution and transition to new sources, also applies to the eventual transition to other forms of energy or means of energy utilization such as the electrification of transportation. Social engineering with environmentalist agendas that are based on shoddy or exaggerated science are not solutions to energy supply. The only thing they can accomplish is to, at least, increase costs and, at worse, cause catastrophic energy shortages. Things will change, but in due time and based on sound economic principles and market forces. Instead of the overnight changes touted by irresponsible politicians and ignorant pundits and influenced by ideologues, transition can comfortably take decades, causing enough "natural pain" without the "shooting ourselves in the foot" variety.

PETRO-APOCALYPSE NOW?

One final observation is merited. It is ironic that the modern generation professes incredulity that the prophet-of-doom-induced mass hysteria of former ages should reveal itself to be perhaps the most paranoid of all. Over recent decades, the popular science–mass media axis has been wrong in its dire warnings of one global disaster after another. Global cooling and a new ice age (in the 70s), mad cows, killer eggs, a whole litany of virus threats, killer bees, Y2K, to name but a few have, so they bleated, threatened millions of lives — even the planet itself. After so many failed predictions you might think they would wise up to the gulf that exists between real science and speculative "consensus" science. Now the same axis of alarmism is equally "sure" about global warming and the early end of our oil-driven civilization. Clearly, when we stop playing the science–conjecture game, we find the hard science facts, just like the massive reserves of oil, are out there — for those prepared to drill, or explore, for them.

And precisely the same can be said for the other great scare of our age, global warm-ism and the incomparably dumb war the elites have declared on the climate and on carbon dioxide. To that issue we now turn.

Notes

1 For the Club of Rome website go to www.clubofrome.org
2 The USGC (United States Geological Survey) 2000, see the executive summary online at http://energy.cr.usgs.gov/WEcont/chaps/ES.pdf
3 Online synopsis at Amazon.co.uk for *The Last Oil Shock: A Survival Guide to the Imminent Extinction of Petroleum Man*, David Strahan, (John Murray), published April, 2007.
4 *The Color of Oil*, Michael Economides and Ronald Oligney, (Round Oak Publishing), 2000.
5 During this period Michael Economides was a senior advisor to YUKOS.
6 For more information go to www.hubbertpeak.com

7   "The World has Plenty of Oil," by Nansen G. Saleri, *Wall Street Journal op-ed*, March 4, 2008.

8   W.N. Schollnberger, "Who shapes the future mix of primary energy? What might it be?" *Oil Gas European Magazine* (International edition of *Erdol Erdgas Kohle*), 32, 1 (2006), 8–20.

9   "The World has Plenty of Oil," by Nansen G. Saleri, *Wall Street Journal op-ed*, March 4, 2008.

10 "Oil Industry Sets a Brisk Pace of New Discoveries," Jad Mouawad, *The New York Times*, September 24, 2009.

11 "BP in 'Giant' New Oil Discovery," BBC News, September 2, 2009.

12 *The Battle For the Barrels: Peak Oil Myths & World Oil Futures*, Duncan Clarke, (Profile Books), p. 165.

13 "Britain to Claim More Than 1 Million Square Kilometres of Antarctica," Owen Bowcott, *The Guardian*, October 17, 2007.

14 "Battleground Antarctica: UK, Argentina and Chile." Available online at: www.neurope.eu/articles/79156.php

15 "Deepwater Oil, Gas Set for Long-term Growth," Judy Maksoud, International Editor, *Offshore Magazine*, October 12, 2007.

16 "Geologists Believe Known Reserves Off Greenland Could Just Be Tip of Iceberg," Robin Pagnamenta and Peter Stiff, *The (London) Times*, December 27, 2007.

17 "The Battle for the New Energy Frontier: The Russian Polar expedition and the Future of Arctic Hydrocarbons," Shamil Midkhatovich Yenikeyeff and Timothy Fenton Krysiek (respectively Research Fellow and Visiting Research Fellow at the Oxford Institute for Energy Studies) published August 2007.

18 "Deepwater Oil, Gas Set for Long-term Growth," Judy Maksoud, International Editor, *Offshore Magazine*, October 12, 2007.

19 "U.S. May Have 115 Billion Barrels of Oil Offshore" (Update 2), Daniel Whitten, Bloomberg.com, April 2, 2009. Available online at: www.bloomberg.com/apps/news?pid=20601103&sid=auwljnsJURDc

20 "Brazil's Companies Announce New Oil Discoveries," (China's) People's Daily Online (English), November 17, 2009. Available online at: www.english.peopledaily.com.cn/90001/90778/90858/90864/6815464.html

21 US Energy Information Administration. See online at http://www.eia.doe.gov/cabs/Kazakhstan/Oil.html

22 "In A Hamstrung Oil Industry, Petrobras Will Rule," Michael J. Economides, *Energy Tribune*, May 27, 2009.

23 "In the Oil Patch, A Tale of Have and Have Not," Thomas Catan and Bernd Radowitz, *Wall Street Journal* (Business), October 30, 2009. Available online at: www.online.wsj.com/article/SB10001424052748704 317704574503500707233912.html

24 "The New Natural Gas Paradigm: 30,000 Trillion Cubic Feet (and Counting)," *Energy Tribune*, November 13, 2009. Available online at: www.energytribune.com/articles.cfm?aid=2592

25 Oil Shale and Tar Sands Programmatic EIS (Environmental Impact Statement) Center. Available online at: www.ostseis.anl.gov/guide/oilshale/index.cfm

26 RAND Corporation's *Oil Shale Development in the United States Prospects and Policy Issues*. J.T. Bartis, T. LaTourrette, L. Dixon, D.J. Peterson, and G. Cecchine, MG-414-NETL, 2005.

27 "Growth in the Canadian Oil Sands: Finding a New Balance," IHS Cambridge Energy Research Associates, published May 2009.

28 "Bakken Formation: Will It Fuel Canada's Oil Industry?" Jerry Langton, CBC News, June 27, 2008 and 3. 4.3 Billion Barrels of Technically Recoverable Oil Assessed in North Dakota and Montana's Bakken Formation — 25 Times More Than Thought in 1995," Press Release from U.S. Department of the Interior-USGS, October 4, 2008.

29 "Massive Oil Deposit Could Increase US Reserves by 10x," *Energy News* Editorial, February 13, 2008.

30 "Nonsense, Peak Oil and Oil Prices," Michael C. Lynch, *Energy Tribune*, December 17, 2009. Available online at: www.energytribune.com/articles.cfm?aid=2739

31 "The Future of Global Oil Supply: Understanding the Building Blocks," report by CERA and authored by IHS CERA senior director, Peter M. Jackson. Report published: November 2009. Available online at: www.cera.com/aspx/cda/client/report/report.aspx?KID=5&CID=10720

32 *The Bottomless Well: The Twilight of Fuel, The Virtue of Waste, and Why We Will Never Run Out of Energy*, Peter W. Huber and Mark Mills (Basic Books), p. 181.

5

The Pseudo-Science War on Carbon and Climate

In questions of science, the authority of a thousand is not worth the humble reasoning of a single individual.

Galileo

It was Charles Mackay who noted the socio-phenomenon that "Men go mad in herds and only recover their senses slowly and one by one." Never, perhaps, has the phenomenon been better exhibited than in the global warming scare.

Perhaps the most insidious aspect of global warming alarmism, conveniently re-named sometime ago, "global climate change," is not the shoddy science. Normal human beings are not well suited or trained to understand the nuances of science, especially the one as complicated and multi-faceted as climate science. But then, climate is so multi-faceted and little understood that we should take the claims of "experts," especially the ones making definitive alarmist statements about what the climate *may* do in future, with extreme caution. The onus is always on "alarmists" to prove their case. Instinctively, therefore, given science's penchant for changing its "consensus opinion," it should not surprise us that the science of climate is currently dominated by highly speculative theories and transient belief, rather than empirical (proven) truth, or even reasonable certainty.

Most are able, however, to understand that "Climategate," upon which we will elaborate later in this chapter, constitutes ethical lapses and shenanigans by unscrupulous scientists and, depending on one's *political* point of view, those events may strengthen negative opinions, or may be ignored. It is telling that almost all liberal groups, environmentalist organizations and social engineers the world over have espoused man-made global warming. Few, however, possess the credentials to grasp the science currently available, and few have actually read any technical papers on the subject.

We do not claim "expert" status, but we do claim to be as informed on the science as most, and thus able to articulate a powerful case against bowing to "consensus" alarmist views on carbon and climate issues. Bottom line: We might as well just take up arms against the wind.

What matters to us all, however, are events such as hurricanes, hurricane intensity, sinking islands, droughts, snowstorms and cold spells (yes, even those are blamed on global warming!) or glaciers melting. Invariably just about everything has been attributed to global warming/climate change and for at least a decade many in the press, many politicians and certainly most environmentalist organizations are unwilling to admit that these events are normal physical phenomena or cycles.[1] What they are immediately ready to do is to attribute all "unusual" events to climate change, which in their rhetoric is entirely anthropogenic. There is a direct line of equations. For example: bad hurricanes equal global climate change equal anthropogenic origin equal carbon dioxide emissions equal world lifestyles must change radically.

Historically, man has always been far more concerned about cooling climates.[2] But, Danish climate scientist Henrik Svensmark and science writer Nigel Calder point out, "Among the thousands of human generations, ours may be the first that was ever frightened by a warming."[3] Indeed, it is hard to credit why less than a single degree of warming (which is what we are talking about) between the 1850s and the mid 1990s should register as a blip on the news-of-interest screen, much less set in transit a whole global multi-billion dollar industry. Given the level of prophetic prediction and sheer blind faith in Anthropogenic Global Warmism (AGW) we ought to perceive AGW-ism as more akin to a religious movement than a scientific one. For one thing is certain, global warmist fears are predicated almost exclusively on speculation and fear about what *may* happen in the future, not what *is* happening now. The projections are based on the much ballyhooed "science," the one that "is all in," espoused by a nebulous "consensus," and claiming that anthropogenic global warming is to blame. But, as we shall see, it is in the beliefs behind AGW-ism that we perceive the movement's apocalyptic nature, and its ultimate appeal to what the great philosopher Edmund Burke defined as "man's inherently religious nature."

Of course, that is not how climate alarmists see themselves. They see themselves as "scientific" and "concerned" to "sound the alarm." The only problem is that their entire belief-system, far from being founded upon observable, proven facts and data — something to which, perversely, they have a surprising antipathy in practice — is rooted entirely in computer programmed models, and thus highly speculative science. Such computer modeled science is today the sole basis for the thesis that the slight warming of the last century MUST be man-made and MUST be on a correlatable upward climb. In these models, more carbon dioxide emissions would certainly mean higher global warming.

As cyclical warming and cooling periods have always been the norm throughout history one has to wonder why they *insist* that the usual parameters of natural temperature variation could not possibly apply today. What it all boils down to is that the twin "infallible" tenets or unassailable doctrines of AGW-ism are: 1) that its chief priests understand the science of climate — when they clearly don't (it's too complicated with many factors, no one does), and 2) that carbon dioxide is the "Great Satan" that must be defeated — when it plainly isn't (and there is, literally, *zero* empirical evidence for it).

Undermine the first tenet, and the house of cards must fall. Undermine the second, and the house must also fall. Empty both of any scientific credibility and you begin to perceive clearly the point Charles Mackay was making about men going mad in herds.

What we propose to review initially is both the science and the scandal of the alleged consensus that has, monstrously, sought to end all public debate. In doing so however, it becomes impossible to avoid one unpleasant but recurring theme, that of a general lack of integrity by alarmist politicians, researchers and journalists alike, reflected in the suppression of non-alarmist counter-evidence and the vicious demonization of "heretics" who disagree with them.

THE SCANDAL OF THE SCIENCE "CONSENSUS"

How many scientists does it take to make a consensus? Answer: 2,500. That is, according to the United Nations who instigated the IPCC[4] to "settle" the issue of whom or what is responsible for a late twentieth-century global warming period. Unfortunately, as it turns out, the 2,500 who famously made up the UN IPCC were *not* all climate scientists — and not all contributing scientists even read all the parts of the report that they were supposed to agree on.

In fact, very few actually peer-reviewed the critical portions of the first UN IPCC report in 1996 that made mankind the CO_2 emitting villain of the peace. Writers Tom Harris and John McLean take up the case:

> *An example of rampant misrepresentation of IPCC reports is the frequent assertion that "hundreds of IPCC scientists" are known to support the*

following statement, arguably the most important of the WG I report, namely "Greenhouse gas forcing has very likely caused most of the observed global warming over the last 50 years."

In total, only 62 scientists reviewed the chapter in which this statement appears, the critical chapter 9, "Understanding and Attributing Climate Change." Of the comments received from the 62 reviewers of this critical chapter, almost 60 per cent of them were rejected by IPCC editors. And of the 62 expert reviewers of this chapter, 55 had serious vested interest, leaving only seven expert reviewers who appear impartial.[5]

If any of us should ever make the mistake of being impressed by numbers, rather than by being *right*, especially when it comes to science, we ask: How many scientists would it take to convince us that a climate "consensus" *never* existed at all?

Back in 2008, Dr Arthur Robinson of the Oregon Institute of Science and Medicine (OISM) picked up exactly this point when speaking to a packed National Press Club in Washington DC. In his address he announced that more than 31,000 scientists had at that point signed the Oregon Petition *rejecting* the IPCC line on man-made emissions and climate change. Acutely aware that claims of a "phoney list" would immediately be leveled, Dr Robinson pointed out that the list had been carefully vetted to confirm that over 9,000 of those who signed held PhDs.[6] But Dr Robinson, a PhD scientist himself, was rightly appalled at the notion of being forced to play the numbers game, explaining, "Science shouldn't be done by poll. The numbers shouldn't matter. But if they want warm bodies, we have them." Impressive as these numbers are however, much of the Western media persists in ignoring them.

In March 2008, over 500 individuals, including leading climate scientists, economists, policymakers, engineers, and other professionals, endorsed the Manhattan Declaration on Climate Change.[7] Sponsored by climate scientists of the International Climate Science Coalition (ICSC),[8] it states: "There is no convincing evidence that CO_2 emissions from modern industrial activity have in the past, are now, or will in the future cause catastrophic climate change." The Declaration calls for governments and others to "reject the views expressed by the UN IPCC, as well as popular but misguided works such as Al Gore's 'An Inconvenient Truth.'" ICSC chairman Professor Tim Patterson said, "Instead of wasting billions restricting emissions of CO_2, a vitally important gas on which all life depends, governments must concentrate on solving known environmental problems over which we have influence." As impressive as the signatories and numbers are, yet again, the Western mass media has, generally, ignored it.

Previously, in December 2007, the US Senate released a report signed by over 400 dissenting scientists.[9] In it scientists expressed a range of views from skepticism to outright rejection of the theory of anthropogenic global warming. Surprise, surprise: yet again the mass media deemed it not newsworthy. Neither did they report that Professor Paul Reiter — a member of the original IPCC review team — was so appalled by what he perceived as the misuse of the review procedure and other distortions of the science when the first report came out, that he demanded his name be removed from the report. Eventually, the UN administration did so, but only after Dr Reiter intimated legal action may be taken. They finally complied and removed his name.[10]

Today, at the end of the first decade of the twenty-first century, the list of climate scientists and other climate-informed dissenters is considerably more extensive and the alleged science consensus now only a figment of elitist mindsets. Even so, to play the numbers game when it comes to science is to miss the point of genuine scientific endeavor entirely. Consensus science has a poor track record. How often have you heard "science" dictate that coffee, butter, and countless other consumables were bad for you, only for "science" to contradict itself weeks later by concluding coffee is in fact good for you? In a bid to give the public the certainty it craves on a given issue, consensus science has far too often substituted speculation and faith for empirical evidence and genuine scientific investigation.

In 2003, scientist and science writer Michael Crichton delivered what ought to be the definitive intellectual blow against the whole notion of "consensus science." In a speech delivered to the California Institute of Technology, Crichton said:

> *I regard consensus science as an extremely pernicious development that ought to be stopped cold in its tracks. Historically, the claim of consensus has been the first refuge of scoundrels; it is a way to avoid debate by claiming that the matter is already settled. Whenever you hear a consensus of scientists agree on something or other, reach for your wallet, because you're being had.*
>
> *Let's be clear: the work of science has nothing whatever to do with consensus. Consensus is the business of politics. Science, on the contrary, requires only one investigator who happens to be right, which means that he or she has results that are verifiable by reference to the real world. In science consensus is irrelevant. What is relevant is reproducible results. The greatest scientists in history are great precisely because they broke with consensus.*
>
> *There is no such thing as consensus science. If it's a consensus, it isn't science. If it's science, it isn't consensus. Period.*[11]

We will return to Crichton's incisive logic and his early grasp of the religious-style nature of his much-beloved discipline of environmental science later.

At the end of the first decade of the twenty-first century, however, one consensus *is today* factually indisputable: *there has been no median global warming since the mid-1990s, and since 2002 the global mean temperature appears to have declined slightly.*

As early as 2008, a peer-reviewed research paper[12] (*Nature 453, 43–45, 1 May, 2008*) even suggested a cooling cycle may take over for the next 20 years. Dyed-in-the-wool AGW advocates like the BBCs meteorologist John Kettley have been forced to concede that globally speaking warming "appears to have stalled."[13] While AGW hardliners refuse the simple explanation of natural cyclical variation, they are currently attempting to dredge up all manner of explanations explaining why not one of their alarmist computer models predicted the current cooling period. But then it wouldn't, would it? If your computer model includes the assertion that man-made carbon emissions are the root cause of global temperature rises and that carbon emissions have inexorably continued to rise, the computer prediction will persist in predicting *further* temperature rises. But the global mean temperature has *not* continued to rise. The natural explanation is that CO_2 emissions are *not* the causal factor when temperature rises. But, once again, the "natural" explanation is not acceptable to AGW-theorists. Too many science grants and personal reputations are now staked on high-profile alarmist predictions.

The reality is that CO_2 emissions are continuing to rise around the world while the global mean temperature has remained static for over a decade, and may even have fallen. That should be enough to "hole" AGW-theory below the waterline. And if we were dealing with real science it would, and the vilification of CO_2 would be at an end (or at least suspended pending further investigation). *But we are not dealing with pure science.* We are rather dealing with science suffused with a strong, anti-human, eco-faith agenda. Facts and data are ultimately, for AGW activists, non-essential elements of their faith.

. Far from denting their faith in climate theory, they cling tenaciously to it, and thus to their reputations, which depend on it. Today, we are in the bizarre position that we cannot predict with any degree of certainty weather patterns for next week, yet some climatologists are trying to tell us that they can predict with certainty climate patterns a hundred years from now.

Indeed, so dire have the long-term predictions of the UK Meteorological Office consistently been in recent years, the BBC has considered sacking them entirely.[14] Yet, the arrogance of those whose faith is in "man-programmed" computer models knows no bounds. As Michael Crichton (in the same speech previously quoted) puts it, "I have to say the arrogance of the model-makers is breathtaking. To predict anything about the world a hundred years from now is simply absurd."[15]

Whatever we may personally believe about global warming, serious science-based pressure has long been building on the UN IPCC to hold their hands up and admit its objectives are political not scientific. As the trickle of "dissident" scientists has become a stream over recent years, leading anti-alarmists, like S. Fred Singer, author of *Unstoppable Global Warming: Every 1500 Years*, described 2008 as the "tipping point," the year when the real science argument decisively swung away from the AGW alarmists. And given the increasingly colder winters with which the northern hemisphere has been hit since 2007 in particular, he clearly has a point. Singer's assertion was borne out within the year when polls in 2009 on both sides of the Atlantic[16] showed plainly that the percentage who no longer accept that man is responsible for warming the planet, has grown to well over half the population. As usual it is only the nation's elites, politicians, social ideologues, and journalists, who lag behind the common sense understanding of the "common man" and the fact-driven reality.

And nowhere does elitist "out-of-touch" arrogance running on as high octane as at the UN IPCC.

THE UN IPCC'S CULTURE OF ANTI-SCIENCE

The UN IPCC itself has set the tone for an ideological, politically-driven scope and a lack of scientific integrity from first to last; beginning with its opening report in 1995 through to the scandal of "Climategate" in late 2009. In 1995, the draft of the first IPCC report said this, "Any claims of positive detection of significant climate change are likely to remain controversial until uncertainties in the total natural variability of the climate system are reduced." It went on, "No study to date has positively attributed all or part of observed climate changes to anthropogenic causes."[17]

All of which smacks of *genuine* scientists wrestling with the reality that, as yet, our understanding of climate variations is wracked with uncertainty, not least in relation to man's role. But now, consider what the IPCC political administrators did *after* the scientists who drafted the original went home. They removed both of the nuanced phrases concerning man's *possible* role, and replaced them with: "The balance of evidence suggests a discernible human influence on climate." It was the latter sentence which appeared in the final 1996 IPCC report and upon that single, dishonest, non-scientific politicized amendment the whole case for anthropogenic global warming now pivoted in a very different direction.

The UN IPCC had spoken. In a post-Cold War world, with the US the undisputed winner and the de-emphasizing of the issues which for decades led the international debate, the UN IPCC filled two other important elements. For many, uncomfortable with the US as the only world superpower, the substitution of the UN in the leadership role was a very positive thing. The other, the elephant in the room, was the implicit assertion that CO_2 emissions, directly connected with wealth and something that clearly separates rich from poor countries, had a far more sinister dimension.

The science was allegedly "in," man was deemed proven guilty, and now it was to be open season on all "heretics" who disagreed with the IPCC verdict. Variously vilified by researchers and journalists alike as "holocaust deniers" and "criminals," even top climate scientists were now depicted as "mavericks" and the jobs of researchers who disagreed were threatened. All of this, stemming from that very first anti-science "sleight of hand" in the first IPCC report in 1996 that showed the IPCC had no compunction in politicizing science for socio-political ends.

In his article "The Sloppy Science of Global Warming,"[18] Roy W. Spencer reminds us how "the practice of science is an unbiased search for truth, right?" He goes on to lament that "unbiased search" has managed to adduce "no solid published evidence that has ruled out a natural cause for most of our recent warming — not one peer-reviewed paper. Spencer notes how the alarmists have made such a big deal out of the "unprecedented" opening of the Northwest Passage as that part of the Arctic ice has receded without mentioning that a warming period back in the 1930s led the Passage to open then too.

He also points out that due to a lack of actual data "scientists instead explore what we have measured: man-made greenhouse gas emissions" — ignoring that water vapor (clouds) is a far more important green-house gas, one we do not understand at all, and one we have no control over. Hence, the obsession with a fairly piddling greenhouse "trace" gas, CO_2. Spencer also points out the other major embarrassment to IPCC AGW theory: that it was just as warm, probably warmer, during the Medieval Warming Period. We know this earlier major warming period has persistently caused AGW-theorists a major headache, as the leaked "Climategate" emails scandal (more shortly) reveals only too clearly. As Spencer comments, "While climate change used to be natural, apparently now it is entirely man-made." Of course, they cannot explain high temperatures in earlier periods in terms of much lower man-made CO_2 emissions. Why would they want to? It doesn't fit their dogmatic theories.

Roy Spencer goes on to point out that it is "surprisingly difficult to separate cause and effect in the climate system" and how it is that today "entire careers (including my own) depend upon the threat of global warming." Spencer fears that politicians have jumped aboard the "Global Warming Express, and this train has no brakes" to such an extent that no amount of actual evidence — remember what we said about facts and data meaning little to AGW activists? — other than a "prolonged period of cooling" will end the "hysteria." And even then there would, Spencer believes, be "cries of anguish from vested interests" that are making a fortune from the AGW taxpayer windfall.

"It is unfortunate," laments Spencer, "that our next generation of researchers and teachers is being taught to trust emotions over empirical evidence. Polar bears are much more exciting than careful analysis of the data. Social and political trends increasingly trump all other considerations. Science that is not politically correct is becoming increasingly difficult to publish. Even science reporting has become more sensationalist in recent years." In short, he perceives that "climate research has become corrupted." Indeed it has, and it all began in earnest on climate when the UN's IPCC first "fiddled the books" by insisting that the science was saying something it was not. Not that the IPCC has cornered the market on climate science corruption.

In his essay "Global Warming: The climate of fear"[19] writer Alexander Cockburn observes how "Climate catastrophism is tied into the decline of the left, and the decline of the left's optimistic vision of altering the economic nature of things through a political program. The left has bought into environmental catastrophism because it thinks that if it can persuade the world that there is indeed a catastrophe, then somehow the emergency response will lead to positive developments in terms of social and environmental justice." And Charles Murray's words about "men going mad in herds" resonate again in Cockburn's next comment: "Here in the West, the so-called 'war on global warming' is reminiscent of medieval madness. You can now buy indulgences to offset your carbon guilt." Cockburn links the "madness" to something far darker. "In today's political climate, it has become fairly dangerous for a young scientist or professor to step up and say: 'This is all nonsense.' It is increasingly difficult to challenge the global warming consensus, on either a scientific or a political level. Academies can be incredibly cowardly institutions, and if one of their employees were to question the discussion of climate change he or she would be pulled to one side and told: 'You're threatening our funding and reputation — do you really want to do that?'"

See what we mean about the thread of lack of scientific integrity running through the whole AGW movement? Its core doctrines and its reprehensible resorting to personal vilification? Should we not wonder why their arguments alone are just not up to scratch — especially when hard questions are leveled? Not that most mainstream journalists chose to pose them. It has consistently been up to climate research "heretics" and astute bloggers to do their job for them.

GLACIERGATE: A CASE STUDY IN UNETHICAL INCOMPETENCE

Not many news reports have been used so effectively to incite fear on entire populations, demand immediate government action and cause concern among people the world over, than the alleged melting of the Himalayan glaciers.

Chapter 10 of the 2007 IPCC report stated: "Glaciers in the Himalayas are receding faster than in any other part of the world, and if the present rate continues, the likelihood of them disappearing by the year 2035 and perhaps sooner is very high if the Earth keeps warming at the current rate. Its total area will likely shrink from the present 500,000 to 100,000 square kilometers by the year 2035."

To put it in starker terms, among other calamities it presaged, India's great rivers would dry out, and all associated agricultural, cultural and religious impacts associated with them. To begin with, the IPCC's geography is appalling. 500,000 square kilometers is probably the area covered by *all* glaciers throughout the world. But it is fascinating how this gem made the IPCC report and how it has spawned, at a cursory count, 7,000 news stories and commentaries.

It has since emerged that the IPCC statement on Himalayan glaciers was entirely fictitious, based as it turns out on thoroughly misleading information from a *2005 report by the World Wildlife Fund*, which itself was taken from an article published in the "eminent" and popular UK science journal, *The New Scientist* in June 1999. That article, "Flooded Out," was written by an Indian glaciologist Syed Hasnain who *speculated* that Himalayan glaciers *could* vanish within 40 years as a result of global warming.[20]

By diabolical coincidence on 20 January 2010, exactly at the time of the writing of this chapter, the IPCC released a statement saying that "estimates relating to the rate of recession of the Himalayan glaciers in its Fourth Assessment Report" were "poorly substantiated" and "well-established standards of evidence were not applied properly." The IPCC had little alternative but to out its "evidence" as "bovine excrement" after a UK *Mail On Sunday* interview with the scientist behind the claim, Dr Murari Lal, admitted it was bogus. Lal admitted that when his claim was repeated in the 2007 Nobel-prize winning IPCC report he knew it had not been verified.[21] Lal's defense was that it was included to "impact policy-makers and politicians and encourage them to take concrete action." And take action politicians duly did. On the basis of the spurious glacier claims, especially that threat of the Himalayan glaciers melting, Rajendra Pachauri's Energy and Resources Institute (much more on him in Chapter 6) was awarded over $500,000 by the Carnegie Foundation of New York and the "lion's share" of a $4 million EU grant funded by European taxpayers for further research.[22] Research into a claim that had no foundation in science whatever.

And yet the IPCC, *despite* their admission has "reiterated its concern about the dangers melting glaciers present in a region that is home to more than one-sixth of the world's population."[23] We will have more to say on allegedly melting poles and glaciers in the next chapter.

KYOTO TO COPENHAGEN: A HOT AIR JOURNEY

The science having been "settled," politicians, green zealots and journalists were now freed from the trouble of having to think or consider new data and facts. Anything that now flew in the face of IPCC orthodoxy was not worth engaging with, and not worth reporting. As Alexander Cockburn had indicated, now the West's socialist-leaning and liberal, planet-saving, elites perceived an unparalleled opportunity for centralizing control in government hands, and pursue social engineering on an unprecedented scale. Everything from what size car you should buy, to how many flights you should take, to what sort of light-bulbs you should use in your home, was now on the freedom-diminishing political agenda. The common enemy was clear: carbon emissions — and man, *read* Western man and for many Americans, who most contributed to them.

Politicians now began jockeying to give a "world lead" in the fight against the planetary enemy: man-made CO_2 emissions. But while grandiose pronouncements proved easy — it costs politicians nothing — it was always going to prove more difficult when it came to international agreements and the economic realities. Despite all the climate bluster, the Kyoto–Copenhagen hot air balloon, designed to bring greenhouse

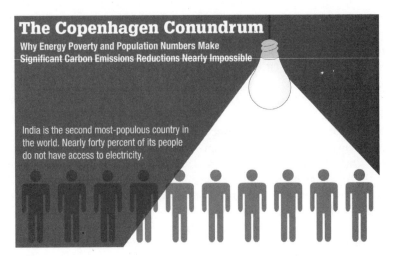

The Copenhagen Conundrum

Why Energy Poverty and Population Numbers Make
Significant Carbon Emissions Reductions Nearly Impossible

India is the second most-populous country in
the world. Nearly forty percent of its people
do not have access to electricity.

Figure 5.1: *Source: Energy Tribune.*

gases, especially man-made CO_2 emissions, under control, was destined to ground itself, with a severe bump.

The Kyoto Protocol, drafted in 1997, finally came into force in 2005. From its inception national leaders were falling over themselves to commit their countries to CO_2 cutting targets. After all, aspirations like windy rhetoric cost nothing. By June 2009, 187 had signed the Kyoto Protocol. Only the US among the major nations refused to sign. For this act of unilateral defiance, the US and the Bush administration were branded "uncaring unilateralists." The truth is, as history shows plainly, it was the US (the only country to not sign) who called Kyoto correctly, and the other 187 (numbers again) who got it wrong. Only the Bush administration faced the reality that it would be signing an economic suicide note. Eventually, the potentially catastrophic economic impact of Kyoto would come home to many leaders in Europe, too.

Today, barely any of those who signed up to Kyoto have any prospect of actually achieving their CO_2 cutting targets. And to do so would mean seriously handicapping domestic industry competitiveness. Take the situation in Europe. Well before Copenhagen, numerous European nations were lining up with CO_2 "sick-notes," demanding a renegotiation of their Kyoto commitments. As the full horror of the costs of cap and trade binding targets had sunk in, European national leaders were finally grasping the industry-busting ramifications.

Europe's industrialists had been warning vociferously enough. But by 2008, it was only when the credit crunch turned up the hearing aids for ideologically poor of hearing Eurocrats that the latter were forced to listen. Suddenly, Germany's so-called Green Chancellor, anti-CO_2 crusader Angela Merkel began turned shades of red, as back-pedaling became the new EU sport. With the reality of a legally binding agreement on CO_2 cuts looming at December's EU climate summit in 2008, the burgeoning list of carbon rebels had grown to include some of the EU's big hitters. By October 2008, Germany and Italy were in cahoots with the former echoing Italy's Berlusconi that any cap and trade measures should not "weigh on the economy."

Italy estimated that the cost of complying with its imposed target would be 25 billion euros ($32 billion) a year. In 2008, a study calculated that Germany could lose up to 300,000 jobs by 2020.[24] German industrialists had consistently called for a moratorium on the climate package and lobbied hard for the Chancellor to cut the political climate rhetoric before the German industry voted with its feet and moved abroad. Essentially, Germany's public support for the Italian position — Germany and Italy are Europe's leading manufacturers — made a 27-state approved EU climate package impossible in December 2008.

Poland and at least eight other eastern European countries with coal-dependent power stations had also lobbied against a non-voluntary CO_2 cutting European Trading Scheme (ETS) regime. Even some last-minute carrot dangling by France, offering the prospect of millions of euros of free carbon emission allowances (halving their emission allowance quota until 2016) failed to head off the fears of the eastern European nations. France and Austria too asked the EU to ease its climate ambitions of 20 percent reduction in CO_2 emissions from 1990 levels and 20 percent of power from renewable sources both by 2020. The writing was already on the wall for the planet-saving Copenhagen Summit in 2009.

Bizarrely, at such a dire world economic juncture, the socialist British government unilaterally moved to consider imposing legally-binding CO_2 targets via a new Climate Bill. Speaking on the Bill before the House of Lords at the end of November 2008, Lord Nigel Lawson, Thatcher's chancellor who presided over one of the UK's most dramatic economic recoveries in the 1980s, and who has authored a book on the economic effects of fighting climate change, delivered a broadside to the notion of self-imposed cap and trade targets. Lawson said, "This Bill will go down in history, and future generations will see it as the most absurd Bill that this House and Parliament as a whole has ever had to examine."[25] According to the UK government's own figures, the UK Climate Bill would cost the country between £30 billion (over $45 billion) and £205 billion (over $305 billion) between now and 2050 to implement. The benefits, however, are calculated to lie between £82 billion (over $123 billion) and £110 billion (over $165 billion).

Consequently, at the Copenhagen Summit in December 2009, world leaders never had a chance of achieving a meaningful "Son of Kyoto" agreement. China and India previously made it more than clear they had no intention of slowing their own hydrocarbon-driven industrialization process. And, quite rightly, they demanded to know by what moral right an industrialized West could deny them the same modernizations they had enjoyed.

The simple fact is that China is opening a new coal-fired power station at the rate of more than one a week and India is fast-industrializing using coal-fired power; a process that will, incidentally, help deliver millions out of their abject poverty. Forty coal-fired power stations are due to come online across Europe itself over the next five years, 26 in Germany alone. At the same time the World Bank has been and is investing massively in coal projects around the world. Why? Because it knows, and thinking individuals cannot deny, that developing nations need cheap energy — and it doesn't come cheaper than coal — to industrialize and overcome mass poverty, just as the West has done. Clean or otherwise, King Coal remains the cheap fuel of choice as the key to industrialization, and will continue to punch very large holes in the CO_2 rhetoric of Western politicians.

Predictably, national economic considerations, not planet-saving ideological geopolitics, dominated in Copenhagen. Described as an "historic summit," so it proved to be . . . for the scope of its failure. In the end the Copenhagen Accord, billed as the "last chance to save the world," made a stunningly pompous statement suggesting that world governments hold a power to perform they plainly do not; the power to "keep global temperature rises to below 2 degrees C (3.6F)." Scientists, however, maintained that such a goal would require a cut of greenhouse gases by at least 50 percent. In short, no legally binding targets were agreed, rendering the Accord meaningless. The war against CO_2 is effectively over. As a representative of one leading charity observed, Copenhagen was "a triumph of spin over substance."

Joseph D'Aleo, an acclaimed meteorologist, is executive director of Icecap (International Climate and Environmental Change Assessment Project). In his article, "12 Facts About Global Climate Change That You Won't Read in the Popular Press,"[26] he sums up, as succinctly as we have seen anywhere, the key elements and real science.

1   Temperatures have been cooling since 2002, even as carbon dioxide has continued to rise.

2   Carbon dioxide is a trace gas and by itself will produce little warming. Also, as CO_2 increases, the incremental warming is less, as the effect is logarithmic so the more CO_2, the less warming it

produces.

3   CO_2 has been totally uncorrelated with temperature over the last decade, and has proved significantly negative in effect since 2002.

4   CO_2 is not a pollutant, but a naturally occurring gas. Together with chlorophyll and sunlight, it is an essential ingredient in photosynthesis and is, accordingly, plant food.

5   Reconstruction of paleo-climatological CO_2 concentrations demonstrate that carbon dioxide concentration today is near its lowest level since the Cambrian Era some 550 million years ago, when there was almost 20 times as much CO_2 in the atmosphere as there is today *without* causing a "runaway greenhouse effect."

6   Temperature changes lead, not lag, CO_2 changes on all time-scales. The oceans may play a key role, emitting carbon dioxide when they warm as carbonated beverages lose fizz as they warm, and absorbing it as they cool.

7   Most of the warming in the climate models comes from the assumption that water vapor and precipitation increase as temperatures warm, a strong positive feedback. Water vapor is a far more important greenhouse gas than CO_2. However, that assumption has been shown in observations and peer-reviewed research to be wrong, and in fact water vapor and precipitation act as a negative feedback that reduces any small greenhouse warming from carbon dioxide.

8   Indeed, greenhouse models show the warming should be greatest at mid to high atmosphere levels in the tropics. But balloon and satellite observations show cooling there. The greenhouse signature or DNA does not match reality, and the greenhouse models thus must greatly overstate the warming — and in a court of law would have to be acquitted of any role in global warming.

9   The sun has both direct and indirect effects on our climate. Solar activity changes on cycles of 11 years and longer. When the sun is more active it is brighter and a little hotter. More important though are the indirect effects. Ultraviolet radiation increases much more than the brightness, and causes increased ozone production, which generates heat in the high atmosphere that works its way down, affecting the weather.

Also, an active sun diffuses cosmic rays, which play an important role in nucleation of low clouds, resulting in fewer clouds. In all these ways the sun warms the planet more when it is active. An active sun in the 1930s and again near the end of the last century helped produce the observed warming periods. The current solar cycle is the longest in over 100 years; an unmistakable sign of a cooling sun that historical patterns suggest will stay so for decades.

10   The multi-decadal cycles in the ocean correlate extremely well with the solar cycles and global temperatures. These are 60 to 70 year cycles that relate to natural variations in the large-scale circulations. Warm oceans correlate with warm global temperatures. The Pacific started cooling in the late 1990s and it accelerated in the last year, and the Atlantic has cooled from its peak in 2004. This supports the observed global land temperature cooling, which is strongly correlated with ocean heat content. Newly deployed NOAA buoys confirm global ocean cooling.

11   Warmer ocean cycles are periods with diminished Arctic ice cover. When the oceans were warm in the 1930s to the 1950s, Arctic ice diminished and Greenland warmed. The recent ocean warming, especially in the 1980s to the early 2000s, is similar to what took place 70 years ago and the Arctic ice has reacted much the same way, with diminished summer ice extent.

12   Antarctic ice has been increasing and the extent in 2008 was the greatest in the satellite monitoring era. We are today running ahead of record pace in 2008.

As D'Aleo laments, "What will it take for the media to let go of their biases and begin doing their job, reporting the truth?" What indeed?

But even as the Copenhagen Summit was about to get under way in December 2009, a storm broke that, once again, raised the issue of the anti-science skullduggery that is endemic at the heart of the UN IPCC machinery, and the AGW movement generally.

THE CLIMATEGATE SCANDAL: THE "GREATEST IN MODERN SCIENCE"

In November 2009, a climate "missile" struck when 1079 emails and 72 other documents from the University of East Anglia's Climate Research Unit's (CRU) computers were released onto the Net.[27] As usual the mainstream media was asleep, which was surprising since the contents proved explosive, auguring a major climate science scandal.

But the furor across the Internet could not be ignored. A scandal that writer Andrew Bolt rightly termed "Climategate," was not just any scandal, it amounted to the "greatest in modern science." What was particularly explosive was the insight it gave us into the science "mafia" running IPCC and in the AGW "show." Reading the emails[28] is a chilling experience, especially when one realizes that some of the authors were also authors of the "definitive" UN IPCC reports, and those who have persistently declared the science to be "settled."

The UK *Daily Telegraph*'s James Delingpole sums up the contents thus, "Conspiracy, collusion in exaggerating warming data, possibly illegal destruction of embarrassing information, organised resistance to disclosure, manipulation of data, private admissions of flaws in their public claims and much more."[29] Here is an excerpt from the CRU's Keith Briffa to the world-famous "manufacturer" of the discredited hockey stick graph (more later), Michael Mann, in response to the latter's support for his role in producing a report for the IPCC. "Your words are a real boost to me at the moment," says Briffa. "I found myself questioning the whole process and being often frustrated at the formulaic way things had to be done . . . I tried hard to balance the needs of the science and the IPCC, *which were not always the same*."[30] So science has one need — presumably for empirical truth — while the IPCC has another?

Elsewhere we learn about the apparently regular manipulation of data evidence: "I've just completed Mike's [Mann] *trick* of adding in the real temps to each series for the last 20 years (i.e. from 1981 onwards) and from 1961 for Keith's to *hide the decline*."[31] Hide what decline, we might ask? Well the context is a discussion of the scientific *fact* that global temperatures have *not* warmed for a decade, indeed they have "declined." The decline they wanted to hide was the one in global temperatures.

But surely, for a scientist, facts are facts? *Why hide facts?* Then we learn of the private doubts of another researcher: "The fact is that we can't account for the lack of warming at the moment and it is a travesty that we can't. The CERES data published in the August BAMS 09 supplement in 2008 shows there should be even more warming: but the data is surely wrong." It seems if the evidence does not fit the theory, the evidence must be changed or suppressed.

Quite a few emails were also taken up with the "embarrassment" caused by the Medieval Warming Period, one even suggesting "it would be nice to try to 'contain' the putative 'MWP.'" Here we have scientists actually discussing "dumping" a fact of history, one that embarrasses their theory. Next, we have enlightening discussions about how best to squeeze dissenting scientists out of the peer-review science process entirely.

In one email the CRU's director (and key IPCC author), Phil Jones, writing to Michael Mann, discusses two scientific papers that deny the link between human activity and global warming. He wants them kept out of an upcoming IPCC report. "Kevin and I will keep them out somehow — even if we have to re-define what the peer-review literature is!" The context of the discussions here is Michael Mann and CRU director Phil Jones discussing putting pressure on the editors of academic journals who might see fit to publish dissenting scientific opinion. Heaven forbid! Mann writes, "Perhaps we should encourage our colleagues in the climate research community to no longer submit to, or cite papers in, this journal?" Jones responds, "I will be emailing the journal to tell them I'm having nothing more to do with it until they rid themselves of this troublesome editor."

The visceral hatred — no other word is adequate — toward climate skeptics is ubiquitous in these memos. When skeptic John Daly died in 2004, for CRU director Jones this was "cheering news." Benjamin Santer, of the US Lawrence Livermore National Laboratory, writing to the CRU about one dissenting climate scientist, states, "Next time I see Pat Michaels [a leading dissenting climatologist] at a scientific meeting, I'll be tempted to beat the crap out of him." One is tempted to suggest that "beating the crap out of something" may be a far more profitable exercise at the CRU?

Reading through the emails, we might have thought someone had hacked into the Soprano family's private computers. But no, we have to keep reminding you, these authors are among the world's leading lights in collating and publishing scientific data for the UN IPCC. They *are* the principal voices of climate alarmism. In fact, the UK's CRU is one of the UN's four global science data collating agencies. In the wake of the "Climategate" revelations, former Thatcher economist Lord Nigel Lawson was the first to call for a public enquiry, one to be headed by a high court judge.[32] By early December an inquiry was set up, by the university.[33] It had the effect, at least, of forcing CRU's director, Phil Jones, to step down. And, above all, *remember* that billions of dollars — mostly taxpayer dollars — *and the entire global climate fight* is predicated on the "scientific" deliberations of such individuals. But let's get back to the data.

THE DATA *IS* THE SCIENCE, STUPID!

Implicit in the emails is a blatant conspiracy to avoid submitting to any requests for data under the UK Freedom of Information Act. Worst of all, subsequent to the email debacle, the CRU turns out to have "inadvertently" dumped its raw climate data for the 1980s. So now we don't even have the means to check their data — data that is alleged to prove a consistent long-term rise in global temperatures during the twentieth century. As Roger Pielke Jnr., professor of environmental studies at

Colorado University, says, "The CRU is basically saying 'trust us.' So much for settling questions and resolving debates in science."[34]

If one leaked document goes to the heart of Climategate, it is what the *New York Times* called an "executive summary."[35] It is taken from a file marked "HARRY_READ_ME." It is the log of one unnamed CRU computer expert, the reverberations from which should echo around the scientific and media world. Writing of his long struggle to make sense of a database of historical temperatures, "Harry" writes:

> "*Aarrgggghhh! Oh [EXPLETIVE] this! It's Sunday evening, I've worked all weekend, and just when I thought it was done I'm hitting yet another problem that's based on the hopeless state of our databases. There is no uniform data integrity . . .*"

Meanwhile, Harry's colleagues are dependent on the same "hopeless databases" and lack of "uniform data integrity" can continue to predict, with total confidence, potential planetary catastrophe.

CLIMATEGATE FALLOUT

Britain's Viscount Monckton, a leading climate skeptic, upped the ante denouncing the CRU and its partners as "not merely bad scientists — they are crooks. And crooks who have perpetrated their crimes at the expense of British and US taxpayers."[36] Even more chilling than the prospective cost of Copenhagen shenanigans, Monckton claims to have seen a draft Danish treaty proposal pre-summit which, on the back of GW theory, would establish an embryonic one-world government. According to Christopher Monckton, this is the ultimate agenda for the green liberal left or "watermelons" as they're nicknamed, who are "green on the outside, red on the inside." The proposal, Monckton says, expected to divert as much as 2 percent of the GDP of rich nations to third world countries, supposedly to compensate them for the environmental evils wrought by Western industrialization.[37]

Even a dyed-in-the-wool AGW alarmist like the UK's George Monbiot was forced to admit to having been badly shaken by the CRU revelations. Monbiot says the scientific data *does* now need "re-analyzing." He laments, "There's no use pretending this isn't a major blow. There appears to be evidence here of attempts to prevent scientific data from being released, and even to destroy material that was subject to a Freedom of Information request." Monbiot even called for CRU's Phil Jones to resign.[38] He wasn't alone. The UN IPCC's own Eduardo Zorita has declared that his colleagues "Michael Mann, Phil Jones and

Stefan Rahmstorf should be barred from the IPCC process." Even the University of East Anglia's Mike Hulme, one of the ten most quoted climate scientists in the world, states: "It is possible that climate science has become too partisan, too centralised." He suggests that because of the IPCC's "structural tendency to politicize climate change science" that "it is also possible the IPCC has run its course." But now the US data is coming under the spotlight, too.

UP NEXT: NASA'S DATA

But the British CRU staff work closely with their US counterparts, those who compile the GISS (Goddard Institute for Space Studies)/NCDC dataset. For two years the GISS data-keepers have also been accused of "hiding data" by dragging their feet on a request under the Freedom of Information Act from Chris Horner, a senior fellow at the Competitive Enterprise Institute (CEI).[39] This is data that has already seen significant amendments forced on GISS staff when the "experts" were found to have variously used poor data by diligent independent scientists and bloggers. At time of writing Horner had informed the NASA's GISS that it has until the end of 2010 to comply, or else he will sue to compel release.

While it's the data itself Horner is seeking, he has also requested release of the chain of emails from scientists discussing anomalies pointed out to GISS staff in the past. Given the current British CRU furor we might not expect GISS staff to be willing to comply. But here's the thing — the NASA and CRU data are collectively the backbone of the consensus science alleged to prove anthropogenic global warming. And the caliber of those involved might be considered, to the say the least, "unscientific." Senator James Inhofe, ranking member of the US Senate's Environment and Public Works Committee, has, additionally, called for a hearing to assess whether the UN IPCC "cooked the science." Even some of the UN's own scientists have called for an enquiry. So will Climategate finally bring reason and an end to speculative science at last to this key issue? It's doubtful; there's way too many vested interests at stake.

REPUTATIONS, MONEY AND POWER

Obama's White House immediately trashed the leaked British emails as "irrelevant." Nor is any inquiry likely to impact what Lord Monckton describes as the world's "class politique." Why? Because too many reputations, too many research grants, too much power-grubbing, is riding on the anthropogenic global warming horse. And that's because there's a great deal of money to be made by it leading proponents, too.

In December 2009, Paul Cheeser, special correspondent for the Heartland Institute, revealed that Michael Mann has received around $6 million for his various predictions, models and reconstructions.[40] Such is the scandal of where all this public money is going, and to what end, that it forms the substance of our next chapter.

In short, there are just too many who have a powerful vested interest to admit that the *real* science does not come close to proving, even supporting, AGW Theory. But then, as Climategate reveals, when it comes to unsound alarmist claims, we are too often not dealing with scientists pursuing empirical truth, nor, as we have seen, with men of high personal moral integrity. Above all, what becomes clear from the evidence is that in dealing with climatism, specifically, and environmentalism, more generally, we are dealing with an ideological movement rooted in faith and speculation, not scientific truth.

ENVIRONMENTALISM AS RELIGION

Earlier we referred to the writings of Michael Crichton and his insight into the value of the term "science consensus." Crichton was also among the first scientists and science writers to recognize the religious nature of the modern environment movement. A movement far more steeped in prophetic pronouncement and eschatological belief than empirical fact. A movement prepared to politicize itself to fulfill its social engineering agenda. A movement more interested in acting for its own ends than in the common interest — and especially the interest of the poorest and most vulnerable in society.

Here's how Crichton saw it already in 2003:

Today, one of the most powerful religions in the Western world is environmentalism. Environmentalism seems to be the religion of choice for urban atheists. Why do I say it's a religion? Well, just look at the beliefs. If you look carefully, you see that environmentalism is in fact a perfect 21st century remapping of traditional Judeo-Christian beliefs. There's an initial Eden, a paradise, a state of grace and unity with nature, there's a fall from grace into a state of pollution as a result of eating from the tree of knowledge, and as a result of our actions there is a judgment day coming for all of us. We are all energy sinners, doomed to die, unless we seek salvation, which is now called sustainability. Sustainability is salvation in the church of environment. Just as organic food is its communion, that pesticide-free wafer that the right people with the right beliefs, imbibe.

> *Increasingly it seems facts aren't necessary, because the tenets of environmentalism are all about belief. It's about whether you are going to be a sinner, or saved. Whether you are on the side of salvation, or the side of doom. Whether you are one of us, or one of them.*
>
> *With so many past failures, you might think that environmental predictions would become more cautious. But not if it is a religion. Remember, the nut on the sidewalk carrying the placard that predicts the end of the world doesn't quit when the world doesn't end on the day he expects. He just changes his placard, sets a new doomsday date, and goes back to walking the streets. One of the defining features of religion is that your beliefs are not troubled by facts, because they have nothing to do with facts.*[41]

Lord Nigel Lawson takes up the theme. "It is not difficult to understand . . . the appeal of the conventional climate change wisdom," says Lawson. "Throughout the ages something deep in man's psyche has made him receptive to 'end is nigh' apocalyptic warnings. We, as individuals, are imbued with a sense of guilt and a sense of sin" even "a sense of collective guilt and collective sin." This, says Lawson, spawns a "new religion of Eco-fundamentalism" whose "new priests are scientists (well rewarded with research grants) rather than the clerics of established religions."[42]

London Mayor and former editor of *The Spectator*, former journalist Boris Johnson commenting on James Lovelock's environmental alarmist blockbuster *The Revenge of Gaia* has written:

> *The more one listens to . . . Lovelock, and the more one studies public reactions to his prophecies, the clearer it is that we are not just dealing with science . . . this is partly a religious phenomenon. Humanity has largely lost its fear of hellfire, and yet we still hunger for a structure, a point, an eschatology, and a moral counterbalance to our growing prosperity.*
>
> *All of that is brilliantly supplied by climate change. Like all the best religions, fear of climate change satisfies our need for guilt, and self-disgust, and that eternal human sense that technological progress must be punished by the gods.*[43]

US writer John M. Ostrowski notes: "the prime threat to Mother Gaia is anthropogenic climate change." He continues, "Like other religions, environmentalism is a human-centered one "which has "a strong emphasis on the end of the world. Fear mongering and predictions of the apocalypse are the primary evangelizing tools of environmentalists."[44]

THE NEW ORTHODOXY

But Ostrowski also points out something else, that for modern environmentalists "humans are the problem," and he quotes Greenpeace co-founder Patrick Moore — a man totally disaffected with the environmental movement — as perceiving former colleagues as "anti-human."

Martin Livermore is an independent consultant on science and policy issues. Writing on an international news website Livermore points out that:

> *The new orthodoxy teaches that mankind is guilty of Original Sin by despoiling Eden (the pre-Industrial world). This guilt must be assuaged by repairing the damage and protecting all other forms of life.*
>
> *For the deepest Greens, the only real solution is the disappearance of our species from the Earth — the ultimate sacrifice — and for many others a much smaller "optimum population of humans is a desirable goal."*[45]

The increasingly unrestrained condemnation of "heretics" is also part of that mythology.

Vanity Fair magazine went so far as to condemn anyone who questioned the new orthodoxy — the "unbelievers" as they put it — to Dante's Hell. (We'll send a postcard!) Environmental activist Paul Watson, famous for his militant "stop the whalers" campaign, confirms the growing orthodoxy that "We are killing our host Planet Earth." Invoking the worst of Malthusianism, Watson has described mankind variously as "a virus" and "the AIDS of the Earth." Watson wants "vast areas of the planet where humans do not live at all and where other species are free to evolve without human interference." He adds, "We need to radically and intelligently reduce human populations to fewer than one billion" and "return to primitive lifestyles."[46] *Note the dark strategy*: "radically . . . reduce human populations."

Christopher C. Horner, Senior Fellow at the US Competitive Enterprise Institute, rightly observes, "When normal humans look at another human, we see a mind, a soul and a set of hands. The Greens see only a stomach." It doesn't take much to make the intellectual link between the "religious" fervor of the anti-Judeo-Christian, anti-human agenda of Secular Liberalism — with its emphasis on abortion, euthanasia, and depopulation — and the unparalleled opportunity the Climate Change Gospel affords it in seeking its ends through political means.

In the book *Toxic Terror*, Charles Wursta, chief scientist for the US Environment Defense Fund, speaking of how the worldwide ban on DDT, which had virtually wiped out malaria as a global killer, was likely to lead to millions of deaths, replied: "This is as good a way to get rid of them as any." Even though scientists had *proved* DDT was *not* carcinogenic, the environmentalists forced a ban through anyway. It is conservatively estimated that over the next four decades between 10 and 30 million people, mostly children in sub-Saharan Africa, died from malaria as a direct consequence of the ban.

A powerful anti-human theme runs through modern environmentalism. And one can only wonder why those promoting such radical "final solutions" are never among the first to demonstrate their *personal* commitment to it.

But something more sinister has occurred in the broader failure to recognize the inherently religious faith nature of AGW-ism. It is the damage being done to trust in science itself while the faith-system that masquerades in its place is leading governments to divert vast quantities of public money into an AGW-created economic chasm — with all the consequences that has for impacting first the very poorest in society.

Neither should we forget the role and abject failure of the Fourth Estate, the media, to do its job and hold both scientists and governments to account.

To these two key contemporary issues we now turn.

Notes

1 It is worth asking *why* alarmists struggle to allow any current climate events to be *normal* climate activity? Change is what climate (the world is made up of many variable mini-climates) does, and has always done. The Vikings who grew crops in southern Greenland and the Romans who grew grapes in the north of England are testimony to the fact. Volvo and Ferrari may manufacture gas-guzzlers today, but we are not aware that their forefathers also drove them.

2 There is in fact no such thing as a "global climate" only a vast array of local or mini climates around the world. When individuals speak of a "global temperature" they are referring to an aggregated mean average temperature taken from numerous temperature readings and satellite readings.

3 *The Chilling Stars: A New Theory About Climate Change*, Henrik Svensmark and Nigel Calder (Icon Books, 2007), p. 30.

4 http://www.ipcc.ch/

5 See "The UN Climate Change Numbers Hoax," op-ed at Australia's

Online Opinion site. Go to http://www.onlineopinion.com.au/view. asp?article=7553&page=2

6 At time of writing in 2010 the figures now stand at 31,486 scientists, 9,029 of whom hold PhDs. Go to http://www.petitionproject.org/

7 Both authors have signed the Manhattan Declaration. Go to http:// www.climatescienceinternational.org/index.php?option=com_content &task=view&id=63

8 http://www.climatescienceinternational.org/

9 In January 2010, that figure had risen to over 700. The report was published by the US Senate Committee on Environment and Public Works (Senate Minority Page). For more see http://epw.senate.gov/public/index. cfm?FuseAction=Minority.Blogs&ContentRecord_id=2158072E-802A-23AD-45F0-274616DB87E6

10 See: http://www.foxnews.com/story/0,2933,258993,00.html However, a fascinating exchange took place when this same allegation was levelled in the Channel 4 documentary "The Great Global Warming Swindle." What is fascinating from reading the Ofcom finding that took a pro-IPCC stance in its assertion that the comment was made to "diminish the authority of the IPCC" and play up Professor Reiter's links with the IPCC. What is wholly ignored, however, is that Professor Reiter's name *was* on the first draft as a contributor and that he had to threaten to get it removed — *no matter what* the status of his links with, or his contribution to, the IPCC report. See: http://www.ofcomswindlecomplaint.net/Misreprestn_Views/ IPCC/ResignationAllegations.htm

11 Michael Crichton, "Aliens Cause Global Warming," speech to the California Institute of Technology, Pasadena PA, January 17, 2003.

12 *Nature 453*, 43–45, 1 May, 2008.

13 "Thanks St Luke's Little Summer for a Quiet Dry Spell," John Kettley, *Daily Mail Online* updated October 17, 2009.

14 "BBC May Dump Met Office After Complaints About 'BBQ Summer' and 'Mild Winter' Predictions," *Daily Mail*, updated January 18, 2010.

15 Michael Crichton, "Aliens Cause Global Warming," speech to the California Institute of Technology, Pasadena, PA, January 17, 2003.

16 A Rassmussusen US poll reported by Newsbusters.org website in "Gore losing war: 59% don't believe man is warming planet," January 19, 2009. Also, "59% of UK population are 'village idiots' says The Times," James Delingpole *Daily Telegraph* blog, updated November 14, 2009.

17 Detailed assessment of various IPPC "amendments" drafts are provided in a Letter to the IPCC (Working group 1) Scientists, by Dr S. Fred Singer at the Science and Environmental Policy project (SEPP) available online at http://www.sepp.org/Archive/controv/ipcccont/ipccflap.htm

18 "The Sloppy Science of Global Warming," Roy W. Spencer, principal

research scientist at the University of Alabama in Huntsville, published *Energy Tribune.com* March 20, 2008.

19 "Global Warming: The Climate of Fear," Alexander Cockburn, *Energy Tribune.com* March 18, 2008.

20 "UN Climate Chiefs Apologize for Climate Error," Matthew Knight, CNN website, January 20, 2010.

21 "Glacier Scientist: I Knew Data Hadn't Been Verified," David Rose, *Mail on Sunday*, January 24, 2010.

22 "UN Climate Panel Blunders Again Over Himalayan Glaciers," *The Times Online*, January 24, 2010.

23 Ibid.

24 "Merkel to Defend German Jobs Against Climate Deal," AFP, December 8, 2008.

25 "Lords Debate Climate Bill, Carbon Racket," *The Register* online site, November 20, 2008.

26 "12 Facts About Global Climate Change That You Won't Read in the Popular Press," Joseph D'Aleo, *Energy Tribune.com* August 18, 2008. *Reproduced in full with permission.*

27 Initial reports suggested it was the work of hackers or even the Russian Secret Service. However, as Junk Science's Steve Milloy later reported: "It has become obvious this archive was not 'hacked' or 'stolen' but rather is a file assembled by CRU staff in preparation for complying with a freedom of information request. Whether it was carelessly left in a publicly accessible portion of the CRU computer system or was 'leaked' by staff believing the FOIA request was improperly rejected may never be known but is not really that important. What is important is that:
1. There was no "security breach" at CRU that "stole" these files
2. The files appear genuine and to have been prepared by CRU staff, not edited by malicious hackers
3. The information was accidentally or deliberately released by CRU staff
4. Selection criteria appears to be compliance with an or several FOIA request(s)."

28 The emails can be viewed online in their entirety at: http://www.eastangliaemails.com/index.php

29 James Delingpole "Climategate: The Final Nail in the Coffin of 'Anthropogenic Global Warming,'" Daily Telegraph online blog, updated November 20, 2009.

30 All of the hacked Climategate emails can be viewed online at www.climategateemails.com/ Italics added to quote.

31 Ibid. Italics added to quote.

32 "Lord Lawson Calls for a Public Inquiry Into UAE Global Warming Data Manipulation," *Daily Telegraph*, November 23, 2009.

33 "Ex-Civil Servant to Head Inquiry Into 'Climategate' Row," *The Times*, December 3, 2009.

34 Roger Pielke Jnr. Blog, "We Lost the Original Data," August 12, 2009.

35 "Email Fracas Shows Peril of Trying To Spin Science," *New York Times* (Science Section), November 30, 2009.

36 "Viscount Monckton on Climategate: They Are Criminals," *Pajamas Media* online news, November 23, 2009.

37 "Copenhagen: A Step Closer to a One World Government?," James Delingpole's *Daily Telegraph* online blog, updated October 21, 2009.

38 "Even Monbiot Says the Science Now Needs 'Re-analyzing,'" Andrew Bolt, *Herald Sun* (Australia) online blog, November 24, 2009.

39 "Researcher: NASA Hiding Climate Data," Stephen Dinan, *Washington Times*, December 3, 2009.

40 "Mann's Mad Money," Paul Chesser, *The American Spectator* (AmSpecBlog), December 2, 2009.

41 "Environmentalism As Religion," speech to the Commonwealth Club, San Francisco, September 2003.

42 Lord Nigel Lawson, *An Appeal to Reason: A Cool Look at Climate Change*, Gerald Duckworth & Co, March 2009.

43 "We've Lost Our Fear of Hellfire, But Put Climate Change In Its Place," Boris Johnson, extended review of James Lovelock's "The Revenge of Gaia," February 2, 2006.

44 John M. Ostrowski, "Environmentalism as Religion," posted at Lew Rockwell.com here: http://www.lewrockwell.com/orig8/ostrowski-john1.html

45 "In Thrall to the Green God," Martin Livermore, BBC online, *Viewpoint*, March 3, 2006.

46 "The beginning of the End for Life As We know it on Planet Earth? There is a Biocentric Solution," Paul Watson, posted at the Sea Shepherd Conservation Society online, May 4, 2007.

6

Greens, Hacks and Greenbacks: The Great Climate Money Scandal

The greatest challenge facing mankind is the challenge of distinguishing reality from fantasy, truth from propaganda.

Michael Crichton

The climate change[1] debate revolves primarily around the use of the world's hydrocarbon energy reserves, their carbon emission role and the role some allege they play in promoting global warming. It has been one of the grandiose narratives of the modern era, marrying both science and philosophical ideas. As we have seen, it is also a narrative that has raised so many red flags over the most unsustainable direst predictions — and the rush to non-viable alternative energy sources — that is no longer believed by the mass of an increasingly skeptic general public.

At the time of writing, a US Gallup survey has revealed that *a mere 28 percent* of Americans now worry "a great deal" about global warming.[2] According to the study, this is because Americans believe that environmental conditions in the US are improving not declining. The polls percentage drop continued the downward trend from a high of 41 percent in 2007 — the year after Al Gore's sensationalist "An Inconvenient Truth" was released — through 33 percent in 2009. The poll should be of concern to an Obama White House fresh from its legislative success on healthcare reforms in March 2010, and which next has imposing carbon cap and trade taxes in its sights. Once again, the Obama administration will have its work cut out. For a public that no longer buys the AGW message, industry and job hitting cap and trade taxes are going to be a hard sell.

As if that were not enough, yet more bad news undermined President Obama's proposed cap and trade legislation. Just days after the health-care success France, the driver of European cap and trade policy, dropped a political climate bombshell, by backtracking on its national commitment. France was due to become the first unilaterally to impose a domestic carbon fuel tax.[3] But with President Nicolas Sarkozy facing an electoral humiliation after a series of defeats in regional elections, his government quietly withdrew the controversial carbon tax proposals, a major plank of the government's environmental policy, and a policy that would undoubtedly have put French industry at a severe international economic disadvantage. On hold "unless there is a European accord," the French announcement may have received little media attention, but its implications for any government thinking of pioneering such a deeply unpopular and crippling domestic and business tax are profound. And once more, it underlines how national self-interest, as at Copenhagen 2009, always trumps international "necessity," even when the fate of the planet is claimed to be at stake. As we said in the previous chapter, the carbon war is over — the alarmists lost. Politicians and journalists are just not as quick as the rest of us in recognizing facts of life.

In reality, neither the science, nor anything approaching a science consensus, exists to support the theory that man-made CO_2 plays a significant role in warming (or cooling) cycles. Nor is there any indication that current and recent warming and cooling cycles are anything other than entirely within the normal and historical parameters of natural temperature variations. All of which begs the stark question: Why are we wasting billions of dollars fighting pointless battles against an enemy that is really no enemy at all (CO_2) to win a fight (to change global climate) that's entirely beyond us? And where is all this finite resource — money — all going?

Equally serious is the potential of jeopardizing energy resources whose continued and affordable supply are vital to the modern world, and especially to developing nations desperate to improve their social conditions. In the rush to divert vast economic, mostly taxpayer, funds into the daddy of all economic Black Holes, we should not forget that it is the poorest in society who are the real losers. To fund the losing battle against carbon emissions and the grandstanding war on climate, all of us are being forced to pay green stealth taxes and increasingly exorbitant and wholly unnecessary hiked energy prices to heat and light our homes, cover our transport costs and, generally, go about our normal business.

It is not the poor who can afford the latest Toyota Prius "celebrity" hybrid car, or vastly expensive LED light-bulbs — neither of which live up to the manufacturers' hype, and both of which use far more energy to manufacture than standard vehicles and bulbs, when genuine like-for-like costs are exposed. Then there is the scandal of the diversion of food crops — again the world's poor pay — into the manufacture of alternative fuels such as ethanol, which again does nothing to the presumed goal, reducing greenhouse gases.

In 2008, Indian writer Deepak Lal writing about recent food price spikes and resulting riots in Indonesia, Mexico, Egypt, the Philippines, and Vietnam, quoted the International Food Policy Research Institute: "While cereal use for food and feed increased by 4 and 7 percent respectively since 2000, the use of cereals for industrial purposes — such as biofuel production — increased by more than 25 percent." Lal's anger as he writes is palpable, "It is not the Third World's burgeoning and increasingly prosperous population that has caused this recent spike in food prices, but it is a by-product of the West's obsession to reduce carbon emissions from using fossil fuels." Literally, our obsession with reducing carbon has diverted vital food crops away from hungry mouths and into Western fuel tanks. For many celebrities and eco-warriors, who so often fail to think through the ramifications of their preferred public policy actions, it is a necessary price to pay to "save the planet."

The scandal of vast and vital economic resources diverted into the phoney war against carbon climate is one that should outrage us all. We have already seen examples of where much government money is being invested in the ultimately doomed renewable revolution. But "the fight" has also made entrepreneurial millionaires out of those who got in early to build wind turbines, solar projects, and to develop biofuels and other speculative alternative energy ventures, using seed-funded government grants. But the money made via the current alternative energy industry will be nothing compared to the money about to be (and in some cases already being) made via the greatest "legalized" speculative finance scam ever: carbon trading, the world's fastest-growing commodity market. A truly "invisible" commodity based on a wholly unproven and highly speculative scientific theory, and even battier economic thinking.

In truth, collating the cost of the folly of fighting, rather than adapting to, changes in climate as man and animals have always done, is beyond us all, such are the vast figures involved. How could we possibly quantify all of the collective global efforts of international, national and local authorities? How can we cost fully all the time and effort put into researching and fighting the *prospective* "impact of global warming"? And what of the cost of the failure of the December 2009 Copenhagen Summit and the international failure to agree on real cuts in man-made CO_2 emissions internationally — without which the fight against climate change truly *is* a lost cause? When real science denies that CO_2 is *not* a pollutant[4] and when the major developing nations are bent on industrializing, *primarily* fuelled by . . . burning fossil fuels.

Even so, it is right to attempt to try to gain some foothold on what is at stake economically, and one intrepid researcher has done exactly that, at least insofar as the cost to the US taxpayer is concerned.

THE CLIMATE MONEY: $79 BILLION
— AND COUNTING (FAST)

By the end of 2009, the US taxpayer had subsidized the American climate industry to the tune of $79 billion — with trillions more to come. According to a recent report, the figures reveal that the US government has established a near-monopsony,[5] that is, a hugely distorting climate science industry in favor of "self-serving alarmism."

Climate Money,[6] written by Joanne Nova and published by the Science and Public Policy Institute (SPPI) in July 2009, was the first report to assess the cost to the US taxpayer of national climate-related policies gleaned from the government's own documents. Report author, Joanne Nova, points to a "well funded highly organized climate monopoly" that she cites as wasting billions of dollars and where no proper science "audit" exists to see where the money went. A familiar refrain when it comes to pay-outs from President Obama's stimulus

Figure 6.1: *Climate Money.*

billions more generally. That audit, she maintains, is instead being attempted by "unpaid volunteers" who have exposed the climate industry's "major errors time and again."

Most scathing is the accusation that the massive public expenditure has "created a powerful alliance of self-serving vested interests" drawn by the prospect of lucrative profits soon to be garnered from carbon trading. Isn't it "self-serving interests" that the Green movement is supposed to be *against*?

Climate Money states that the US government has "poured in $32 billion for climate research — and another $36 billion for development of climate-related technologies" over the last 20 years. Yet, "after spending $30 billion on pure science research no one is able to point to a single piece of empirical evidence that man-made carbon dioxide has a significant effect on the global climate." The report makes the telling point that a burgeoning industry employing thousands and receiving billions in free government handouts simply has no "real incentive to 'announce' the discovery of the insignificance of carbon's role."

Nova also perceives a "ratchet effect," whereby *pro*-AGW (anthropogenic global warming) theory is "reported, repeated, trumpeted and asserted" while *anti*-AGW findings, often the work of unfunded, retired scientists, "lie unstudied, ignored and delayed." The SPPI report shows how it is largely left to unfunded bloggers and scientists to expose major errors like that perpetrated by Michael Mann's now infamous and discredited Hockey Stick Graph. The report also cites how, once again, it was left to "unfunded volunteers" to expose how 89 percent of the NOAA's (National Oceanic and Atmospheric Administration) temperature sensors were in sites polluted by being too near to heating and air conditioning outlets, car parks and other artificial sources of heat. A bizarrely basic error, yet these are the sites upon which the NOAA relies for its "reliable readings and national statistics."

THE CULTURE OF *AD HOMINEN* ATTACKS

Next up, *Climate Money* rounds on the culture of demonizing *ad hominen* attacks aimed at those who question alarmist orthodoxy. In particular, the report highlights the vilification of "Big Oil" and, what it calls, the "Exxon Blame-Game." Nova's report reveals that while Exxon Mobil gave a mere $23 million, spread over ten years, to climate skeptics, *climate alarmism was funded to the tune of $2 billion by the US government*. Yet as stark as the funding difference is, it is ExxonMobil that has been, and still is, attacked mercilessly for "distorting the debate."

Nova draws the ironic conclusion that those who attack ExxonMobil, "are inadvertently drawing attention away from the real power play and acting as unpaid agents for giant trading houses and large banks." Something she notes "could sit a little uncomfortably with greenies and environmentalists." As Nova says, "The side show of blaming Big Oil hides the truth: that the real issue is whether there is any evidence, and that the skeptics are a grassroots movement that consists of well respected scientists and a growing group of unpaid volunteers."

Describing the culture of *ad hominem* attacks as a "form of censorship," the SPPI report identifies that: "Not many fields of science have dedicated smear sites for scientists. Money talks." The point is underlined when we learn that scientist-smearing *Desmog* is a funded wing of the PR consultancy group Hoggan and Associates, which acts on behalf of groups with a vested climate interest. *ExxonSecrets* turns out to be funded by Greenpeace, an organization that "lives off donations to 'save the planet.'"

GREENS AND GREENBACKS: AN UNHOLY ALLIANCE

Citing the World Bank, the report notes that turnover of carbon trading has doubled from $63 billion in 2007 to $126 billion in 2008. "Not surprisingly," comments the report's author, "banks are doing what banks should do: they're following the promise of profits, and hence urging government to adopt carbon trading."[7] Bart Chilton of the Commodity Futures Trading Commission is quoted as predicting carbon trading will become a $2 trillion market and the "largest commodity market in the world." Richard Sandor, chairman and CEO of Climate Exchange plc, predicts the market will eventually "total $10 trillion a year."

No wonder this "entirely new fiat currency has banks and financial institutions 'wholly in bed' with a scientific theory." Nova believes that climate science itself has become critically important to the new "self-sanctioning circle of vested interests." She continues, "The stealthy mass entry of bankers and traders into the background of the scientific 'debate' poses grave threats to the scientific process" which increasingly "hinges on finding that human emissions of carbon dioxide have a significant role in the climate." Unwittingly, green planet-saving eco-warriors and many environmentalists are in bed with an unholy alliance that is working to boost further the coffers of global bankers and financiers who, on another day, they would likely "throw rocks at."

The SPPI report concludes with a plea to recognize that "the process of science can be distorted (like any human endeavor) by a massive one-sided input of money." It's a plea for science to be released from the "vice like grip of politics and finance" allowing "more attention to be paid to empirical evidence." It demands we "get serious about auditing science" and deplores our failure to grasp that "monopolistic funding tests the fabric of the way we do science." While report author Nova believes, "the truth will come out in the end" she begs one final and crucial question: "How much damage will accrue while we wait for volunteers to audit the claims of the financially well-fed?"

FOLLOW THE MONEY

Climate Money is the first audit report on the US Climate Industry, and it succeeds in sending up a major warning flare to the US taxpayer — indeed to every taxpayer around the globe. We would like to have seen a short section in it covering the lamentable role of much of the mass media which, while having access to all the same figures, have rejected their traditional skeptical role and fallen in with the climate "mob." Goodness knows what their failure and clamor for "action now" has added to the economic costs.

But the report does achieve its aim of highlighting the growing international financial scandal. It does so first by revealing how an industry backed by $79 billion in public funds has singularly failed to make out even a baseline case for the carbon-climate link — *the industry's raison d'etre*. Second, by revealing how the US government, among others, is backing a wholly biased scientific "horse," one promoting the very antithesis of how scientific enquiry works best. And, in all of this, consider also the inordinate and largely unnecessary impact on energy prices — and the economic disenfranchising that can mean for Joe Average, citizen.

As if diverting vast public funds into an economic abyss with no discernible benefit to the environment were not enough, we find that the AGW industry has created a raft of climate millionaires; most uncomfortably, those at the vanguard of campaigning advocacy over the direction of government policy — advocacy and policy from which they are able to profit.

THE CLIMATE MILLIONAIRES

This is the story of the former politician, the ex-railway engineer and the discredited scientist. All three number among the chief priests of global warming theory and climate alarmism.

They are in turn, Al Gore, in the running to become the world's first carbon billionaire, Dr Rajendra Pachauri, chairman of the UN IPCC, and Michael Mann, discredited hockey stick "manufacturer," lately accused (via Climategate) of manipulating climate data, and would-be suppressor of alternative scientific opinion.

Mann aside, we should note that neither Gore nor Pachauri have any qualifications in climate science.

AL GORE INC.

We do not suggest, as many others have done increasingly, that Al Gore (or for that matter Pachauri or Mann) does not have what, for him, are genuine environmental concerns. Our business is *not* speculation as to motive. Instead, we pursue hard facts and examine how we, as public and especially taxpayers, might ethically view them. Gore got a BA in Government from Harvard before dipping his toes into journalism and law school then dropping out to run for public office. Hardly the qualifications, we might think, for *the* world's leading spokesman on climate science.

Since losing the election to George W. Bush in 2000, Al Gore has reinvented himself as an extremely successful businessman. According to financial disclosure documents released before the 2000 election, the Gore family's net worth was $1–2 million. By the beginning of 2008 the Gore family's net worth had jumped to well over $100 million, with Gore owning a multi-million dollar home in a plush section of Nashville, a family home in Virginia, and a multi-million dollar investment in a San Francisco condo/hotel.[8] How did he do it? Mainly, "in what may be the greatest brand makeover in history."[9] But, essentially, much as any other would-be capitalist entrepreneur has the right to do, by making some astute business investments — and at $175,000 a shot speaking fee certainly helped.

Over 60, Gore is today a Nobel Peace Prize winner (for his climate advocacy), an Academy Award winner (for his documentary "An Inconvenient Truth"), and a bestselling author (for his climate books). But it is as a businessman that he has excelled. After his election defeat he became an advisor to Google in 2001, receiving stock options worth (in early 2008) around $30 million. In 2003 he joined the board of Apple, receiving stock options valued (again in 2008) at around $6 million.[10] Like any of us, Gore is entitled to make money by investing in legitimate business enterprises, at least where there are no blatant conflicts of interest. But the conflicts of interest for Gore, moral if not criminal, come thick and fast.

In 2004, Gore launched Generation Investment Management (GIM), a London-based investment management firm with a key focus on environmental and sustainable factors. It is this overlap between Gore's role as chairman of GIM and his role as a key climate spokesperson and advocate, lobbying his Democratic buddies to pass cap and trade legislation, that could make Gore the world's first carbon billionaire.

The Competitive Enterprise Institute has stated that they believe policies Gore advocated before the US Senate in January 2009 "will make him and his friends extremely wealthy at the expense of consumers." GIM already owns a 10 percent stake in the Chicago Climate Exchange (CCX) which in turn owns half the European Climate Exchange. Whichever way we cut it, Al Gore clearly has a very real business interest in promoting government controls through the issuing of carbon credits. Republican representative Marsha Blackburn of Tennessee has openly pointed out that Gore stands to benefit personally and massively from energy and climate policies he has been consistently urging Congress to adopt.[11]

And Gore is already making big money through other such investments. In 2008, GIM loaned Silver Spring, a small Californian firm $75 million to develop energy-saving technology. They make hardware and software to improve the electricity grid system. In November 2009, it proved a highly astute investment when the US Energy Department announced $3.4 billion in smart grid grants. $560 million of that figure went to companies associated with Silver Springs.[12] Gore and his associates could easily recoup their investment many times over in future years. The links between Gore's business and advocacy to government run deeper still. It was Gore's environmental groups and other green activists who helped draft the prospective US Climate Bill. It has been widely acknowledged by legislators that the Waxman-Markey Bill relied heavily on the proposals put forward by the US Climate Action Partnership's (USCAP) proposals as its blueprint for legislation.

As the hearings for the Bill got under way in late October 2009, Myron Ebell, climate and energy policy director for the Competitive Enterprise Initiative, told legislators, "The authors of the draft bill have invited the beneficiaries of what could turn out to be the biggest transfer of wealth from consumers to special interests in American history to write the rules for this legalized plunder." It was reported that the Bill includes a provision that benefits Duke Energy Corporation, a founding member of USCAP. Al Gore's World Resources Institute is a founding member of USCAP.[13]

DR RAJENDRA PACHAURI'S "GLOBAL CONSULTANCY"

Dr Rajendra Pachauri wields enormous influence as the chairman of the UN's IPCC. He was ubiquitous in the media in the days before Copenhagen 2009, and was the main architect of the UN's last — now much pilloried, yet Nobel Peace Prize winning — climate report in 2007. In December 2009, a UK *Daily Telegraph* report[14] accused Pachauri of making a fortune from his innumerable business links with carbon trading companies around the world. The writers, Chris Booker and Dr Richard North, also questioned how the BBC could refer to Pachauri as "the world's top climate scientist" when he is "a former railway engineer with a PhD in economics" who "has no qualifications in climate science at all."

Booker and North describe how Pachauri has "established an astonishing worldwide portfolio of business interests with bodies which have been investing billions of dollars in organizations dependent on the IPCC's policy recommendations." Pachauri occupies a long list of posts where he acts as director or advisor to innumerable bodies across the climate industry. The furor over Pachauri's apparently blatant conflicts of interest began after Australian Senator Stephen Fielding and former scientific advisor to Margaret Thatcher, Viscount Lord Monckton handed an open letter to Pachauri after the latter had given a lecture at the 2009 Copenhagen Summit. The letter ostensibly demanded the removal of a prominent and highly misleading graph[15] from the 2007 IPCC report — a graph Pachauri had used in his Copenhagen address. Further, the letter went on to question why, in the report, Pachauri had not declared a litany of personal interests in organizations that stood to profit from its findings. The letter duly called for Pachauri's dismissal from the IPCC.

The Telegraph reports that "since Pachauri became a vice-chairman of the IPCC in 1997" his Delhi power base at the Tata Energy Research Institute (TERI) has "vastly expanded its interests in every kind of renewable or sustainable technology." Renamed simply The Energy Research Institute, the links with Tata nevertheless remain with various divisions of the Tata Group now expanding into projects such as its $1.5 billion in vast wind farms. Booker and North reveal that the TERI empire has spread into the US and Europe and that "TERI Europe, based in London, of which he [Pachauri] is a trustee (along with Sir John Houghton, another key figure in the early days of the IPCC) is currently running a project on bio-energy, financed by the EU." Another TERI project involves the use of German and UK taxpayer cash to study "how India's insurance industry, including Tata, can benefit from exploiting the supposed risks of exposure to climate change."

Listing a wealth of interesting business and lobbying links between Tata (North America) and corporate sponsors as diverse as the World Wildlife Fund, Amoco Oil, and Monsanto, the world's largest GM producer, Booker and North state: "But this is peanuts compared to the numerous other posts to which Dr Pachauri has been appointed in the years since the UN chose him to become the world's top climate-change official."

The list includes an appointment in 2007 to the advisory board of a San Francisco-based venture capital company, where his remit involves providing the firm with "access, standing and industrial exposure at the highest level." In 2008, he became advisor on renewable and sustainable energy to the Credit Suisse Bank and the Rockefeller Foundation. He joined the board of the Nordic Glitnir Bank to help with its Sustainable Future Fund and became chairman of the Indo-China Sustainable Infrastructure Fund. Also in 2008, he became director of the International Risk Governance Council in Geneva set up by EDF and E.ON, two Euro giants in electricity, to promote "bio-energy." Pachauri also serves as a "strategic advisor" at the New York investment fund Pegasus, as chairman to the Asian Development Bank, on the climate advisory board of the Deutsche Bank, and as director of the Japanese Institute for Global Environmental Strategies.

Along with a further list of roles on influential government bodies back home in India — and the above lists are by no means exhaustive — the key to all of the above is his advocacy over the apocalyptic threat from global warming and the need to control carbon emissions. Booker and North report TERI's latest newsletter as quoting Pachauri "telling the US Environmental Protection Agency that it must go ahead with regulating US carbon emissions without waiting for Congress to pass its cap and trade bill."

Leaving aside the small issue of Pachauri's apparent suggestion that the EPA circumvent the provisions of the American Constitution, it spotlights a staggering list of conflicts of interest. How much Pachauri receives from this vast array of highly lucrative commercial interests — and he won't tell us — is anyone's guess. Whatever the figure, it ought to disqualify him from the key role of IPCC chairman. And it is not just his business deals that are causing concern, so too is his (and the IPCC's) general incompetence.

In the previous chapter we learned of "Glaciergate" and the UN IPCC's blunder in utilizing a bogus scientific report for its key 2007 report — a report which gained the Nobel Peace Prize for the IPCC, and significant kudos for the IPCC's chairman, Pachauri. As we now know, the report and claim over a Himalayan meltdown by 2035 was a total sham. As *The Times* article, one of those exposing the blunder, pointed out, "The IPCC was set up precisely to ensure that world leaders have the best possible scientific advice on climate change." Yet, when criticism of this claim was previously made to Pachauri, he initially dismissed the criticism as "voodoo science." As we heard earlier, the claims of 2007 — including the central bogus claim about the Himalayan meltdown — was subsequently used by Pachauri's TERI group to obtain massive research funds from the US Carnegie Foundation and the European Union.

Over recent years, Pachauri's scientific credentials and competence have come under serious scrutiny, so too, the list of blatant conflicts of interests between his IPCC role and his climate legislation advocacy.

PROFESSOR MICHAEL MANN: TRUTH-OBFUSCATOR GENERAL?

At the time of writing, Professor Michael Mann, at the heart of global warming research and the machinations of the IPCC, is under investigation by Penn State University where he works, accused of fraud and perpetuating a hoax, a direct consequence of the Climategate emails leak. The hoax in question: overstating the impact of man on climate change and then trying to cover it up. So central is the professor to the key tenets and theories of anthropogenic global warmism that some have dubbed it "Mann-made global warming."

The fact is that Mann is somebody who attracts mega-funds to Penn State for his research work. With such large grants at stake it may be thought that an internal inquiry is likely to whitewash the case against Mann. Stephen Bloom, a local Cumberland County attorney states, "Penn State has such a vested interest in keeping the big research dollars that are flowing in as a result of global climate change research they're doing now, it's hard to imagine how Penn State can truly take an independent look at the situation." Matt Brouillette of the Conservative Commonwealth Foundation has called for an independent investigation by lawmakers to investigate Mann before acting on his research data to instigate legislation. And Brouillette reminds us that the stark evidence of the Climategate emails suggest Mann has, "bullied critics, he has destroyed data, that he has engaged in behaviour not becoming of a true academic in pursuit of accuracy and truth."

And what science clarity *has* Mann contributed to the issue of global warming? Well, most famously, his now discredited "hockey stick" graph, an iconic illustration that has helped enormously to cement

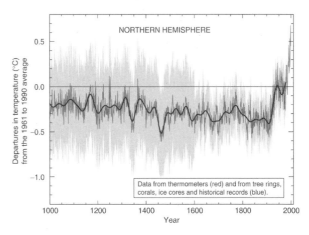

Figure 6.2: Michael Mann's famously discredited 'Hockey Stick' Graph obscures the reality of the Medieval Warming Period and the Little Ice Age.[16]

the faith of the media and public in the science behind AGW beliefs. Essentially, what Mann's graph purported to show was a straight trend line of temperatures over the past 900 years with a steep upturn (hence the hockey stick analogy) over the past 100 or so years (clearly intended for everyone to conclude: AGW). However, diligent work by Stephen McIntyre and Ross McKitrick in 2003 revealed Mann had manipulated the figures to show a linear straight line that effectively eliminated the Medieval Warming Period and the Little Ice Age, thus eradicating the visual impact of *natural* global temperature variation.

As we have indicated, Mann's research brings in millions for the university. Yet, even as Mann was under investigation by Penn State University, he received a substantial further grant of $541,184 from the Obama administration. Tom Borelli, PhD, director of the National Center's Free Enterprise Project said, "It's outrageous that economic stimulus money is being used to support research conducted by Michael Mann at the very time he's under investigation by Penn State and is one of the key figures in the international Climategate scandal." Referring to Mann's apparently "agenda-driven science," Borelli rightly notes, "It's shocking that taxpayer money is being used to support a researcher who seemingly showed little regard to the basic tenet of science — a dispassionate search for truth."[17] By "little regard to the basic tenet of science" Borelli is referring to, as Mann himself called it in the Climategate emails, his "trick" of attempting to hide the Medieval Warming Period entirely as well as dumping data, bullying journal editors and generally obscuring the scientific truth.

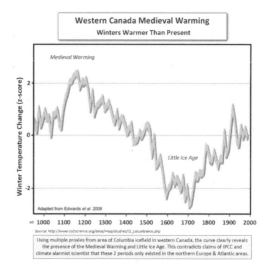

Figure 6.3: A strange looking hockey stick. How Mann's graph obscures the reality of global temperature variations over recent centuries. *Source Icecap.*

Quite simply, we wonder how a researcher with such a proven, by the Hockey Stick Graph fiasco and Climategate, anti-science, truth-obfuscating agenda could be eligible to receive *any* public research funds.

THE CULPABILITY OF THE MAINSTREAM MEDIA (MSM)

Question: How could the scandal of the climate money billions have happened, sanctioned by the IPCC's brand of dodgy science? *Answer:* It could not have succeeded had mainstream journalists and editors not failed in their duty to question it. Instead, most of the mass media and innumerable editors and journalists, chose instead to take the side of climate alarmism, abandoning entirely the role of asking hard questions of those with authority and power.

Today the MSM is in severe decline. We are not surprised and have no sympathy for its current plight. Both of us as writers have found it incredibly hard to get energy and climate facts and data into the mainstream media. Quite simply, if it did not fit the radical populist green agenda most editors simply did not, and many *still* do not, want to know.

It has been alleged that while journalists are fearless in their questioning of politicians, they are inherently more afraid to question scientists. If that is so, then they have no real business doing what they do. And some are blatant about their abandonment of the ethics of journalistic principles when it comes to genuine debate on unproven social theories:

> *I would freely admit that on Global Warming we have crossed the boundary from news reporting to advocacy.*
>
> —Charles Alexander, *Time* magazine science editor.

> *Not only do journos not have a responsibility to report what sceptical scientists have to say, they have a responsibility not to report what these scientists say.*
>
> —Ross Gelbspan, former editor, *Boston Globe*.

We know from personal experience that the inclinations of Alexander and Gelbspan have dominated across the MSM for over a decade. Hardly the spirit of an investigative, skeptical, and truly free democratic press, we might think. And it is not as if the global news majors have even been able to make up their own minds as to whether the planet is warming or cooling. *Newsweek* and *Time* (see illustration), for instance, have proved to be among the chief alarmist propaganda sheets. Yet here's what *Newsweek* trumpeted just four decades ago:

> *Because of increasing dust, cloud cover and water vapor, the planet will cool, the water vapor will fall and freeze, and a new ice age will be born.*
>
> —*Newsweek* magazine, January 26, 1970.

We would say they are a little confused. Wouldn't you?

International columnist and writer P.J. O'Rourke once noted, "Some people will do anything to save the earth, except take a science course."

Figure 6.4: *Time* magazine April 3, 1977 (poor reproduction here due to a raft of similar ice age warning covers from the 1970s being deleted from the *Time* website).

It seems that includes a majority of the modern environmental movement and a sizeable proportion of the Western journalistic profession. Not that the decline of the standards of the Western journalistic ethic is necessarily a recent phenomenon. Just a few decades ago, writer Graham Greene observed, "A petty reason . . . why novelists more and more try to keep a distance from journalists is that novelists are trying to write the truth and journalists are trying to write fiction."

And we don't have to look far for evidence of the increasingly abysmal standards of the Fourth Estate when it comes to how they have contributed to the myth of a science consensus on global warming and, worse, systematically attempted to put an end to all legitimate scientific debate. Let us just take one example: the MSM's headlining of dubious research — such as that we have seen over the allegedly melting Himalayas and ice caps.

MEDIA TRUTH, NOT ICE CAPS, IN MELTDOWN

Eco-warriors and media hype aside, the fact is, at the beginning of 2009, the world's ice mass had been expanding *not* contracting. Which will surprise evening news junkies fed a diet of polar bears floating about on ice floes and snow shelves falling into the oceans. But if a whole series of reports on ice growth in the Arctic, the Antarctic and among glaciers are right, then it is truth in the mainstream media that's in meltdown, not the polar ice caps.

The problem for the MSM is: no ice cap meltdown, no rising waters. No disappearing islands, no reason for alarm. In short, no sensationalist angle, no story. Worst of all, getting *yet another* global apocalypse wrong: no credibility. Clearly, the MSM has a significant stake in running sensational warm-mongering headlines. Not to mention a neat sideline in disparaging those who have the temerity to disagree.

And there's nothing more the modern climate alarmist media loves than a "melting Arctic" ice cap story. So why not stories from the far larger expanse of ice that could have been called the "melting" Antarctic? Well it might have something to do with the fact that the Antarctic ice grew to record levels[18] *in 2007* — and has continued to grow and thicken.[19]

THE ANTARCTIC

Climate scientist Dr Ben Herman, past director of the Institute of Atmospheric Physics and former head of Atmospheric Sciences at the University of Arizona, notes that for the media:

What happens in the Arctic may be an indicator of what will happen in the rest of the world. How about what happens in the Antarctic then? Since its ice area has been increasing, is this also an indicator of what might be happening in the rest of the world?[20]

The FACT is that the majority of Antarctica has cooled over the past 50 years and ice coverage has grown to record levels.[21] Take the well-publicized collapse of a 160 square mile block of the Wilkins Ice Shelf in Antarctica in March 2008. For the alarmist media this was conclusive proof of the dramatic global warming effects. *The Los Angeles Times* ran "Antarctica Collapse," referring to the "rapid melt of the Wilkins Shelf."[22] The *Sydney Morning Herald* ran "The Ice Shelf Hangs by a Thread"[23] and the leftwing *Salon* online news site ran the ludicrous "Bye-bye, Antarctica?"[24] But Icecap's Joseph D'Aleo, former first Director of Meteorology at *The Weather Channel* and Chief Meteorologist at Weather Services International, was more prosaic, giving the incident a little more perspective than is common in the popular press. D'Aleo wrote[25] that the collapse was the equivalent, given the enormity of Antarctica, of "an icicle falling from a snow and ice covered roof." He added, "The latest satellite images and reports suggest the ice has already refrozen around the broken pieces. In fact the ice is returning so fast it is running an amazing 60 percent ahead of last year when it set a new record." Noting the ludicrous media hype, D'Aleo laments, "Yet the world is left with the false impression Antarctica's ice sheet is also starting to disappear."

Climate scientist Dr Ben Herman gives us real context when he adds an appropriate footnote: "It is interesting that all of the AGW (anthropogenic global warming) stories concerning Antarctica are always about what's happening around the western peninsula, which seems to be the only place on Antarctica that has shown any warming." Herman asks, "How about the rest of the continent, which is probably about 95 percent of the land mass, not to mention the record sea ice coverage recently."[26]

Former Colorado State Climatologist and senior scientist at the University of Colorado in Boulder, Dr Roger Pielke Sr, speaking in 2008, was severely critical of the "typical bias that many journalists have." Pielke noted, "The media has ignored the increase in Antarctica sea ice cover in recent years, with at present, a coverage that is one million square kilometers above average." Pielke added, "Unfortunately, it appears that most journalists just parrot the perspective of the first news release on these climate issues, without doing any further investigation. If this is inadvertent, they need to be educated in climate science. If deliberate bias, they are clearly advocates and the reporters should be clearly and publically identified as having such a bias. In either case, the public is being misinformed!"[27]

In December 2006, Dr Duncan Wingham, Professor of Climate Physics at University College London and Director for Polar Observation and Modelling, presented evidence that showed "Antarctic thinning was no more common than thickening." Wingham and his colleagues found that 72 percent of the Antarctica ice sheet was growing at the rate of 5 millimeters per year. Most significantly, Dr Wingham commits media heresy when he states: "That makes Antarctica a sink, not a source, of ocean water." According to their best estimates, Antarctica will "lower global sea levels by 0.08 mm per year."[28] MSM sacrilege.

Statisticians Dr Bjorn Lomborg, author of *The Skeptical Environmentalist* and professor at the Copenhagen Business School, and Fleming Rose, observed that the media covers only the "2 percent of Antarctica [that] is dramatically warming and ignores the 98 percent that has largely cooled over the past 35 years." Lomborg and Rose also round on Al Gore who "points to shrinking sea ice in the Northern Hemisphere, but doesn't mention that sea ice in the Southern Hemisphere is increasing."[29]

And for those for whom the UN IPCC is always the last word on all things climate, Dr Madhav L Khandekar, retired Environment Canada scientist and an expert IPCC reviewer, says, "In the Southern Hemisphere, the land-sea mean temperature has slowly but surely declined in the last few years." He adds, "Several other locations in the Southern Hemisphere have experienced lower temperatures in the last few years" the result of "surface temperatures over world oceans slowly declining since mid-1998."[30]

Fair enough. But the Arctic at least *is* in total meltdown, *right*? Truth is, it just isn't that simple. October 2008 saw the fastest Arctic sea ice extent growth ever recorded. Remember when the MSM reported it? No? Neither do we.

THE ARCTIC

During October and November 2008 the extent of Arctic ice was 28.7 percent greater than during the same period in 2007. According to data published by the International Arctic Research Center (IARC/ JAXA) October 2008 saw "the fastest ever growth" of Arctic Sea ice since records began. Not good news for doomsayers like Dr Mark Serreze of the National Snow and Ice Data Center. Alarmist Dr Serreze had gone on record predicting an ice-free North Pole in the summer of 2008.[31]

The Arctic has indeed undergone some warming in some areas, especially Greenland, a warming that culminated in a summer temperature high of 5°C in 2007. The gradual melt has opened up the prospect of navigable seaways and a rush for the Arctic's energy-rich deepwater reserves. The reality is, however, warming periods are nothing new to the Arctic. When the Vikings settled Greenland they grew crops in temperatures higher than those of today.

The media has also made much of the potential opening of the Northwest Passage. What it leaves out is that similar weather patterns prevailed in the 1930s when two boats, the Nascopie and Aklavik, famously met up in the Passage in 1937. In October 2008, a study by Ohio University confirmed that current Arctic warming patterns mimic those in the 1920–40s. By July 2008, the Arctic ice had increased by nearly half a million square miles over the same first half year period in 2007. A NASA study published in the peer-reviewed *Geophysical Research Letters* in October 2007 had already noted that thinning Arctic ice was more likely the result of "unusual winds" that had blown "older thicker" ice into warmer southern waters. In other words, the Arctic warming experienced more recently may well be the result of the unusual strength of winds, not man-made warming.

According to the National Snow and Ice Data Center's own figures, world sea ice in April 2008 reached "unprecedented" levels for the month of April. The World Meteorological Organization (WMO) went on to declare 2008 the coolest since 2000.[32] Moreover, the WMO reports that the fall in the global mean temperature since 1998 is not just affecting the polar ice caps either, it is also affecting glaciers elsewhere.

THE GLACIERS

In October 2008, after a particularly bitterly cold Alaskan summer, glaciologists began reporting that Alaskan glaciers, particularly those at Glacier Bay where the shrinkage had mainly been, began advancing for the first time in years. Glaciologist Bruce Molnia of the US Geological Survey said, "In mid-June, I was surprised to see snow still at sea level in Prince William Sound." He added, "On the Juneau Icefield, there was still 20 feet of new snow on the surface in late July. At Bering Glacier, a landslide I am studying did not become snow free until early August."[33] In short, 2008 was the first time since records began that Alaskan glaciers *did not* shrink during the summer months.

In late November 2008, reports from Norway showed that Alaska's glacier experience was being replicated there, too. Hallgeir Elvehoy of the Norwegian Water Resources and Energy Directorate (NVE) reported that the magnitude of glacial growth appeared to have been underway for two years.[34] In 2008, glacier growth was also reported in Canada[35] and New Zealand.[36]

Here is how the dubious research-media nexus works to feed public angst with popular myths, such as those associated with the Arctic's "endangered" polar bears. First, a small research group goes to Greenland and notes fewer polar bears living in a particular region than in previous years. A poorly researched report is duly published, along with a sensationalist headline warning of the imminent extinction of polar bears. Cue endless news flicks with "lonely" polar bears on scant ice floes — when, in fact, "surfing" ice floes is what polar bears do for fun. They like to swim — yes, they can swim — and ride ice floes when the summer arrives. Don't we all? Next, *real* science researchers return *to the same area* to check the previous reports and find, in fact, that a small amount of warming led the polar bears to adapt, as polar bears do, and move further up the coast, where they are today *thriving* in larger numbers than in previous decades. Successive research reports are now published in an attempt to set the record straight. But to no avail, or they appear in a tiny paragraph on page 17. Consequently, the popular myth, not the scientific truth, is now lodged in the public consciousness. If anything is under threat of extinction, it is media truth, not polar bears, courtesy of the collusion of bad science and lousy journalism.

The facts adduced here represent just the tip of an under-reported iceberg (pun intended). But the fact that the ice mass is anything but in meltdown is plainly of seismic importance in the climate debate. Even so, many media organizations continue to have a major stake in freezing out the truth — having sold their journalistic soul for a mess of warm-mongering pottage.

LIES, DAMNED LIES AND BBC CLIMATE REPORTS

When the global warming alarmist house of cards finally collapses, exposing the pseudo-science/scare-journalism that has helped perpetrate the world's greatest scientific hoax, among the first led out into the public square for ritual humiliation ought to be the science and environment correspondents of the major networks, the popular press and, particularly, the "world's broadcaster," the BBC.

In the case of the BBC, first, for submitting fraudulent CV's to BBC

Human Resources, claiming they actually knew *something* about science. Second, for asserting, as public service broadcasters, that they were "only reporting what scientists were saying." They will claim they were "only following orders" after news editors "water-boarded" them, destroying their "testicular fortitude" forcing them to concoct a cornucopia of journalistic drivel to feed the public angst. Anything, but accept responsibility for their own stories. But the truth is, we have suffered a panoply of dire warnings of global apocalypse rooted in everything from swine flu to SARS to the mad cow disease (including their allegedly "toxic farts"), till the daddy of all media scare scams: warm-mongering.

So science is turned on its head. Carbon dioxide is consistently reported by the MSM as a "pollutant," and all exhaling humans are dubbed "toxic." Faith, not science, now prophesies that "higher CO_2 emissions cause global warming" — even though the actual data show that the small degree of recent global warming ended in 1998, *while CO_2 emissions continued (and continue) to rise.* Planet Gore-ism propaganda has found a ready home displaying its wares via the "world's broadcaster," the BBC. Next, an epidemic of teenage sleep-denying stress is brought on by viewing science-fiction horror flicks, entitled "An Inconvenient Bunch of Statistical Crap," as media-induced hysteria invades our schoolrooms.[37] And the evening news presents us with a steady procession of reports warning us that if we don't sell our SUVs and buy light-bulbs that'll eventually lead to mass eye problems, dire prognostications will befall us. We will see the end of the Gulf Stream, the demise of islands (various), the loss of both polar ice caps and the bulk of the world's population — not to mention the nightly re-runs of those cuddly polar bears floating about on over-sized ice cubes.

In June 2008, in the wake of Japanese scientists disputing the UN IPCC's anthropogenic warming orthodoxy,[38] the Japanese government put forward what the BBC's Environment Correspondent Richard Black called "weak 'climate' targets."[39] And right here, writer/blogger Maurizio Morabito helpfully provides us with stark numerical evidence of Black's — thus the BBC's — biased reporting. Morabito says: "The article is made up of 469 words. Of those, 249 make up 'neutral' sentences (54%). Negative comments are made of 156 words (34%). Only 58 words (13% . . . a mere three sentences!!) are left to explain the reasons for the Japanese government's decision."[40]

It wasn't so long ago — April 2008 to be precise — that the actions of another BBC science reporter, Roger Harrabin, epitomized the shameful lack of integrity in BBC climate news reporting. Having had the temerity to speak the truth — that global warming appeared to have peaked in 1998 — Harrabin actually went as far as *changing the news* to accommodate the anger of a single angry climate activist who had harangued him on his blog for the comment. It is well worth reading the full sordid account.[41]

Then there was Susan Watts, BBC TV's *Newsnight*'s science editor, who solemnly informed the British public that "scientists calculate that President Obama has just four years to save the world." It was unclear, at the time, whether she meant from climate catastrophe or a prospective Republican White House. Watts later confirmed, via her blog, that she was in fact referring to comments by Dr James Hansen. For the uninitiated, Hansen is the resident "end-is-nigh" alarmist at NASA's Goddard Institute for Space Studies — a man whose science advocacy has become such a serious embarrassment that his NASA colleagues have been publicly queuing up to skewer him.[42]

In "BBC Abandons 'Impartiality' on Warming" Chris Booker provides other examples of Watts' "bizarre" reporting, including editing Obama's inaugural speech "to convey a considerably stronger impression of what Obama has said on global warming than his careful wording justified." Booker also reminds us that, "as late as August 28, 2008, it [the BBC] was still predicting the Arctic ice might soon disappear."[43] By the end of the year, as we have seen, reports showed the Arctic Ice had grown by 30 percent from the previous year. Then there was the controversy over an "impartial" BBC devoting 15 hours of live TV airtime to the Live Earth/Al Gore musical "propaganda" show in 2007. A gig that featured that old chestnut favorite — you guessed it — a giant poster of Michael Mann's infamous "hockey stick" temperature graph. "One of the most discredited artifacts in the history of science," as Booker points out.

Okay, so why pick on the BBC? Haven't they had enough troubles playing down internal reports[44] *that confirm* their ideologically leftwing and liberal biases? True enough. But the BBC loves to call itself, as we have noted, the "world's broadcaster." It can afford to be so, as it has a distinctly unfair advantage over most of the opposition: it is wholly government-funded and thus supposed to be — irony on irony — a public service broadcaster. But its scientifically-challenged science/enviro correspondents, as Dr Richard North's excellent 2006 report "The BBC's Climate Change Meltdown" (mentioning Harrabin and Watts by name) notes, "give us every sign that they think sceptics are fools or knaves or both."[45]

The BBC, replete with its increasingly shabby moral reporting values, is now a growing player in the American[46] and Canadian[47] markets too. The fact is, there was a time when "end is nigh" placarders and other much-loved eccentrics, operated at the margins of society. Today, they have plainly moved indoors, gained a degree in journalism and assumed key editorships in major newsrooms; not least at the BBC. When the time cometh, only the highest profile ritual humiliation will do. Of course, by then, they will no doubt have moved on to new globally-threatening science-fiction narrative.

AGW AND PROPAGANDA

French philosopher Jacques Ellul, in his landmark book *Propaganda: The Formation of Men's Attitudes*,[48] warned: "To be effective, propaganda must constantly short circuit all thought and decision." This is the role the MSM seems, through its sound-bite journalism, to have adopted throughout the climate debate, as the quotes of former key editors (see above) reveal. We also note the powerful element of "centralization" that is vital to the propagandist's cause. We have seen how the social engineers of the environmental movement aim for greater centralized government control — which is why AGW alarmism appeals far more to the left than to the right. Ellul observes, "One can propagandize for centralization because modern man firmly believes in the strength of a centrally administered state."

As Ellul points out, "The aim of propaganda is no longer to modify ideas, but to provoke action. It is no longer to change adherence to a doctrine, but to make the individual cling irrationally to a process of action. It is no longer to lead to a choice, but to loosen the reflexes. It is no longer to transform an opinion, but to arouse an active and mythical belief."

As one reads Ellul's insights into propaganda it is amazing just how closely they resonate almost precisely with the cheerleading of the "free" Western press in the AGW debate. Ellul notes, "The propagandist does not necessarily have to worry about coherence and unity to his claims. Claims can even be varied and contradictory." Remember what we said earlier, about there being a distinct lack of concern over facts and empirical evidence among AGW advocates?

Ellul could have been talking about the work of the modern MSM science correspondent when he concludes: "The propagandist uses a keyboard and composes a symphony." As psychologist F.C. Bartlett accurately observed, the goal of propaganda is not to increase political understanding of events, but to obtain results through action. Let's face it, on that score bad scientists and journalists have combined to *inglorious* effect. If the effect and consequence of the appalling level of science reporting has contributed to the myth that global temperatures are anything other than within natural variation and that CO_2 is a pollutant and is not a key factor in temperature rises, the role of the MSM has proven singularly culpable.

Worse still, ultimately, it has proven an enemy of the truth.

Notes

1 We should not allow environmental alarmists to confuse the issue as they dance from foot to foot using the terms "global warming" and "climate change" interchangeably. At the time of writing, the northern hemisphere was just coming out of one of the worst global freezes for decades. During such times, unsurprisingly, the term "global warming" is quickly replaced by "climate change" by eco-activists. Thus, any climate variation, warm or cold can be laid at the door of "global warming." But the fact is that there has been no global warming at all for a decade or more. The entire climate activist "house of cards" stands or falls on its central thesis that man-made CO_2 is the chief cause of either AGW or climate change. With no "global warming" taking place and with CO_2 (man-made and otherwise) inexorably rising, that thesis must wither on the vine.

2 See the Gallup website at: www.gallup.com/poll/126716/Environmental-Issues-Year-Low-Concern.aspx

3 "France Backs Down on Carbon Tax," *Associated Press*. Go to: http//online.wsj.com/article/SB100014240527487048961045751395135138 42550.html

4 Even though the US Supreme Court in a truly momentous and bizarre "anti-science" moment voted five to four that it was a pollutant.

5 A market dominated by a single buyer. A monopsonist has the market power to set the price of whatever it is buying (from raw materials to labor). Under perfect competition, by contrast, no individual buyer is big enough to affect the market price of anything. *Source: The Economist*.

6 For the full report online go to: http://scienceandpublicpolicy.org/originals/climate_money.html

7 In fact, in the wake of the Copenhagen Summit fiasco and the international failure to agree binding CO_2 cutting targets, evidence of the banks getting cold feet and pulling out of the carbon offset markets surfaced in January 2010. See: http://www.guardian.co.uk/environment/2010/jan/24/carbon-emissions-green-copenhagen-banks

8 "Al Gore's $100 Million Makeover," Fast Company.com, December 19, 2007. Go to: www.fastcompany.com/magazine/117/features-gore.html

9 Ibid.

10 Ibid.

11 "Al Gore Could Become the World's First Carbon Billionaire," *The Daily Telegraph*, November 3, 2009.

12 "Al Gore's Green Investments Prompt Conflict of Interest Row," *The Guardian*, November 3, 2009.

13 "Junk Scientist Al Gore Denies Conflict of Interest in Global Warming Investments," *Gateway Pundit* online, November 3, 2009.

14 "Questions Over Business Deals of UN Climate Change Guru Dr Rajendra Pachauri," Christopher Booker and Richard North, *Daily Telegraph*, December 20, 2009.

15 The bogus graph features no less than three times in the IPCC's 2007 report. It is bogus because it relies on made-up figures from the discredited data of the Climate Research Unit at the University of East Anglia. The graph has been shown to be overlain with four separate colored trend-lines, each with a start-date carefully selected to give the false impression that the rate of warming over the past 150 years has itself been accelerating, especially between 1975 and 1998. When the lines are separated out and can be seen more clearly, however, the graph ingeniously obscures the fact that the warming rate from 1860–80 and again from 1910–40 the warming rate was exactly the same as the warming rate from 1975–98.

16 Graph can be downloaded from the pdf at: www.grida.no/climate/ipcc_tar/wg1/pdf/WG1_TAR-FRONT.PDF

17 The National Center for Public Policy Research press release "Economic Stimulus Funds Went to Climategate Scientists," January 14, 2010.

18 "A New Record for Total Antarctic Ice Extent," *Icecap* online, September 11, 2007.

19 "Revealed: Antarctic Ice Growing Not Shrinking," *Watts Up With That?* Online science blog, April, 18, 2009.

20 "Media Hype on "Melting Antarctic Ignores Record Ice Growth," Senator James Inhofe's United States Senate Environment and Public Works Committee (House Minority Leader's Page), March 27, 2008.

21 http://earthobservatory.nasa.gov/IOTD/view.php?id=6502

22 "Antarctic Ice Shelf Fast Collapsing," *Los Angeles Times* (publishing an original report from Reuters), March 20, 2008.

23 "Ice Shelf Hangs By a Thread," *Sydney Herald*, March 27, 2008.

24 "Bye-bye, Antarctica?" *Salon* online news, March 26, 2008.

25 http://icecap.us/images/uploads/MISLEADING_REPORTS_ABOUT_ANTARCTICA.pdf

26 http://epw.senate.gov/public/index.cfm?FuseAction=Minority.Blogs&ContentRecord_id=f1f2f75f-802a-23ad-4701-a92b4ebbccbf

27 Ibid.

28 "Polar Scientists on Thin Ice" (The Deniers — Part IV), Lawrence Solomon, *National Post*, February 2, 2007.

29 "Will Al Gore Melt?" Fleming Rose and Bjorn Lomborg, *Wall Street Journal* op-ed, January 21, 2007.
30 "Scientific Consensus 'not represented' in the IPCC Documents: Scientist," *The Hill Times Online*, August 13, 2007.
31 "EXCLUSIVE: Scientists Warn There May Be No Ice at the North Pole This Summer," *The Independent*, June 27, 2008.
32 "2008: Coolest Year of This Century," *WorldNetDaily* online, December 16, 2008.
33 "Bad Weather Was Good For Alaska Glaciers," *Anchorage Daily News*, October 14, 2008.
34 "Glaciers in Norway Growing Again," *Daily Tech online*, November 27, 2008.
35 http://www.canada.com/ottawacitizen/news/story.html?id=cda7b596-d5e8–4a50-bf5d-66a42c45ab0c&k=47765
36 http://wattsupwiththat.com/2009/05/02/new-zealand-glacier-findings-upset-climate-theory/
37 A British judge ruled that Gore's DVD presentation "An Inconvenient Truth" being shown in British schools contained eight serious statistical errors.
38 "Japanese Report Disputes Human Cause for Global Warming," *Daily Tech* online, January 14, 2009.
39 "Japanese Set 'Weak' Climate Target," BBC online, June 10, 2009.
40 "Numerical Evidence of Richard Black's (and the BBC's) Biased Climate Reporting," *The Unbearable Nakedness of Climate Change* blog, June 10, 2009.
41 Go to Jennifer Marohasy's excellent political and environmental blog site at http://www.jennifermarohasy.com/blog/archives/002906.html
42 "Dissing Hansen," Peter C. Glover, *The American Thinker* online, February 2, 2009.
43 "BBC Abandons 'Impartiality' on Warming," *Daily Telegraph*, January 31, 2009.
44 "BBC 'Must Become More Impartial,'" BBC online, June 18, 2007.
45 The full report can be downloaded at: http://www.iea.org.uk/files/upld-book340pdf?.pdf
46 http://www.bbcamerica.com/
47 http://www.bbccanada.com/
48 *Propaganda: The Formation of Men's Attitudes,*" Jacques Ellul, (Vintage) revised edition 1973, p. 27.

Part Three: Future World

7

Trans-Nationalism and the New World Order: A Warning

If the people fear the government, there is tyranny.
If the government fears the people, there is liberty.

Thomas Jefferson

If the abject failure of the Copenhagen Summit in 2009 sounds a global alarm, it should not be over prospective planetary apocalypse. While the Grand Narrative of man-made climate alarmism was driving the push for international binding carbon emission targets, the real sub-plot at Copenhagen was a different target: democracy itself. The necessary corollary of a trans-national, legally-binding, accord envisaged at Copenhagen for the lofty purpose of "saving the planet," of necessity, would require a new world order, a one world governance. And, in the Danish capital, the social engineers were pursuing an unparalleled opportunity.

Former British Prime Minister Margaret Thatcher, writing in 2003, foresaw the danger plainly enough: "Since clearly no plan to alter climate could be considered on anything but a global scale, it provides a marvellous excuse for worldwide, supra-national socialism."[1] Above all, what Copenhagen showed is how the latest media-hyped global threat can be instrumental as an argument to circumvent the normal democratic process and arrogate power to a more "clearer-seeing" few, in a time of crisis and for the "common good."

Murray N. Rothbard, however, saw the argument in starker terms: "The necessary consequence of an egalitarian program is the decidedly inegalitarian creation of a ruthless power elite."[2] So what would the consequences of the "egalitarian" program to be enforced by the new world order have meant had the socialist centralizers succeeded in Copenhagen?

WHATEVER HAPPENED TO "REPRESENTATION OF THE PEOPLE"?

First, major nations like China, India, Brazil, and others could forget about industrializing, a process that would, as it did in the West, help bring millions out of poverty. Just as in the West, the industrialization of these nations would depend almost entirely upon the use of cheap and efficient *hydrocarbon* resources to perform the economic miracle they are all working for. Something Copenhagen, with its emphasis on inadequate renewable energy, would have militated against. And why *should* the populations of China, India, etc. forego the same industrialized miracle enjoyed in the West? Second, only the elites, the politicians and the media, in particular, actually profess belief in man-made global warming as the polls in the West (see chapters 5 and 6) increasingly show.

Yet, the political elites have a very real stake in making the global warming alarmist case. It offers the prospect of unprecedented central-izing power, by which all manner of social engineering projects could be implemented. Why else would the United Nations and the European Union — *neither* a democratic institution — work so assiduously to promote themselves as supra-governmental power elites? Whatever happened to the concept of power resting with the "representation of the people"? When it comes to utilizing the Global Warming narrative for ideological ends, leftwing social engineers, to adopt Jeffersonian terms, prefer socialist "tyranny" to democratic "liberty."

Had Copenhagen reached an accord, the climate alarmism bandwagon could really have rolled. Public Enemy No. 1 being human-emitted CO_2, a full frontal assault against capitalism would have followed.

Heavy industry would have been first in the firing line, forced to buy carbon credits, hiking domestic energy bills still further, adding costs to transport and prices generally, doing little or nothing for the environment, while massively boosting government income. All of which would enable yet more enormous subsidies to be poured into highly inefficient renewables projects, a cornerstone of left-wing social engineering.

Quite simply, the new world order, established to "govern" this massive forced redistribution of wealth, would have gained a level of global power social engineers in previous generations could only dream about. But it would all have been short-lived, as, without any incentive to capitalize and create real jobs and economic wealth, the whole socialist edifice would eventually soon crumble. We only need look to how the centralization of socialist power in Russia and China brought each to its economic knees.

With the intuitive insight of one who had seen both the fledgling French socialist and American capitalist revolution take shape, the great French philosopher Alexis de Tocqueville saw that democracy is an essentially individualist institution standing in irreconcilable conflict with socialism. "Democracy extends the sphere of individual freedom," said de Tocqueville in 1848, "socialism restricts it. Democracy attaches all possible value to each man; socialism makes each man a mere agent, a mere number. Democracy and socialism have nothing in common but one word: equality. But notice the difference: while democracy seeks equality in liberty, socialism seeks equality in restraint and servitude."[3] And, in the 1940s, F.A. Hayek made the point that, "Although we had been warned by some of the greatest political thinkers of the nineteenth century [and he names de Tocqueville and Lord Acton] that socialism means slavery, we have steadily moved in the direction of socialism."[4]

Who, other than anti-democratic social engineers, could disagree? Today the 27 *unelected* Commissioners of the EU have *imposed* a new uber-president and a new supra-bureaucracy on the people of Europe; so much for the notion of a "democratic Europe." How could this possibly have happened, other than by a creeping, centralizing, de-democratization? It is as if the people of Europe had been inoculated against notions of individual liberty and freedom. Perverse, when one considers that Europe has been only too familiar with the diktats of socialist tyrannies run by elites with such appalling results in previous centuries. President Obama may believe America should move his country along a European socialist path, but he would do well to listen to the stark realities of what such a socialist direction brings in tow. As Margaret Thatcher observed, "During my lifetime, most of the problems the world has faced have come, in one fashion or other, from mainland Europe, and the solutions from outside it."[5]

Energy is the world's most precious commodity. Period. Control energy resources and you control the lifeblood of even the most developed of nations. And that is what, effectively, the Copenhagen Summit could have achieved once it had control of the climate-associated issues, especially actively declining vital hydrocarbon energy use. And if there should be any lingering doubt about the link between the politics of energy and climate change, and the prospect many Greens perceive in the overthrow of the "old world order," socialist zealots are open enough in their mendacious approach to achieving their goals:

No matter what if the science is phoney, there are collateral environmental benefits, Climate Change provides the greatest chance to bring about justice and equality in the world.[6]

> —Christine Stewart, former Canadian Environmental Minister.

Some go further:

Isn't the only hope for the planet that our industrialized societies collapse? Isn't our responsibility to bring that about?

> —Maurice Strong, Senior Advisor to former UN Secretary-General Kofi Annan, and founder of the UN Environment Program.

For many eco-zealots, nothing less than the destruction of over-arching industrialized society will do. For them, capitalism, the cornerstone of the industrialized edifice, must be dislodged.

I think if we don't overthrow capitalism we don't have a chance of saving the world ecologically.

> —Judi Bari, Earth First!

Nor should any lack of scientific justification be allowed to stand in the way:

A global warming treaty must be implemented even if there is no scientific evidence to back the greenhouse effect.[7]

> —Richard E. Benedick, President of the Committee for The National Institute for the Environment (NIE).

Incidentally, Richard Benedick's actual NIE remit is, "to improve the scientific basis for environmental decision-making by insulating science from politics." But hey, who reads their own job description these days? And here is the irrepressible Benedick again, this time on the type of "detailed" and "clear" international treaty he and many modern environmentalists demand from Copenhagen-style summits:

"Don't worry about the blandness of the final [Global Climate] treaty, because it has hidden teeth that will develop in the right circumstances."[8]

THE DNA OF THE NEW WORLD ORDER

It should not be surprising that the environmental *bête noire* of the Capitalist Beast is Big Oil. Oil, as coal before it, has lately been (literally) the driver of the monstrous capitalist beast. To that end, alarmist climate advocates have maintained that Big Oil has "wickedly" funded a massive disinformation campaign aimed at subverting the truth about climate catastrophe. But having debunked that particular media myth in Chapter 6, whatever financial investment Big Oil may or may not have made into funding in the climate debate, it is plainly dwarfed by the mega-bucks fuelling the AGW-activist movement and its supporters.

Indeed, the truth is that Big Oil and Big Energy generally *has acquiesced* in the face of the environmentalist onslaught, and they now run PR campaigns extolling the virtue of their green credentials, especially alternative energy research and projects. Knowing that most of these alternative energy projects are highly uneconomic (much of the cash coming from government) the question is, why? Well, Big Energy long ago realized it was swimming against the PR tide. In the case of Big Oil, it was often the equivalent of diverting money into a "loss-leading" advertisement campaign. In the case of the power utility companies, they could attract enormous government subsidies and were empowered to hike prices on the basis of charging a green levy to customers, the chief reason why we *see* so many wind farms today. Far from being of proven value to national energy production, they remain heavily subsidized "facts on the ground" that, for some, convince them of an energy value that is illusory.[9]

But another anti-capitalist beast has arisen to aid the new world order, the UN Environment Program's Agenda 21; its chief architect being Maurice Strong, a committed socialist. Strong is a key mover in the concerted effort to impose draconian global environmental policies. And the philosophy of Agenda 21 can be seen to become thoroughly suffused into the leaked "Danish text," the proposed draft accord for the Copenhagen Summit in 2009.

In an earlier quote in this chapter, we heard how Strong promotes the actual collapse of industrialized societies. Addressing the Rio Earth Summit in 1992, Strong stated, "Current lifestyles and consumption patterns of the affluent middle class — involving high meat intake, use of fossil fuels, appliances, air-conditioning, and suburban housing — are not sustainable."[10] Strong and his political friends mean business too, as Malthusianism once again raises its ugly head with the US, capitalism's leading exponent, attracting the usual approbations at such gatherings.

Paul Ehrlich, professor of Population Studies at Stanford University (as ever) goes even further:

A massive campaign must be launched to de-develop the United States. De-development means bringing our economic system into line with the realities of ecology and the world resource situation.[11]

The Population Bomb,[12] published in 1968, predicted that in "the 1970s and 1980s hundreds of millions of people will starve to death in spite of any crash programs embarked upon now. At this late date nothing can prevent a substantial increase in the world death rate . . .." One would think that Ehrlich, the author of this alarmist book, would have either learned the fallacy of his thinking, or would have been publicly discredited. Instead, and this is emblematic of what we are confronted with, he is still considered a ribald hero by the social engineers.

Radical solutions, all of them based on an inbred hatred of industrialized societies, and the US in particular, and an underlying theme of elitist hatred for mankind in general, abound from leading eco-activist academics:

Global sustainability requires the deliberate quest of poverty, reduced resource consumption and set levels of mortality control.

—Professor Maurice King

In a 1970 *Economist* editorial, Ehrlich leaves us in no doubt he perceives mankind as a species of vermin: "The extinction of the human species may not only be inevitable but a good thing . . . This is not to say that the rise of human civilization is insignificant, but there is no way of showing that it will be much help to the world in the long run." And Ehrlich pulls no punches in consistently casting humans — and fellow Americans in particular — as a cancer on the plant.

You (and we) might consider cheap energy important for mankind — given, as we saw in Chapter 1, that energy use promotes greater social prosperity. Not least that the most vulnerable and poorest among us should receive the genuine benefits cheap energy offers by way of "the basics," — heating homes, helping cook, transport to work and beyond. But eco-activists have no compunction about demanding the cost of energy rise ever higher to discourage the use of hydrocarbons, even though the poorest suffer most. But Ehrlich is unrepentant, "Giving society cheap, abundant energy . . . would be the equivalent of giving an idiot child a machine gun."

Try telling that to the Victorians; that impressive generation of industrious and visionary scientists and engineers who took the "machine gun" of "cheap, abundant energy" and created the greatest anti-poverty Industrial Revolution the world has seen. And try telling the generations who benefited directly via the Industrial Revolution, seeing their families not only pulled out of social poverty, but able to live longer, healthier, less polluted lives, as a result. And if you want further evidence of how such elitist eco-thinking influences the influential and powerful today:

> *If I were reincarnated I would wish to be returned to earth as a killer virus to lower human population levels.*
>
> —Prince Philip, Duke of Edinburgh,
> patron of the World Wildlife Fund.

Not surprisingly, we can see why so much media hype is influenced by it, too:

> *A total population of 250–300 million people, a 95 percent decline from present levels, would be ideal.*
>
> —Ted Turner, media mogul, founder of CNN, and major UN donor.

Needless to say, when it comes to rectifying the planetary malaise, Ehrlich, Turner, and their eco-zealot friends, including Al Gore, are not putting *themselves* forward for "mortality control" programs, you understand. Nor are they themselves willing to lead by example giving up the benefits of their *own* (literally) high-flying, industrialized-sponsored, lifestyles.[13] As with most radical modern eco-theorists, *their* elitist moral solutions are only for the rest of us, the plebeians.

We have sought here merely to give a flavor of the anti-human, suggestively sociopathic, nature and thinking of leading environmental academics and their political and media allies. But Google the views of many leading green ideologues and you will find far more. Indeed, whole websites exist (and we acknowledge our thanks for their help) to warn of what those in politically-influential positions actually believe and preach, and in the highest political circles. Key individuals like Maurice Strong, who offered up the radical environmental blueprint that became the subtext to the Copenhagen Summit in December 2009.

The fact that so many world leaders were prepared to sign up to its anti-democratic agenda, and sign away parts their own nation's sovereignty into the bargain, shows just how far radical, anti-capitalist, anti-free trade environmental ideologies are driving modern geopolitics in the climate debate. And through it prepared to arrogate control of key national energy security to a supra-national oligarchy; a process inaugurated at the launch of the "world saving" Club of Rome[14] in the 1960s.

THE CLUB OF ROME

In April 1968, a small international group of professionals from the fields of diplomacy, industry, academia and civil society met at a villa in Rome. Their self-ordained mission is to discuss what they consider the "dilemma of prevailing short-term thinking in international affairs and, in particular, the concerns regarding unlimited resource consumption in an increasingly interdependent world." Participants subsequently agreed to spend the next year "raising the awareness of world leaders and major decision-makers on the crucial global issues of the future."[15] And so the Club of Rome was born. It was with the publication of the Club's first commissioned report *The Limits of Growth* in 1972 that the "originality" of their thinking became clear. Today, the Club of Rome website informs us: "In recent years, the Club of Rome has embarked on a whole new range of activities and has modernised its organisation and its mission. Its commitment to finding new and practical ways of understanding global problems and plans to turn its thinking into action are as strong as ever."[16] A review of members reveals a string of participants highly placed in the United Nations, the European Commission as well as senior scientists and influential businessmen from all over the world. All fine and dandy, that such high-ranking officials and representatives should be concerned to plan a better future? We'll let you decide.

Here are just a few quotes — and stick to the order below when reading — it will give you a clearer idea of the nature of the pompous philosophical mindset that drives the power-grubbing members of the Club of Rome:

> *The earth has a cancer and the cancer is Man.*
>
>   —Club of Rome, *Mankind at the Turning Point.*

> *We are on the verge of a global transformation. All we need is the right major crisis.*
>
>   —David Rockefeller, Club of Rome executive manager.

> *In searching for a new enemy to unite us, we came up with the idea that pollution, the threat of global warming, water shortages, famine and the like would fit the bill.*
>
>   —Club of Rome, *The First Global Revolution.*

All these dangers are caused by human intervention and it is only through changed attitudes and behaviour that they can be overcome. The real enemy, then, is humanity itself.

—Club of Rome, *The First Global Revolution.*

The resultant ideal sustainable population is hence more than 500 million but less than one billion.

—Club of Rome, *Goals for Mankind.*

In nature organic growth proceeds according to a Master Plan, a blueprint. Such a "master plan" is missing from the process of growth and development of the world system. Now is the time to draw up a master plan for sustainable growth and world development based on global allocation of all resources and a new global economic system.

—Club of Rome, *Mankind at the Turning Point.*

A keen and anxious awareness is evolving to suggest that fundamental changes will have to be take place in the world order and its power structures, in the distribution of wealth and income.

—Club of Rome, *Mankind at the Turning Point.*

And, just in case, you might still be under the illusion that our view and yours would actually count for something when it comes to "jointly" deciding what is for the common good:

Democracy is not a panacea. It cannot organize everything and it is unaware of its own limits. These facts must be faced squarely. Sacrilegious though it may sound, democracy is not longer well suited for the tasks ahead. The complexity and the technical nature of many of today's problems do not always allow elected representatives to make competent decisions at the right time.

—Club of Rome, *The First Global Revolution*

But what is the point of a "private" radical agenda if you don't have the global platform to promote it in much more subtle, socially acceptable, language, say, adopting the positive language of greater environmental "sustainability"? And what better platform of influence than that of the UN's world-government-in-waiting?

Heard enough? In fact, such is the rank arrogance to which the Club of Rome's members appear oblivious — as elitists tend to be — we are reminded of an apt literary analogy that illustrates the syndrome wonderfully:

> *"What does an ass like you know about things of that sort? You know you're no good at thinking, Puzzle, so why don't you let me do your thinking for you?* (Shift to Puzzle, p. 12)

> *"It's because I'm so wise that I'm the only one Aslan is ever going to speak to. He can't be bothered talking to a lot of stupid animals. He'll tell me what you've got to do, and I'll tell the rest of you."* (The Ape to the other animals, p. 32)

—Quotes taken from C.S. Lewis' *The Last Battle*, *The Chronicles of Narnia*.

THE UN'S "AGENDA 21"

Earlier we quoted Maurice F. Strong, a Canadian and a former petroleum engineer turned leading eco-activist politician who can be credited for advancing the globalist radical environmental movement, particularly through his work at the United Nations Environment Program (UNEP) and, above all, as the chief architect of its *Agenda 21*.[17]

A long-time advocate of increasing the UN's authoritative role in world affairs, Strong became Secretary-General of the UN's Conference on the Human Environment, and then the first executive director of the UNEP and special advisor to the UN Secretary-General. It was Strong,

Figure 7.1: *Time* magazine cover, April 3, 2006.

remember, who believes, "The only hope for the planet [is] that our industrialized societies collapse? Isn't our responsibility to bring that about?" At the senior echelons of the UN, Strong was now well placed to begin to implement his agenda.

We have already heard from Strong's opening address at the 1992 Rio Conference (Earth Summit II) where he advocated that "consumption patterns of the affluent middle class . . . are not sustainable. A shift is necessary toward lifestyles less geared to environmentally damaging consumption patterns." Strong had hoped that a full-fledged Earth Charter, literally a blueprint to which nations should adhere, would result from the 1992 event. The best he could achieve, however, was the introduction of Agenda 21, "a comprehensive plan of action to be taken globally, nationally and locally by organizations of the United Nations System, Governments, and Major Groups in every area in which human impacts on the environment."[18] Agenda 21 thus laid the groundwork for a future Earth Charter, one with teeth.

Interestingly, Terry Melanson reports how Strong invoked some curious pseudo-religious New Age language in his Rio address. He reports Strong as saying, "it is the responsibility of each human being today to chose between the forces of darkness and the force of light." Melanson notes how these particular terms appear to invoke earlier quotes made by Alice Bailey and Blavatsky that alluded to the "forces of darkness" as the "outdated Judeo-Christian faith." Melanson further notes that "force of light (Lucifer) in their view is the inclusive new age doctrine of a pagan pantheistic New World Religion." He further quotes Strong as saying, "We must therefore transform our attitudes and adopt a renewed respect for the superior laws of divine nature."

With the backing of David Rockefeller, current head of the Rockefeller Foundation, Strong went on to set up what is today the Earth Council Alliance to facilitate the outworking of Agenda 21 and lay the groundwork for the future enforcement of its Earth Charter. Strong has stated that, "The Charter will stand on its own. It will be in effect, to use an Anglo-Saxon term, the Magna Carta of the people around the Earth. But, it will also, we hope, lead to action by the governments through the United Nations."[19]

But a further, somewhat stunning, self-incriminating, revelation comes from the pen of a key Strong backer, David Rockefeller himself.[20] In Rockefeller's *Memoirs* published in 2002, on page 405, he makes a curiously enlightening statement when he openly asserts that he, Rockefeller, is in actually part of a "secret cabal working against the best interests of the United States . . . conspiring with others around the world to build a more integrated political and economic structure

— one world, if you will."[21] As much as we have here gone out of our way to stick to the facts and avoid any suggestion of conspiracy, we think it more than interesting that one of the world's leading billionaires should feel so insulated from public and media approbation that he feels able openly to espouse personal involvement in a "secret cabal" working against his own country, and for an anti-democratic agenda. "Curiouser and curiouser," said Alice.

Henry Lamb, in his 1996 exposé *The Rise of Global Governance*, takes up the running. "Strong has worked diligently and effectively to bring his ideas to fruition. He is now in a position to implement them." Lamb explains, "Education programs to teach the "global ethic" have been underway by UNESCO and by UNEP for more than 20 years. That the US government, through its representatives to the various UN agencies, has not already crushed this global governance agenda is a testament to the effectiveness of the UN's education program." Lamb next claims Strong and Co. intended to replace the Economic and Security Council (ESC) with a new Economic and Social Council.[22] "The new ESC would consist of no more than 23 members who would have responsibility for all the international financial and development activities. The IMF, the World Bank, and the WTO — virtually all finance and development activities — would be under the authority of this body. *There would be no veto power by any nation* (italics ours). Nor would there be any permanent member status for any nation."

Nor would there be any place in Strong's New World Order for either democracy, it seems, or for dissent — especially affording legal protection to "whistleblowers." As Lamb states, "The Commission [on Global Governance] believes that the UN should protect the 'security of the people' inside the borders of sovereign nations, with or without the invitation of the national government. It proposes the expansion of an NGO 'early warning' network to function through the Petitions Council to alert the UN to possible action."

In 2005, Strong's influence, temporarily at least, took a backward step as the culture of lack of integrity and conflict of interest, that dogs the enviro-elites, was evoked yet again. In July 2005, Strong was dismissed from his post as a top envoy for North Korea when his involvement in the UN oil-for-food scandal broke. It was alleged that Strong accepted a personal check for just under $1 million from Korean-born businessman Tongsun Park. Tongsun Park was eventually charged in July 1997 with influence-peddling for Saddam Hussein. The money was in fact to purchase a stake in Cordex Petroleum Inc., a company controlled by Strong.[23]

At the time of writing, Strong lives in China, having taken up the role of President of the Council of the United Nation's University for Peace. He is also an active chairman of the Advisory Board for the Institute for Research on Security and Sustainability for Northeast Asia. But a visit to the Earth Council Alliance website reveals clearly Strong remains as active and as influential as ever on the world stage in pursuit of "sustainable" projects and the new world order.[24]

So what does this fascinating excursion into the shady world of the prospective New World Order and self-ordained "cabalists" tell us? Well, everything, as we know how the key elements of thinking behind Club of Rome and Agenda 21 moved center stage, to be played out as the subtext to the 2009 Copenhagen Summit.

TRANS-NATIONALISM AND COPENHAGEN 2009

The red flags warning of the anti-democratic agenda pervading the Copenhagen Summit in December 2009 began going up when a copy of the pre-summit "Danish text" was leaked to the UK's *Guardian* newspaper.[25] Former major policy advisor to Margaret Thatcher, Lord Christopher Monckton, publicly highlighted paragraph 38, Annex 1 of the Copenhagen draft which called for a United Nations-created "government" responsible for taxation, enforcement and economic redistribution.[26] In other words, the establishment of an embryonic world government, a long-term ideological goal for Big Government social engineers since the collapse of the Berlin Wall and the communist ideal. A "government" that could, post Copenhagen, impose an international cap and trade system, and could enforce the payment of the "climate debt" the developed nations "owe" to the developing nations.

In the event, Copenhagen's agenda failed, though not through any want of commitment as political leaders, including Barack Obama and Gordon Brown, strove to support the signing of an accord that would, ultimately, cede key elements of national sovereignty to an unelected global oligarchy. Indeed, the draft document itself was reported to be the work of a group of individuals known as the "circle of commitment" which included representatives from the US, UK and Denmark. The ultimate failure of Copenhagen, ultimately, stands eloquent testimony to the vital importance of continuing *national* economic self-interest — thank goodness. Faced with signing a potential economic — not to mention personal political — suicide note, leaders of the developed states baulked. Equally, faced with the socio-engineering authority and control the proposed draft would place in the hands of the developed nations, the developing nations, too, baulked. In the event, and highly ironically, it was Communist/socialist China,[27] via an unwavering refusal to abandon its coal-fired driven industrial economic miracle, that rescued democratic leaders from themselves.

China — one of the world's biggest polluters — has been using the "global warming" movement to shift attention from genuine environmental problems and from burdening its own economy, while managing to encourage others, especially the US, to burden theirs.

The logic for many leftwing politicians is both compelling and heaven-sent. Not only have imperialist and capitalist countries exploited the rest of the world and its resources for over a century, in particular oil and gas, the use of those forms of energy, so vital to economic prowess, has also endangered the planet. Emission of CO_2 is the ultimate sin from the rich countries and a symbol of inequality. The Obama administration, radically changing course from its predecessors, has adopted the global climate change rhetoric, and all that it implies.

China, by far the world's fastest growing major economy and, as of 2008 the world's biggest emitter, destroys the bliss of the new international order that is supposed to come from a carbon constrained world. Theoretically, Communist China would want to join in anything resulting in the reduction of American hegemony, but in this case it is chary of the economic threat this particular idea would inflict upon itself.

Ever Confucian, China had been paying lip service in fighting global climate change, and had been saying whatever the rest of the world liked to hear, until just before the Copenhagen Summit. China ratified the Kyoto Protocol in 2002 and, in September 2009 at the UN Climate Summit in New York, China's President Hu Jintao spoke about the "international responsibility on climate change" and China's strategy on carbon reduction. That attitude was called "sincere and inspiring" by leading climate policy advocates.

What many did not know, however, was that less than a month before President Hu made his New York speech, China had already stated its position on climate change policy at the meeting of the National People's Congress on August 24, 2009. China proclaimed that with the "financial aid and technical support from the developed nations," it will take proper actions toward emission control "according to the national situations while continuing its economic development."

Shortly afterwards, when China was pushed to make specific emission cuts at the UN climate talks in Bangkok in October, China's top climate representative, Yu Qingtai, had a public spat with delegates from the US and Europe and walked out of the meeting. Yu pointed out that poor countries are the "victims of climate change," and that rich countries are largely responsible for centuries of pollution, and that it is unfair to expect all countries to play a role in combating global warming. At last, China, a nation culturally unwillingly to be confrontational, stood up to counter the Westerners.

In what has been defining the chasm between sclerotic Europe, that has little to lose, and China, Karl Falkenberg, the European Commission's Director-General for the Environment, criticized China by saying that nothing would be gained by focusing on per capita emissions and raised a frequently repeated bogeyman. "We know that consequences of climate change are seen more dramatically as of now in the developing world so continuing to argue (there is) almost a human right to pollution, as I heard from my Chinese colleague, is not the way we need to go about it."

What China was really interested in was how to win more emission rights at the Copenhagen climate negotiating table. Emission rights and energy use are development rights, Ding Zhongli, an academician and the Vice President of the Science Academy of China, had claimed. China's emissions per capita was 2 metric tons per year in 1990, the GDP was only about $600 billion in the same year. In 2008, the emissions per capita was increased to about 5 metric tons per year with the GDP growing to $4.4 trillion.

Emissions per capita in China are a little above the world average of 4.5 metric tons per year, but only two-thirds of those of Europe and less than one-third of the US. Energy use for China is central to its economic development and the seeking of the higher quality life style enjoyed by Westerners. According to the US EIA projections, China's emissions per capita in 2030 will be about 8 metric tons per year, the same as those of Europe in 2030. Assuming that by then the Chinese population increases to 1.6 billion from 1.3 billion in 2009, the total emissions will be 11.04 billion metric tons, compared to 6.72 billion metric tons in 2007. If China were to agree to cut its emissions by complying with the Kyoto Protocol, instead of the even more rigid Copenhagen proposal, China would have to reduce its emissions per capita to a preposterous 1.36 metric tons per year in 2030. Nothing like this could ever happen.

As Zachary Karabell, author of *Superfusion*, puts it, "For the last decades, as China's economy kept growing at unprecedented rates, most Western analysts kept discussing when it would crash. Now with China surging ahead through this [financial] crisis, all they can discuss is, when will China stall?" China knows all too well that its rise to world economic prominence has made a lot of Westerners uncomfortable. From the Central Government to academia, there is a growing belief in that country that the climate change rhetoric is a tool of Westerners to stop China from growing stronger. Strangely, and for different historical reasons, China and the US find themselves in similar predicaments, even if the Obama administration has ideologically positioned itself squarely in the camp of reducing America's wealth. This is something that China will *not* do. With China's obvious position, a truly international and meaningful Copenhagen "accord" was doomed from the outset.

However, the proposed Copenhagen draft would have given control of an enormous global climate slush fund to an unaccountable — to any electorate — body of global trans-governance. That body would have been made up by a number of groups including the World Bank, much as the Club of Rome advocated. Antonio Hill, climate policy adviser for Oxfam International warned, "It [the draft] draft proposes a green fund to be run by a board but the big risk is that it will be run by the World Bank and the Global Environment facility and not the UN."[28] The "Global Environment Facility" in question is in fact a partnership of 10 agencies including the World Bank and the UNEP. Remember the latter? Set up by Maurice Strong, the fairly autonomous department that now seeks to implement Agenda 21? And UNEP, incidentally, remain active participants in the elitist, anti-democratic, Club of Rome, as the latter's website confirms.

Using the political legitimacy global warming alarmism affords, the socialist left today perceives an unprecedented opportunity to work for their long-established twin goals: the destruction of democratic capitalism (so we/you have no say) and national sovereignty (so our national leaders have no say, either).

What was at stake in Copenhagen was not just the governance of an enormous climate slush fund. It was, above all, the instigation of draconian governance run by an unelected elite able to exert powerful control over the use of the world's chief commodity: energy.

TRANS-NATIONAL GOVERNANCE: "NONSENSE ON STILTS"

Most anthropologists acknowledge that the "family" unit is the cornerstone of all civilized society. The nation-state is thus the family unit scaled up to governable social community proportions. At the level of the nation-state it still remains possible to adopt representative government on behalf of the social "family"; given that family's shared language and culture, including a prevailing philosophy or religious belief that underscores the culture's "one-ness," its identity. As much as the romantic notion of a "world family" might appeal to some, in practice the concept of the prospective governance of that one world "family" soon breaks down when any attempt is made to integrate the diversity of language, philosophy/religion and culture into a coherently governable whole.

That is not to say, that international or trans-national co-operation, goals and accords are not desirable nor achievable, plainly they are. But that is a far cry from forcing peoples of varying cultures and beliefs into a "melting pot" of global governance that can act for the "common good" on law, justice, education, free trade, not to mention a people's understanding of freedom and liberty. Hence governance, in a one-size-fits-all arrangement, can never work — without replacing democracy with a powerful centralized tyranny, that is.

And this is precisely why the trans-national efforts of the UN and the EU have been consistently stymied in their grandiose intra-national designs. The fact is, on the international stage, the nation state — and national self-interest — still (at present) rules. But perhaps, only just, as the assault on democracy and democratic capitalism, via the energy-climate wars in particular, will remain a key political issue. What is often maddening is the apparent fixation of globalist social engineers to attack the most successful, most law-abiding and some of the least corrupt countries in the world, headed by the US, while looking away from the transgressions of dozens of countries with abysmal human rights records, rampant corruption and run by despots with impunity. They turn moral right and wrong on its head.

Margaret Thatcher's reticence about the entire EU trans-national governance project is highly instructive. She noted that its leaders' has always been "hyperbolic." Thatcher warned that the EU's "attempts to play a role on the world stage have been universally embarrassing." Most damning of all about the EU project, Mrs Thatcher observed, "Perhaps the most significant shortcoming of the fledgling super-state is that it is not, and will not be, indeed ultimately cannot be, democratic . . . The Commission and the Parliament share the same federalist agenda — and it is not democratic."

Mrs Thatcher went on to note the attempt of those enthusiasts who want to establish a European Constitution preferring the expression "United States of Europe." A comparison with the US that Thatcher warned thoroughly misrepresents the signal differences between the two. "The parallel," she stated, "is deeply flawed and deeply significant. It is flawed because the United States was based from its inception on a common language, culture and values — Europe has none of these things." Thatcher said, "By contrast, 'Europe' is . . . a classic utopian project, a monument to the vanity of intellectuals, a programme whose inevitable destiny is failure; only the scale of the final damage done is in doubt."[29] And Hayek describes the inevitable outcome whenever collectivist ideology and democratic capitalism clash: "If 'capitalism' means here a competitive system based on free disposal over private property, it is far more important to realize that only within this system is democracy possible. When it becomes dominated by a cóllectivist creed, democracy will inevitably destroy itself."[30]

In his essay "Conserving Nations"[31] modern philosopher Roger Scruton makes a powerful case against the elitist desire for increasing trans-national supra-governance. Scruton points out that, "The case against the nation state has not been properly made, and the case for the transnational alternative has not been made at all." Scruton warns, "We are on the brink of decisions that could prove disastrous for Europe and the world, and that we only have a few years in which to take stock of our inheritance and to reassume it." Like Margaret Thatcher, he perceives, "Moreover, every expansion of the jurisdiction beyond the frontiers of the nation state leads to a decline in accountability." Listing the lack of accountability over European Union policies and actions, and throughout the departments of the United Nations, Scruton states, "Accountability, in short, is a natural by-product of national sovereignty which is jeopardised by transnational governance."

Scruton further makes his point by citing the key example of how the idea of human rights associated with the Universal Declaration of Human Rights incorporated into the UN Charter should, for instance, be "taken with a pinch of salt." Why? "Rights do not come into existence merely because they are declared. They come into existence because they can be enforced. They can be enforced only where there is a rule of law. Outside the nation state those conditions have never arisen in modern times." For Scruton, as for us, "The nation state is accountable to all its citizens since it owes its existence to the national loyalty that defines its territory and limits its power. When embedded in the law of nation states, therefore, rights become realities; when declared by transnational committees they remain in the realm of dreams — or, if you prefer Bentham's expression, 'nonsense on stilts.'"

All of this becomes only too relevant when we consider what took place in Copenhagen in December 2009. Had the anti-democratic, anti-capitalist socialist, "egalitarian" agenda succeeded in the Danish capital, the resulting unelected oligarchy would have had no truly "representative" legitimacy; other than that of the self-aggrandizing political elite freed from all constraint of accountability before a disenfranchised people. If the fiasco in Copenhagen taught us anything, it should be that there are those who have no compunction in co-opting the latest Grand Narrative global threat to advance their own ideological aspirations for power.

You would think, given the history of French, Russian, Chinese, German, and Cuban socialist "experimentation," it is a lesson we would all have learned well. But the subtext of the debacle in Copenhagen reveals only too clearly that the current collusion between planet-saving climate activists and the prospective socialist new world order only confirms the truth of the new century's ideological maxim: Green is the New Red.

Notes

1 Margaret Thatcher, *Statecraft: Strategies for a Changing World* (Harper Collins), p. 449.

2 Murray N. Rothbard, quoted at The US Independent Institute's *On Power. org* online site.

3 "Discours pronouncé a l'assemblée constituante le 12 Septembre 1848 sur la question du droit au travail." Œuvres completes d'Alexis de Tocqueville, vol. IX, 1866, p. 546.

4 F.A. Hayek, *The Road to Serfdom*, (Routledge Classics), p. 13.

5 Margaret Thatcher, *Statecraft: Strategies for a Changing World* (Harper Collins), p. 320.

6 Quoted by the *Calgary Herald*, December 14, 1998.

7 Richard Benedick quoted by Dixy Lee Ray in her book *Trashing the Planet* (1990).

8 Richard Benedick quoted by *The New York Times*, June 14, 1992.

9 In fact, in recent years the oil majors, realizing that when the subsidies run out most of their "green" projects are simply uneconomic, have been dumping their renewable energy programs entirely to re-focus on their "core business." This includes oil majors Shell and BP.

10 Maurice Strong address to the Rio Earth Summit 1992, as quoted in "Leaked Copenhagen Document: Third World to be Systematically De-developed, World Bank to Rule Global Climate Slush Fund," John Vidal, *The Guardian*, December 8, 2009.

11 Paul Ehrlich and Anne H. Ehrlich, *Population, Resources, Environment*, (W.H. Freeman, San Francisco, 1970) p. 323.

12 Paul Ehrlich, *The Population Bomb*, (Buccaneer Book, December, 1995).

13 See: "Green Hypocrisy at 30,000 feet," Peter C. Glover, *TCS Daily*, October 5, 2006. Go to: www.tcsdaily.com/article.aspx?id=100506B

14 The Club of Rome website is at: www.cluboframe.org

15 See *The Story of the Club of Rome* and other documents at www.club ofrome.org

16 See documentation at www.clubofrome.org

17 Go to: www.un.org/esa/dsd/agenda21/

18 Agenda 21, published by the Division for Sustainable Development, UN Department of Economic and Social Affairs at www.un.org/esa/dsd/agenda21

19 Ibid.

20 At time of writing in his 90s and is currently patriarch of the Rockefeller clan.

21 Our thanks go to Dr Dennis Cuddy, PhD for this fascinating revelation in his article "The Rockefeller Plan: Part 5," at the NewsWithViews.com website, February 9, 2009.

22 The Economic and Social Council was duly formed and began to meet on an annual basis in 1998.

23 According to the report, Park was given the money "in a cardboard box" by Saddam Hussein's then no. 2 Tariq Aziz in a bid to win the Iraqi regime favorable treatment from the UN. The independent enquiry eventually ruled that the relationship between Strong and Park raised troubling questions regarding conflict of interest among UN officials.

24 We wish to acknowledge our gratitude in this section for information regarding Maurice Strong *et al.* to the "Soldier for Liberty" website at: www.soldierforliberty.wordpress.com; and to Judi McLeod, editor at: www.canadafreepress.com for her article "United Nations and Its Carefully Managed One World Order," November 24, 2008.

25 "Leaked Copenhagen Document: Third World to be Systematically Developed, World Bank to Rule Global Climate Slush Fund," John Vidal, *The Guardian*, December 8, 2009.

26 "Obama's New World Order," Jeffrey T. Kuhner, *The Washington Times*, October 25, 2009.

27 In truth, it is highly debateable just how "communistic" modern China actually is. Since China took over control of the capitalistic colony of Hong Kong some insist that, in reality, it was Hong Kong, economically speaking, that "took over" China.

28 "Leaked Copenhagen Document: Third World to be Systematically Developed, World Bank to Rule Global Climate Slush Fund," John Vidal, *The Guardian*, December 8, 2009.

29 Margaret Thatcher, *Statecraft: Strategies for a Changing World* (Harper Collins), pp. 342, 358, 359.

30 F.A. Hayek, *The Road to Serfdom*, Routledge Press, p. 73.

31 Roger Scruton's essay "Conserving Nations," from his book *A Political Philosophy: Arguments for Conservatism* (Continuum), pp. 5, 20, 21, 29 and 31.

8

Russia's Energy Imperialism and the Threat of Future Conflict

The difference between a welfare state and a totalitarian state is a matter of time.

Ayn Rand

After the end of the Cold War, a curious grey mood engulfed the West, first Europe and then, more than a decade later, the United States. Perhaps, the victors proved once again what history has taught repeatedly; that many nations are far more lively and vigorous when they are waging wars or campaigning. Once victory is assured however, a nation's hunger for an edge and a better life can too easily evaporate, along with the ravages of war. Entire empires collapse or, worse yet, linger towards a slow and painful death, almost right after what should be their moment of crowning glory.

It is perhaps human nature to feel guilty of success, and in the narrative we already followed in this book, nothing shows this more vividly than in the sizeable portions of western society that many politicians appear willing to lessen or even destroy. Western modern lifestyle and the energy use that drives it have been at the cross-hairs for many ideologues. Social engineering calls for a global society that employs many euphemisms such as "equitable," one that dictates "wealth re-distribution." Much of the global warming rhetoric, it turns out, has little to do with the science or even what to do about the world temperature itself, but instead it relates directly to the destruction of the capitalist system generally, and US power in particular.

It is easy to see the brewing of such ideas in Europe because of traditional but ageing philosophical thought. It is hard to envision those ideas taking hold in the US for any lasting period of time both because of the nation's relative youth and its leadership position in the world but also because of its own ideological foundation, far more socially conservative than in Western Europe. In modern parlance the US could be labeled "right of center." As radically left wing as the Barack Obama administration appears to be, it should be considered as a major aberration only made possible because of a latterly unpopular Republican president in George W. Bush, the worst economic crisis since the Great Depression right before the election, and an extraordinarily charismatic candidate.

Under Barack Obama, the US, the undisputed victor of the Cold War, was lowered to a level that would seek "international consensus," to work "within the United Nations" and to ask for forgiveness for a myriad of specified and even unspecified past ills, done not just by the US but by the entire West. Nothing symbolizes the new dynamics of the relationship between European liberals and their new American friends more than the Nobel Peace prizes awarded first to Al Gore for his climate work and then to Barack Obama, the latter nominated just a week after taking office obviously for no other accomplishment than the fact that he was not George W. Bush and for the "change" he appeared to represent. Energy use, types of energy use and climate issues were central to all this.

Interestingly, the loser of the Cold War, Russia, saw a resurrection of sorts and, not surprisingly, riding exactly on the same energy sources that have been used to berate the lifestyle and the very nature of the US and Western Europe.

RUSSIA'S NEW IMPERIUM

An ogre of a giant looms to the East of Europe, occasionally in the shape of a country, other times in the shape of a company, the two often indistinguishable. Russia and Gazprom are poised to devour the whole of Europe and its Asian neighbors, riding quite effectively on the back of oil and gas.

Gazprom's influence inside Russia and especially outside of the country has been underestimated and, astonishingly, not discussed enough. By far the largest owner of natural gas reserves and the largest supplier in the world, six times the second, Royal Dutch/Shell, in 2010 the company was supplying over a quarter of Europe's natural gas, and was aggressively looking to greatly increase that share. Gazprom has been the flagship of former Russian President Vladimir Putin's strategy, and the battering ram to break down defenses of what can arguably be called energy imperialism. The Russian state owns 50 percent plus one share of the company, and almost all of the company's top executives are devout Kremlin loyalists. The current Russian President Dmitri Medvedev was Gazprom's Chairman. He replaced Putin, who became

Prime Minister, replacing Victor Zubkov who became Gazprom's Chairman. You get the picture.

Gazprom, springing from the old Soviet Ministry of Gas has been huge from the very start, but after the 2004–05 dismantling of Yukos and Sibneft, Gazprom got into the oil business as well by taking over Sibneft, now called Gazpromneft.

Gazprom and natural gas are heaven-sent for Russia and are used to cover up gaping national deficiencies generating a massive influx of cash from energy-hungry neighboring countries. That income provides the trappings of power that a dysfunctional economy and a highly corrupt state could not otherwise muster. The company has the largest gas reserves in the world by a wide margin: 1,172 trillion cubic feet (Tcf) of recoverable gas reserves, a 60-year supply based on current production. Even with far more stringent US reserves definitions, which apply economic (time value of money) and license criteria, the number is still enormous, 781 Tcf, at least four times the reserves of the US. Gazprom reserves-to-production (RP), ratio is one of the largest in the world. For example, in the US the RP ratio has been less than 10 for decades. The US industry is far more efficient and drills and develops gas as needed using more sophisticated technology.

Inefficient or not, Gazprom's performance has been imposing, producing 19.3 Tcf of gas in 2008, roughly equal to the US production of 19.5 Tcf. The company is also a major oil producer with 870 thousand barrels of oil and condensate[1] per day. In addition to gas and oil production, Gazprom has another unique asset in Russia, a monopoly on gas transportation and distribution. In 2008, Gazprom's activities accounted for 10 percent of Russia's gross domestic product.

But not everything is rosy and quite a bit of it bodes major difficulties if not calamities in the future. Over the last few years Gazprom has experienced a large gap between its stagnant production and internal and external commitments. The incentive and the capital to expand production are simply not there. Russian internal per capita consumption is huge, larger than the US by almost 25 percent. But prices have been practically giveaways, in some cases less than $1 per million Btu, one-tenth to one-fifth of the price earned internationally. Increasing domestic prices has been Gazprom's answer, understandably a politically explosive issue for Russian consumers.

It was Gazprom's cutting of gas supplies to the Ukraine in early 2006 that first caused a furor in Europe. The incident occurred when the Ukraine refused to accept gas price increases from $65 to $230 per 1,000 cubic meters, at par with prices paid by western European countries. Of course, gas supply to the Ukraine, which was drawing a tiny portion of the flowing gas, was not the issue. The nervousness in Europe was that cutting the flow of gas to Ukraine also meant painful gas deficits to a freezing Europe. The Ukraine dispute was not the end. It opened the floodgates for a barrage of gas price hikes, targeting friends and foes of Russia alike.

The Ukrainian natural gas affair was like the trumpet ushering in the sovereign. Hints of a new Russian Empire, this time riding on oil and gas, projected hegemony over its neighbors, from East Asia to Europe. Putin was the new Tsar and most Russians, starved for power after the Soviet collapse, loved him. Western niceties of democracy, human rights and freedom of the press were never really big deals in Russia. Corruption, which according to Transparency International puts Russia between Nigeria and Indonesia, does not seem to bother the newly internationally relevant Russians.

Gazprom has been the primary vehicle for the new imperium. Far beyond the lesser former satellite states such as Ukraine, Belarus, and the Baltic countries, Russia has resorted to divide-and-rule tactics, dangling the same natural gas carrot over China, Japan, Germany, and Britain. Moreover, it is being coy over the ultimate destination of future energy pipelines, poised to reward or punish, depending on concessions and acquiescence.

Russian geopolitics, always shaped by energy sources, takes several hues. For example Russia buys lots of discounted gas from Turkmenistan for its own use, allowing Gazprom to spare Russian natural gas resources to be sold outside the country at a huge premium. Russia and Turkmenistan recently signed a 25-year contract calling for Turkmenistan to increase its gas supplies piped to Russia from 0.17 Tcf to 2.3 Tcf per year. Coincidence? This is exactly the amount Gazprom has agreed to sell to China beginning in 2011.

But big challenges lurk for Gazprom and Russia. With constant claims by many that the company cannot meet gas promises in both Europe and Asia in the near future, Gazprom has brazenly announced that it will spend $420 billion on projects by 2020 to bring more natural gas to market. Nearly half of the investment will go to pipeline transportation, while up to 30 percent will go to exploration and production.

Gazprom ambitions keep ratcheting up. The company announced it may build a second liquefied natural gas (LNG) terminal near Vladivostok on the Pacific Coast for Asian exports. Outrageously and with little chance of this actually happening, Gazprom claimed that the first LNG tanker load will be shipped to China in 2010.[2] The gas will be piped from the energy-rich Sakhalin Island where numerous disputes are brewing between Gazprom, its other state-owned competitor Rosneft, and western super majors ExxonMobil and Royal Dutch/Shell.

Gazprom, at least at the rhetorical level, oozes confidence and has set very ambitious goals for expanding its energy empire, while attempting to assuage any remaining doubts on its capabilities. CEO Alexei Miller said at the St Petersburg Economic Forum in June 2008: "Our international business ties and our joint projects have turned Gazprom into a global company. We will rigorously abide by all our long-term contract obligations. The size of our reserves permits us to confidently state that Gazprom is able to meet any solvent consumers' demand for gas, in domestic and foreign markets alike."[3]

Miller has been on the stratospheric rhetorical path. In July 2008, he predicted that crude oil prices could reach $250 in the foreseeable future, and that as a result Gazprom's market capitalization would exceed $1 trillion by 2014. No other major energy company executive even came close to such predictions, but then again, nobody has the same power to make their predictions come true.

Pushing further, Miller has been suggesting the creation of OPEC-2, a smaller, core group of energy-producing countries which might have a greater effect on both crude and natural gas prices. Russia has been trying to persuade Iran and Qatar to join this gas cartel in a move highly criticized by the US and the European Union. Russia hopes to be admitted to the original OPEC, and this move has been delayed only because of the 2008 economic crisis, the reduction in oil demand and the collapse of oil prices. Alexei Miller staunchly defends this "OPEC-2" strategy: "The main task of the forum, in contrast to OPEC, isn't the setting of daily production quotas, but questions of long-term strategy and investment plans in the gas industry."

America is trying to fight two wars, one in Iraq and another in Afghanistan and along with almost all western powers is trying to contain radical Iran. Almost pointedly, Alexei Miller and Iranian Energy Minister Gholamhossein Nozari have agreed to develop Iran's South Pars gas field and drill in Iranian oil fields. With little worry about the politics of religion and radicalism, of which Russia has become a victim on occasion, there is a deepening alliance between Iran and Russia, with the latter unabashedly trying to capitalize on the former's energy riches. This is taking place while the rest of the world recoils at the Iranian threat. Despite the fact that nearly every country has shied away from investing in Iran, Russian radio station Ekho Moskvy reported in 2009 that Gazprom could replace French oil company Total's projects in Iran.

The situation is now transparent and blatant, not unlike a Khrushchev era missive stating: world beware; the energy-invigorated Russian bear is at bay. After the collapse of the Soviet Union and its resulting economic calamity, it was up to Putin through Gazprom to redefine Russia's position in the world. Russia's abundant oil and gas resources have already managed to accomplish what nuclear weapons and 50 years of Cold War were unable to do.

But while the seeking of power is central to Russian culture and Gazprom is the obvious vehicle, reality sometimes thwarts ambition, at least temporarily. Gazprom's market capitalization in January 2009 dropped to as low as $85 billion, though it eventually recovered to around $120 billion. This for a company that CEO Alexei Miller boasted, less than a year earlier, was on its way to become the first trillion dollar company. Meanwhile, clues as to the geopolitics of future oil and gas supplies can be gained by reviewing the construction and direction of energy pipelines.

THE PIPELINE WARS

Our guess is that Vladimir Putin's favorite Beatles song is *Back in the USSR*, given "neighborhood difficulties" with former states, especially Georgia and the Ukraine, over energy supplies.

While the 2008 war between Russia and Georgia was ostensibly over nationalist elements in South Ossetia and old grudges (remember that Stalin was a Georgian), the hostility was mostly about Russia's newfound power as an energy imperialist state. Georgia had refused to play along like other former Soviet states. If anything, its independent attitude had been a giant irritant to Russia ever since Vladimir Putin used oil and gas to project hegemony over the region and, by extension, into all of Europe. At the same time, the tiny country of just 4 million people had been trying to ward off the giant to its north by seeking membership in the North Atlantic Treaty Organization (NATO) or the EU.

In the post-Cold War era, the US and Russia-dependent Europe had both been reduced to pleading for calm. But a look at the map makes the conflict's issues quite transparent. Oil and gas can come from Russia into Europe by tanker through the Black Sea from its massive terminal in Novorossiysk, or by pipelines through Belarus and Ukraine. There are also plans for a subsea pipeline in the Baltic. These routes give Russia huge leverage — almost an energy monopoly — over both the transit and the destination countries. Over 25 European countries now depend on Russia for as much as 75 percent of their oil and gas needs.

Georgia was eager to act as a spoiler, and European countries were even more eager to comply while trying to avoid incurring the wrath of the hand that feeds them.

The first important event was the construction of the Baku-Tbilisi-Ceyhan oil pipeline, that started in 2002 at a time when Russia was politically weaker. The 1,776 kilometer line connects the oil-rich Caspian with southern Europe in what was to be an energy corridor for European oil and gas supplies. The pipeline is designed to carry 1 million barrels per day from Azerbaijan's Caspian oil fields to the export terminal Ceyhan via Tbilisi, with Georgia acting as a very important transit country. That did not sit well with Russia, being bypassed from oil exports to Europe. The pipeline, funded by Western oil companies and banks to the tune of $3.2 billion, was commissioned in 2006. What gave Russia fits, and still does, are other possibilities that could affect its control — for example, underwater pipelines that could be built across the Caspian linking Kazakhstan or Turkmenistan. The latter newly enrolled among the world's gas-rich superpowers.[4]

But Russia was particularly irked over talk of a gas pipeline — similar to the existing oil pipeline, again linking Azerbaijan and Turkey and points beyond, Baku-Tbilisi-Erzerum through Georgia. This would give Georgia independent power over energy supply and would create

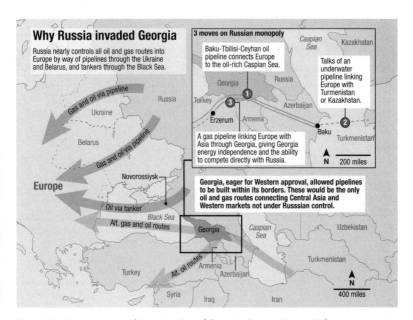

Figure 8.1: Russia's energy-driven invasion of Georgia. *Source: Energy Tribune.*

an alternative route to — the holy grail of Russian geopolitics — Gazprom's transit monopoly.

In 2006, Gazprom, flexing its muscles, manipulated the former Soviet states by setting new records in gas export prices practically every month. It was clear that the geopolitical climate in Eastern Europe would be severely damaged. In fact, double and triple increases in gas prices were imposed on Russia's neighbors. First it was the Ukraine then Belarus, then Armenia, all threatened with gas supply interruptions until new contracts with huge price increases were signed. They had no other choice but to surrender to Gazprom's terms and conditions. Georgia resisted the Russian might, and that predictably ended in war. Within days from the start of military hostilities Russian jets devastated Georgia's key Black Sea energy staging post, the port of Poti and the Georgian oil pipeline, part-owned by BP, which supplies 1 percent of the world's oil needs, pumping around 1 million barrels of crude oil a day to Turkey.[5]

Things did not deteriorate suddenly. The conflict between Russia and Georgia has a long history, such as the attempt made by Moscow in the 1970s to impose the Russian language as the official language of Georgia, a move that provoked such rioting that the Kremlin was forced to backtrack. These chronic tensions intensified with the election in 2004 of Mikhail Saakashvili, who refused to accommodate Russia's ambitions to control his country. Then, Georgians discovered and expelled alleged Russian spies. In return, Russia's president Vladimir Putin stirred a crass witch hunt against Georgians in Russia, while Gazprom threatened to cut off Georgia's gas supplies unless it agreed to an aggressive price hike from $110 to $230 per thousand cubic meters.

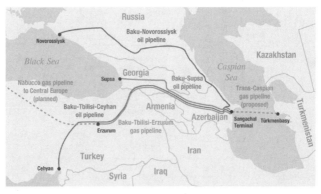

Figure 8.2: Pipelines designed to bypass Russian territory. *Source: Energy Tribune.*

Following the threat, Gazprom's blackmail was blatant, in effect saying, "The Georgians could compensate for the gas price increase by trading off some assets." For example, Armenia paid Gazprom with its transportation network. Armenia had seen the writing on the wall and kept the same price for gas supplies, $110 per thousand cubic meters. But they relinquished control of their gas network in the bargain. And as we mentioned above, the construction of gas pipelines via Georgia would inevitably create an energy supply route that was an alternative to Russian oil and gas, threatening Russia's energy stranglehold on the vast south European markets. Russia could not tolerate this possibility. The war was punitive and brutal. Both the local "neighborhood" and European customers beyond had been warned. Next up was the Ukraine.

Russo-Ukrainian disputes over natural gas and transit supplies to and through the Ukraine turned serious in March 2005. Russian claims that the Ukraine was diverting gas in transit to the EU for its own domestic use was later admitted by the Ukraine. Russia responded by cutting off supplies to the Ukraine on 1 January 2006. In the event, the dispute was resolved and supply restored three days later. But another dispute erupted in October 2007 over Ukrainian gas debts culminating in Russia restricting supplies of natural gas to the Ukraine in March 2008. The unresolved issue of the size of Ukraine's gas debts festered until in January 2009 the restricted supply to the Ukraine resulted in a major reduction in gas supplies to 18 European countries which received gas from Russia via the Ukraine.

This second Russian–Ukraine gas crisis came three years after the first and this time involved cut-offs to Bulgaria, Romania, Turkey, Austria, the Czech Republic, and Greece. It does not really matter that gas soon started to flow again. Europe's dependence on a country that is willing and able to push the continent into freezing cold and darkness was the crucial issue, and Russia seemed to relish that role. The protracted gas dispute with the Ukraine and the 2008 summer invasion of Georgia were both manifestations of Russian energy-fuelled hegemony.

The Georgian and Ukrainian affairs have solidified the new Russian empire riding on oil and gas, and projecting dominance over its neighbors from East Asia to Europe. In July 2008, Gazprom offered to buy all of Libya's exportable gas supplies.[6] Russia's brash move to further control the European energy markets was hard to disguise since Libya is Europe's only credible and neighboring alternative supplier.

It should be understood, however, that energy imperialism and the use of Gazprom will not necessarily bring economic prosperity for Russia. For the Russian leadership, power is far more important. In fact, the international economic crisis and the stand-off with Ukraine drove Russia's core business of gas export to a stand-still. As a result, in January 2009, Gazprom exports dropped by almost 75 percent leading to over-production and a decline in overall gas sales by 16.5 percent for Gazprom, and 10.5 percent for Russia generally. It proved to be a record, post-Soviet era, drop in gas activity. In trying to dominate the Ukraine, Russia "shot itself in the foot" and in the middle of the high-demand season. This event alone drove down the country's GDP by almost 1 percent, which all told declined by 7.9 percent, according to the Russian Statistics Bureau, Rosstat.

Meanwhile, Europeans act like helpless sitting ducks. With no energy alternatives to speak of, an assertive Russia breathing on them, and flaccid domestic policies influenced greatly by Green parties, European countries may become the victims of the old dictum: be careful what you wish for, you might just get it. And this is the lessening of a muscular America leading an assertive western alliance.

Indeed, the feebleness of European efforts to break the stranglehold of Russian energy imperialism is nowhere better exemplified than in the EU's backing (with the US) of its "great pipe hope" for diversification away from Russian energy dependence: the much-vaunted Nabucco Pipeline. A pipeline project that, yet again, is highly revealing how nationalism — in this case German — trumps trans-nationalism every time, when energy security is at stake.

THE NABUCCO CONSPIRACY

The $10 billion Nabucco[7] pipeline story reads like a Bourne-style political thriller. Since its conception in the early 1990s, the introductory narrative has been full of international intrigue geared to helping Europe plot its escape from the "tyranny" of Russian energy supremacy. But almost two decades on we are still not at chapter one and the future remains uncertain, in no small part due to the sabotaging efforts of the EU's anti-Nabucco "fifth column": Germany.

Confusion over the importance of the project was revealed in a two-day EU economic crisis summit in Brussels in March 2009 when Nabucco was first removed[8] and then reinstated[9] on the EU priority energy project list. Construction remains scheduled to begin in 2011. Though German objections to Nabucco's inclusion in the EU's 5 billion euro "anti-crisis" energy stimulus package were overcome, the summit allotted 200 million euros, 50 million less than the originally slated. But while Nabucco has survived that round of disagreement, its troubles were, and are, far from over.

Figure 8.3: *Source: Energy Tribune.*

Conceived to pump natural gas from Central Asia to Europe bypassing Russian territory, Nabucco is perceived by the Eurocracy as essential to weaning Europe of its Russian oil and gas dependency. But addiction to Russian energy sources is proving hard to kick, with problems over viable sources of gas persistently plaguing the Nabucco project. Turkmenistan's enormous reserves were considered one option. But Turkmenistan's natural gas distribution operation is largely managed by Gazprom. Whether the country's latest massive gas discovery at the South Yolotan-Osman field will come under Russian management too, or whether the gas will eventually head west or east — Turkmenistan is developing growing links with China — is still unclear. For the gas to head west would also mean building an additional Trans-Caspian link. Then there are the security problems associated with running the pipeline through transit nations, especially Turkey and Georgia.

Iran has more than enough gas to keep Nabucco busy, and Tehran, with the world's second largest reserves of natural gas, is keen to buy into the lucrative European market. But Nabucco badly needs a reliable provider, and Iran's notoriously unreliable production track record and the uncertain geopolitical situation over its nuclear intentions, have proved powerful barriers to new investment. Equally, Russia and Iran have developed a growing energy alliance. With its European aspirations thus stuck in the geopolitical mud for the foreseeable future, Iran too has turned its eyes east, and has been cutting energy deals with Beijing. It is true that Iraq's prime minister, Nouri al-Maliki, has offered to supply roughly half of the pipeline's gas requirements, some 15 billion cubic meters per year. This would give the Nabucco project a welcome boost, but this offer remains, as yet, theoretical, and very much subject to the vagaries of new energy developments in Iraq.

Meanwhile Nabucco's competition, the Gazprom-backed Nord Stream (linking Russia and Europe via the Baltic) and South Stream (linking Russia to Italy and Austria) pipeline projects are forging ahead. Indeed the Nord Stream project cleared its final hurdle towards construction in February 2010 when Finland issued a permit deeming the pipeline environmentally safe for the Finnish area of the Baltic which it will traverse.[10]

So concerned have some European energy experts become over Nabucco's prospects that they even pushed to offer Russia's Gazprom a stake in the project. Just how such a move would advance Europe's energy diversification away from Russian energy dependence, *the whole point of the Nabucco project*, no one has yet said. According to one report, a formal invitation to take a stake in Nabucco was received by Gazprom in early March 2009.[11] Not surprisingly, Gazprom — holding all the important energy cards — declined, citing the Nord and South Stream projects as their strategic priorities. In a TV interview, Alexander Medvedev, Director-General of Gazprom Export and the Deputy Chairman of the Board, could not resist rubbing in the hard facts. "Unlike Nabucco, we have everything we need for this project to materialize," he said. "We have gas, the market, experience in implementing complex projects, and corporate management."

By the end of 2009, such was the confusion over EU policy on Nabucco that the Azerbaijani State Oil Company too, so far Nabucco's sole projected gas provider, was threatening to sell its gas to Asian countries instead. But even if Azerbaijani gas is, ultimately, forthcoming that would still leave a natural gas deficit of 23 billion cubic meters.[12] Furthermore, issues concerning the pricing and transit policies of countries through which Nabucco is due to pass are still unresolved. Nabucco is supposed to be transporting gas to Europe by 2014. Most analysts now believe that this date is highly optimistic with many believing Nabucco is already a lost cause.

But even with these basic geopolitical factors aside, the Nabucco project reveals how the coherence of EU energy policies are consistently undermined by national self-interest, the issue we addressed in the previous chapter, even among the "federation" of European states.

THE RUSSO–GERMAN "SPECIAL RELATIONSHIP"

Germany has been at the center of efforts to remove Nabucco from the EU's priority energy projects. Though France, Italy and the Netherlands too wanted Nabucco downgraded for economic reasons, it is the Germans who have consistently been its strongest opponents. At the March 2009 summit in Brussels, German ministers argued that as Nabucco was set for construction in 2011, EU funds allotted to the project would be spent too late to be considered an economic "anti-crisis" measure, defeating the aims of the summit. Germany's Chancellor Merkel made it clear that she was only prepared to support projects that would have a "substantial stimulating effect" on the economy in 2009 and 2010. Merkel also argued that sufficient private investment was already available. The German objection was ultimately undermined, however, when the EU Czech presidency, in 2009, came up with a final proposal that Nabucco cash subsidies should be spent up to the end of 2010. It seems apparent that the economic and energy interests of Germany, Europe's largest economy, differ substantially from EU's regional interests. So much then for an EU that speaks with "one voice."

To achieve power, Angela Merkel was forced to cut a deal with the German Green Party to phase out all of its 20+ nuclear power plants. That political pact left Germany even more dependent on Russian hydrocarbon imports than other parts of Europe. So while Germany provides tacit support to the EU's championing of energy diversification, it has steadily pursued a pragmatic policy geared to building even closer national energy ties with — and dependency on — Russia. The Nord Stream pipeline will link Russia and Germany directly via the Baltic.

It just happens that former German Chancellor Gerhard Schroder is Chairman of the Nord Stream Shareholders' Committee. And Herr Schroder has been earning his Nord Stream pay check. While Gazprom owns a controlling 51 percent of Nord Stream, German energy majors E.ON and BASF, through Wintershall Holdings, own 20 percent each. Dutch company NV Nederlandse Gasunie — remember it was The Netherlands who sided with Germany to get Nabucco downgraded at the 2009 summit — holds the other 9 percent. That Nabucco threatens Gazprom's energy, and thus Vladimir Putin's geopolitical interests, is clear. With gas exports to Europe having declined by 40 percent since the beginning of 2009, Gazprom has found in Germany, at the very heart of the EU, a major ally to further its interests. It is a growing relationship that might go a long way to explaining Germany's surprisingly strong opposition, even threatening EU vetoes, to Georgia's and the Ukraine's United States-backed bids for NATO membership.

Given the EU's sense of urgency in achieving greater energy diversification, it now finds itself caught in a pincer movement of external geopolitical realities and internal national self-interest. The EU may yet be forced to admit defeat and raise the white flag over Nabucco, allegedly Europe's energy "salvation." But however the Russo-EU energy plot-line plays out, Germany, Europe's largest economy, is revealing only too clearly that sticking to the Eurocratic official text is one thing, conspiring with Vladimir Putin over the subtext — national self-interest and energy security — is another. The rest of Europe, take note.

Meanwhile, as Europe procrastinates over Nabucco, Russian energy hegemony is forging an "energy axis" in the Caspian-Central Asian area with China (a burgeoning market for its energy; we will review China's needs for energy in Chapter 9) and Iran. In addition, we are seeing Russian influence advance with an axis of energy militant nations around the world, in particular, heavyweight energy producers like Venezuela.

RUSSIA, VENEZUELA, AND IRAN: THE RISE OF THE ENERGY MILITANTS

Nearly five decades after the Cuban Missile Crisis, the Russians, buoyed by energy revenues, are once again trying to increase their influence, far away from their own neighborhood. On 11 September 2008, two Russian long-range bombers arrived in Venezuela, along with a contingent of Russian warships. The jets and 1,000 Russian troops were there to begin training exercises with Venezuelan forces. Although this visit did not go smoothly, even involving a fist fight between Chávez's bodyguards and Russian sailors, it did send a political message to the southern hemisphere.[13]

Much of Venezuela's modern weaponry is Russian made, the result of a $3 billion arms deal between the two in 2006 that allowed Hugo Chávez to purchase 53 helicopters, 24 jet fighters, and various antimissile and antiaircraft systems, along with 100,000 AK47 assault rifles. A more recent arms deal calls for Venezuela to buy Russia's Varshaviankaclass or Kiloclass submarines. Chávez, never at a loss for blustery rhetoric, declared after the Russians' arrival: "Yankee hegemony is finished."[14]

The reaction of the US to all this has been rather muted. Indeed, the US, heavily committed militarily to other parts of the world, including Iraq and Afghanistan, could hardly afford to pay adequate attention to Chávez. But while the international community came to expect erratic behavior from him, it was Russia that surprised many. After the invasion of Georgia, it appeared that Russia was thumbing its nose at the US in Latin America. Prime Minister and former President Vladimir

Putin, after he renationalized the energy industry, has found in Chávez a soul-mate, a "hermano" who shares his animosity toward the US, although the reasons for their animosity may differ.

Chávez's ascent was not surprising. After years of corrupt Venezuelan governments failing to live up to popular expectations Chávez rose to power because of his charismatic promises, characteristic of the populism that, historically, has prevailed in Latin America, where Che Guevara is a cult hero and Fidel Castro remains an admired leader. With Vladimir Putin and Iran's Mahmoud Ahmadinejad, Chávez shares an ideology loaded with empty nationalism and class warfare, with anti-Americanism as the cornerstone, tapping into the people's jealousy and frustration over their own national failures. Dissatisfaction with the Anglo-Saxon dominance of international business and pop culture sometimes takes whimsical turns. Support for autocratic regimes often becomes the face of collective inferiority complexes.

Chávez would be a comical figure were it not for high oil prices, which have papered over his shortcomings and prolonged his eventual day of reckoning. The trouble with ideology and fanaticism is that they are not particularly good management tools. Today, Venezuela has perhaps the unhealthiest economy in Latin America. All productive sectors have been thwarted. "Statization" has been used to strip companies of any profitability. Petroleum, telecommunications, and utilities came under strict state control. But Chávez didn't stop there, continuing on to absorb the cement and steel industries. Productive lands have been confiscated and artificial price and wage controls have been imposed. Food shortages are at epidemic proportions and, not surprisingly, people are hoarding. A rigid system of foreign exchange controls has led to high levels of corruption. There is virtually no investment in infrastructure and deterioration is evident everywhere.

Venezuelan developments in 2010, including a nationwide electrical crisis and the emergence of a more unified political opposition led by a very active student movement, suggested that Chávez's rule might not even survive until 2012, when his presidential term ends. The reason for this is that his three main pillars of support: abundant oil income, the loyalty of the armed forces and the unconditional following of much of the poor, all appear badly weakened. The decline in oil prices has obliged him to get into considerable new national debt that in 2010 stood at some $100 billion. The armed forces have been increasingly restless as less money means less privileges or new weaponry for them. The poor were getting frustrated due to the low quality of public services and the shortages of the most essentials requirements: food, water, and electricity. Even if Chávez were to leave office in 2010 his government actions would take decades to remedy.

The country's economic predicament may not be the worst part. Even more palpable is the social animosity. Chávez has directed such a venomous attack on the middle class that this has led to a counter-reaction. The polarization between Democrats and Republicans in the US pales compared to that between Chavistas and their opponents. Chávez openly speaks of his revolution as a class struggle. His speeches are full of hatred against the middle class and this, in turn, has created deep resentment against his regime among half of the country's citizens, mostly middle class but also including sectors of the poorer classes that no longer share his political ideology.

Anticipation of the regime's unavoidable unraveling is countered by uncertainty over the alternative. Some of the more thoughtful anti-Chavistas reluctantly admit that it may be better to wait until the presumed end of the nightmare, at the prospective end of his term in 2012. Any crisis (such as a small drop in oil prices due to a US or global recession, or food riots) could lead to the frightening possibility of a civil war or to the prospect of an even worse military dictatorship.

Chavismo is such an anachronistic version of socialism that, after the monumental collapse of social engineering (in the USSR) and the end of the Cold War more than two decades ago, one would have thought it could not resurface. By equating government support with patriotism, Chávez has practically eliminated the possibility for any smooth transition. That's why one anti-Chavista hoping for a smooth exit asked pessimistically, "Can you imagine Chávez voluntarily passing the presidential sash to anybody else?"

In both Russia and Venezuela oil revenues have an overwhelming political impact and both countries depend for their hydrocarbons on clients that are their political adversaries. This represents an important geopolitical reality.

During the Russian military visit to Venezuela, Hugo Chávez warned that if the US attacks his country, Venezuela would cut off all oil supplies. The threat is not idle. Venezuela is the fourth largest provider of US crude oil at just over 1 million barrels per day, approximately 11 percent of US crude imports. A sudden cut off of Venezuelan crude could produce a temporary crisis and an abrupt and significant rise in the global price of oil. Although tensions between the US and Venezuela will probably remain long lasting there are increasing indications that the dependence of the US on Venezuelan oil is lessening, mostly due to the deterioration of Venezuelan oil production capacity brought about by the politicization of the state-owned oil company. Venezuelan exports to the US in 2010 have decreased by about 300,000 barrels per day in 2008–09, a shortage that the US has been able to compensate with imports from other producers.

Even with Barack Obama at the White House, Chávez continued his antics. In November 2009, while receiving the Iranian President Mahmoud Ahmadinejad in Caracas at a state reception with full military honors and pomp, Chávez used three words to characterize Ahmadinejad, each with pause for applause: "Leader. Brother. Comrade."

It was in character with the Obama administration to say very little when thuggish leaders like Chávez and Ahmadinejad got together in America's neighborhood and with Chávez praising his "brother, who is resisting like a mountain the intentions of imperialism and colonialism." The recipient of Chávez's adulation, Ahmadinejad, is a bona fide international pariah with nuclear ambitions and brutal suppression of his own people.

The Venezuelan experience made it more important than ever for the US to promote more global oil production capacity, by pressing its allies in the Middle East, something that President Reagan understood all too well, and which precipitated the fall of the Soviet Union, or to develop its own hydrocarbons resources. The reduction in oil prices following the 2008 economic crisis is a two-edged sword for oil supply. On the one hand, lower prices may make investment less attractive; on the other, the lowering of exploration and drilling costs should encourage such activities in the US offshore and the Arctic. A proper national energy policy should have seen to it. Unfortunately, the Obama administration, mired in global climate rhetoric, has had precious little substantive comments on America's real energy dilemma and future oil and gas supplies. It is a sign of naïveté and profound ignorance of the oil industry for American politicians to belittle the impact of incremental domestic production. In a low-margin business like the oil industry, an over or undersupply of one percent can mean a 50 percent impact on the price of oil.

Figure 8.4: Iran's President Mahmoud Ahmadinejad and Venezuela's Hugo Chavez (right). Brothers in arms.

A NUCLEAR IRAN?

However, nowhere is the threat of energy-associated conflict more immediate than in Iran, where an international stand-off persists, at time of writing, over that country's fast-progressing uranium enrichment program. The international community, including the US, Israel, even China and Russia, is deeply worried as Iran persists in its claims that it only wants the use of uranium for domestic electricity production. However, those claims ring hollow for several reasons.

First, Iran is sitting on some of the world's largest reserves of both oil and gas. Its gas reserves are second only to Russia's. Through years of neglect of its energy infrastructure and a lack of refinery capacity, however, Iran is forced to import much of the petroleum products it needs for domestic, especially automobile, consumption. But the question remains: why would a country with the world's second largest gas reserves, be investing so heavily in a nuclear program when it could, and should, just as easily invest in petroleum refining capacity and a gas-fired power infrastructure?

The global community has offered Iran every conceivable alternative to aid in a nuclear program aimed at boosting electricity production that does not involve weapons-grade uranium enrichment. But the hard-line Islamist regime has not only rebuffed foreign assistance that other nations would have jumped at, but has gone out of its way to antagonize the world community by insisting that, sanctions or no sanctions, the country will pursue its course and develop enriched (weapons-grade) uranium. Such a development would provide the Islamist regime with nuclear weapons capacity, and what it most craves: a quick-fix superpower "equalizer" status, a status that would make Iran a major player on the world stage.

What makes Iran's nuclear program particularly dangerous is the fact that the country's president has made it abundantly clear that a clear goal for the Islamist regime is to "wipe Israel off the map." What must be borne in mind is that Iran is run by a group of religious zealots who are ideologically committed to the destruction of the state of Israel — zealots who are fast approaching achieving the means to carry out that very specific threat. There is already abundant evidence that Iran is a terrorist-sponsoring state, and exactly the sort of state no one would, could, or should trust with a nuclear device. Iranian revolutionary guards have already been shown to have been fighting alongside Hezbollah fighters in southern Lebanon,[15] Hamas receives much of its weaponry and other aid from Iran,[16] and Iraq's Shia-backed terrorist insurgency has been almost exclusively Teheran-sponsored.

Although punitive actions are the only type of pressure available to the United Nations and the world community, there is no evidence that sanctions have had, or are having, any effect on Iranian foreign policy. If anything, the Iranian regime regularly brags about its latest progress on uranium enrichment. Among external observers the greatest hope is that the unrest among the middle classes and the youth will eventually bring down the medieval regime.

Iran is one of the Middle East states most difficult to understand, even by those of us that have visited the country and have dealt with Iranians for years both inside and, especially, outside the country. Without question — and this may shock many — Iranians are the most pro-American, pro-Western society in the Muslim world. Many are highly sophisticated and quite modernized; a significant fact, set against some of the societies in the immediate region. The persistent hold of the Islamic regime creates both an enormous stifling effect inside the country but also a sample of what could happen elsewhere, if Islamism takes hold. The Iranian regime simply cannot survive its own internal pressure for long without ratcheting up the brutality of its repression. Unfortunately, there is plenty of evidence for that already.

Israel, watching Iran with growing alarm, may not feel it has the time to wait and see how Iran's internal conflict plays out. In fact, due to the polarization inside the country the Iranian regime may want to appear more militant by accelerating its nuclear program, to appeal further to its supporters. While Iran's threat may be something of an armchair debate for the world at large, it is not so for Israel. For this country the threat is all too real and growing more immediate by the month. If the Iranian regime is not brought down by its own citizenry, or if it persists in its nuclear policy eschewing diplomatic efforts to prevent it, the prospect of war with Iran via an Israel or US-led nuclear attack (it would take bunker-busting nuclear warheads to take out much of Iran's nuclear infrastructure) is real enough. However, as devastating as such a conflict would be for relations with other Islamic regimes, such a conflict could not be defined as an "energy war" per se, that is, a war primarily concerned with energy security — our chief concern here.

A more immediate issue impacting the world's energy security in the event of either a war with Iran, or a political decision by its regime, would be a move by Iran to close the Straits of Hormuz. The reality is, five of the six countries in the world possessing more than 75 billion of proven oil reserves, are inside the Persian Gulf: Iran, Iraq, Kuwait, the United Arab Emirates, and the biggest of all, Saudi Arabia. It would prove catastrophic for the world's energy supplies.

The production capacity of these energy-rich states is far higher than their current levels. With more than 55 percent of world reserves they produce 25.4 million barrels per day, about 28 percent of the total world production of 85 million barrels per day. These five main players, together with some smaller neighbors, manage to export 18.2 million barrels per day by tanker. Whimsical recent claims about a Saudi Arabian oil production "twilight" notwithstanding, the region, mired in war and hostility is grossly underperforming in energy production, due to instability in Iraq and the biting sanctions against Iran. How many people know that Iran, with the world's second largest natural gas reserves is actually a net importer of gas? With almost all its important gas reservoirs located offshore, Iran, being under sanctions, has not been able to procure the right technology to exploit them. Being a radical Islamic republic carries a large penalty.

The Straits of Hormuz tell a compelling story. Along with the Straits of Malacca and to a far lesser extent, the Bosporus, they represent the world's most vital geopolitical energy choke points. Hormuz is in a class by itself. Of the total world oil consumption, about half, 43 million barrels per day, is moved by tanker, trans-nationally. Of this, some 17 million barrels per day pass through the Straits of Hormuz. The US imports about 10 percent of its oil needs from this area, China about 15 percent. But neither comes close to the degree of Japanese dependence; Japan imports 77 percent of its oil from the Middle East. The alternative of Russian oil moving east through pipelines currently under construction is both debatable and years away, due to numerous geopolitical problems. Japan must be shaking in its boots for any Israeli military action in the Middle East. Even a temporary closure of the Straits will make previous oil price spikes look like a picnic.

Of course, Iran will not sit still in the case of an Israeli attack and will lash out in the only way that it thinks it can, by hurting Israel's patrons. According to Reuters AlertNet Fact Box, "Iran has already admitted deploying anti-aircraft and anti-ship missiles on Abus Musa, an island strategically located near the Strait's shipping lanes." A second series of retaliation will likely be a large escalation of attacks against the US military in Iraq.

Closing the Straits of Hormuz would cause the price of oil to shoot to over $200 overnight, perhaps even more. Almost immediately the Strategic Petroleum Reserves of the US, European countries, and China would trigger releases. Re-opening the Straits would become an international priority and the United States Navy, with the overt support of Europe and China, could be marshaled, in a massive show of force, to police the waterways. And there would be a precedent to a re-opening action as it happened on previous occasions when Hormuz was closed. Twice before in 1984 and 1987 in the "Tanker War" between Iraq and Iran, oil shipping through the Straits dropped by a quarter forcing the US to secure the shipping lanes. So if the US and Europe, the only ones with the capability to do so, move quickly, as Iran's nuclear ambitions are neutralized, world energy supplies could be secured since Iran is unlikely to receive meaningful regional support from neighbors lacking sufficient military or political punch.

Meanwhile, Israel has watched the ineffectual diplomatic posturing of the UN and EU with growing concern as Iranian enrichment of uranium has continued apace. But Israel also understands something the UN, the EU, and even some US generals, appear not to grasp: how a Western-backed Israeli military strike to stifle *Shia* Iranian ambitions is likely to play out *beneath* the public façade of the usual Middle East *Sunni* Arab leadership rhetoric. In the West, we easily forget that Sunni and Shia Muslims have been at each other's throats for centuries. Since 2007, over twelve Sunni Middle East states,[17] as nervous about Iranian regional nuclear ambitions as Israel, have lined up to declare their own intention to develop nuclear power. A predominantly Sunni Middle East does *not* seem to want a nuclear Iran any more than do Israel and the West.

While the UN and EU leadership remains angst-ridden that an Israeli or US air strike would ignite a "conflagration across the Middle East," the political reality, we believe, is likely to be more prosaic. Sure enough, young hotheads will be out on the streets of Middle East capitals. And, for the sake of Arab and Muslim solidarity before the "decadent Western" media, regional Arab Muslim leaders will make lots of sabre-rattling noises decrying Israeli and/or US actions. But, as the former US ambassador to the UN John Bolton dryly observes about such an eventuality, "There'll be public denunciations but no action." We would go further. If we were to listen more carefully to any ensuing non-Iranian Islamist political rhetoric, we would detect an enormous collective sigh of relief from Riyadh to Amman to Cairo.

But, in the world of potential future energy-associated conflicts, the Middle East is not the only game in town.

RUSSIA'S GREAT ARCTIC GAME

If Russia's armed conflict with Georgia revealed anything it is that Vladimir Putin does not play by the international, diplomatic rules. Take the Great Arctic Game. In May 2008, Russia met with the four other Arctic-bordering nations (Canada, Norway, Denmark — through its sovereignty of Greenland — and the US) and agreed to abide by UN adjudication — what we will call Plan A — as regards the potential of carving up Arctic territory and mineral rights. Unfortunately, the UN's track record in resolving complex territorial disputes and defusing associated potential conflicts is a lousy one. Putin knows this. He knows too that the US has yet to sign up to the 1982 UN Law of the Sea Convention.

One may think, therefore, given the uncertain geopolitical realities and the importance of an energy-rich Arctic that all five nations would have a clear Arctic back-up policy, a Plan B, should the UN route fail. Plainly, Russia is already running with one: a pre-emptive power play designed to create "facts on the ground," or, as we shall see, in the air and in the icy Arctic waters. What is all too apparent is that the four NATO states have *no* Plan B. They need to get one — and here's why.

In 2001, Russia showed it wanted even more when it filed a claim that the 1,200-mile underwater Lomonosov Ridge, stretching from Siberia to Ellesmere Island in Canada, was an extension of the Siberian continental shelf. In August 2007, Russian explorer Artur Chilingarov followed up by planting a Russian flag on the seabed, directly beneath the North Pole. The world headlines that followed made the point that the PR stunt was predicated upon yet more Russian seismic surveys that, they claimed, further confirmed their territorial rights over the ridge. While the UN Commission has repeatedly rejected the Russian seismological and sonar evidence, it is the increasing Russian military and civil presence in the region that is causing Russia's Arctic neighbors growing concern. Concern only heightened by Russia's military incursion into Georgia, and Vladimir Putin's blatant willingness to use energy supplies as a political weapon, as with Georgia and the Ukraine.

All the signs are that Putin may be prepared to let power, not international law, determine "prospecting" rights in the Arctic. Awash with petrodollars, the Kremlin has invested heavily in military hardware and technology. Russia's navy has already resumed a military presence in the Mediterranean and Atlantic. This followed the reinstatement of long-range strategic bomber flights over the Pacific, Atlantic and, increasingly, the Arctic Ocean. Norway has reported significant extra Russian air activity to the north. In August 2008, Canadian Foreign Affairs Minister David Emerson told CTV's *Question Period*, "We've seen increased activity in terms of Russian over-flights of Canadian airspace. The Americans are seeing the same thing around Alaska." In September 2008, in an interview with the BBC, a senior US coastguard commander warned of the real risk of conflict in the Arctic unless international borders were resolved.

Russian nuclear icebreakers, far more powerful than the oil-fuelled ships of the NATO nations, already "rule" much of the Arctic waterways. Russia's production line of icebreakers, suspended when the Soviet Union collapsed, has also been reinstated and the Arctic fleet has been overhauled. This included the introduction of an impressive new 25,000 ton icebreaker, *Victory's 50th Anniversary*, launched in 2007 to commemorate Russia's victory in WWII. It has already undergone successful trials in the Barents Sea and in Arctic waters.

If any lingering doubts remained over Russia's aspirations in the Arctic, President Dmitry Medvedev has laid them to rest. In a passionate speech in September 2008 to Russia's Security Council, Medvedev said, "We must finalize and adopt a federal law on the southern border of Russia's Arctic zone." He added, "This is our responsibility, and simply our direct duty, to our descendants. We must surely, and for the long-term future, secure Russia's interests in the Arctic."[18] As headlines around the world reported it, Medvedev's speech presaged further unilateral action.

The international response to all this has been, at best, piecemeal. A joint operation between the US and Canada conducted in the summer of 2008 aimed, for the first time, at extending their respective Arctic claims. Canada has initiated what it called a "major military build-up in the north." The Bush administration had expressed an urgency to sign up formally to the UN Convention but, as yet, the Obama White House has not done so. Meanwhile, forays by US icebreakers have increased. In August 2007, the Danes launched an Arctic expedition to gather evidence to support Denmark's territorial claims. Norway — who is cooperating with Russia in a separate offshore hydrocarbon project — has been conspicuously silent on the issue but has reported increased Russian air activity to the north.

In short, the response to increased Russian military and civil activity has been geared almost exclusively in support of Plan A — resolution via the UN Commission. What the Big Four need to wake up to is the urgent need for a version of Russia's pro-active policy, one *also* rooted in the old adage "possession is nine-tenths of the law."

WHAT IF "HELL" FREEZES OVER?

What is often missed in the Great Arctic Game is that much of the Arctic Ocean is ice not land. Thus accurate mapping of the tectonic plates and delineating new borders is no mean task. This might make a round-table settlement, especially one that suits Russia, nigh on impossible. But other factors too could impinge on how the Arctic's Great Game is played out.

Will the Arctic Thaw Continue? A report published by the EU in March 2008, expressed concern over the "international instability" that the "rapid melting of the Arctic" could cause. The EU, of course, is already urgently seeking energy diversity to wean itself off reliance on Russian oil and gas imports. But the EU and the previously cited Oxford Institute reports are both predicated on the assumption that the thawing of the Arctic ice *would* continue. Recent climate data suggest, however, that the world may have already entered a new cooling cycle. In August 2008, predictions of an ice-free Arctic before the summer, were confounded when NASA's Marshall Space Flight Center published photos showing what appears to be a 30 percent *increase* in Arctic ice between 12 August 2007 and 11 August 2008. If this and other data do portend a cooling trend, deepwater energy extraction in warmer climes may yet prove a more attractive proposition.

The sheer cost of extraction will make international cooperation vital. Many experts thought the Arctic's resources would never be tapped, partly because of the horrendous cost involved. Laying pipelines in Canada's Mackenzie Delta and in Alaska to exploit natural gas reserves, for example, costs around $1.5–2 million per mile. Laying pipelines in more northerly, offshore deepwater areas is expected to cost around four to five times that figure. Even a resurgent Russian petrodollar economy might balk at going solo on those figures.

Then there is the need for technological cooperation. Flexing one's military muscle to *de facto* annex the North Pole is one thing; having the proven technology to perform deepwater extraction in such a hostile environment is another. As the Oxford Institute paper points out, Norway's Statoil and Norsk Hydro have "unsurpassed expertise" in offshore drilling and the Anglo-American super-majors have "experience in extreme northern conditions." In short, the Russians would need help.

None of the above factors help settle the central issue of territory and mineral rights, of course. But what Canada, the USA, Norway, and Denmark must consider is a more coherent Plan B; a plan that does not simply lay all its Great Arctic Game cards on the green baize of the UN's table. The Kremlin may hold good cards in the Arctic Great Game, but Russian bluffing about geological rights should not allow Putin to continue creating "facts on the ground" wherever he likes, if future energy conflicts in the Arctic are to be avoided.

Instigating a Plan B of their own may put the four NATO nations on thin ice with the UN. But, by being bullish yet non-threatening they could help to settle the game and produce a peaceful settlement, albeit an uneasy one, something even an ultimately clear UN Directive on Arctic territorial claims is unlikely to achieve. A more pro-active attitude on their part may not resolve the Lomonosov Ridge issue, but it would at least mean all five nations assuming respective sovereign responsibility for land, mining and, yes, conservation rights on reasonably friendly terms.

After all, extracting up to a quarter of the world's untapped hydrocarbons in such a treacherous environment should focus minds on cooperation, not confrontation — a vital attitude whenever humans pioneer *any* new frontier.

Notes

1   A low-density mixture of hydrocarbon liquids that are present as gaseous components in the raw natural gas produced from many natural gas fields.
2   "Gazprom will Ship Gas to Asia in Bid to Curb Reliance on Europe," Anna Shiryaevskaya, *Bloomberg.com*, August 5, 2009.
3   www.forumspb.com/eng/archive/spief2009archive/prog/
4   "Turkmenistan Joins the Natural Gas Elite," Peter C. Glover, *Energy Tribune*, December 8, 2008. Go to: www.energytribune.com/articles.cfm?aid=1046
5   "The Pipeline War: Russian Bear Goes for West's Jugular," UK *Daily Mail*, August 10, 2008.
6   "Gazprom Offers to Buy All of Libya's Oil and Gas Exports," Lucian Kim, *Bloomberg.com* Updated July 9, 2008.
7   Nabucco is short for Nabucodonosor, English "Nebuchadnezzar."
8   en.rian.ru/world/20090317/120598679.html
9   www.novinite.com/view_news.php?id=102133
10   "Nord Stream Wins Final Clearance," *The Moscow Times (Business)*, February 15, 2010.
11   "Gazprom Turns Down Invitation to Join Nabucco Project," *Ria Novosti*, March 17, 2009.
12   "Is the Nabucco Pipeline Worth Investing In?," *Minyanville.com*, January 4, 2010.
13   "Russian Navy's Visit to Venezuela Filled with Mishaps," Human Events, December 18, 2008.
14   "Russian Bombers Land in Venezuela," BBC News online, September 11, 2008.
15   "War Dead Flown to Iran," *New York Sun*, July 24, 2006.

16 "Hamas Commander Assassinated in Dubai 'Helped Smuggle Weapons Into Gaza,'" UK *Daily Mail*, February 15, 2010.

17 "Sunni States' Fear of Iran Trigger Middle East Nuclear Race," Peter C, Glover, *World Politics Review*, November 7, 2007.

18 "Medvedev Wants Russia to Set Arctic Sea Borders," Reuters, September 17, 2008.

9

China, India and the Race for Energy Security

> *Don't be afraid not to follow the herd — because where the herd's gone, the food is already eaten.*
>
> Bob Dylan

While the president of the United States and many European leaders have been stewing in their politically-correct, spiced by hysteria, juices, fiddling around with commercially inadequate and non-viable wind, solar and other alternative energy projects[1] the Chinese have been on a global mission — to secure control of vast quantities of the world's oil and gas to fuel their fast-developing economy.[2]

The plain fact is — and many Western leaders have not grasped it — that oil will continue to account for 40 percent of world energy demand 25 years from now and total world energy demand will increase by at least 50 percent over that same period, the lion's share of which will go to China. Nor have many Western leaders, still mired in the rhetoric of Kyoto and Copenhagen, grasped that by 2035, fossil fuels, oil, gas, and coal will *still* account for 85 percent of world energy demand, a contribution percentage largely unchanged from the situation in 2010. The reality is that, over the next several decades, the combined contribution of wind, solar "advanced biofuels" etc., is unlikely to account for more than 1–2 percent of world energy demand.[3]

Those figures put the political eco-rhetoric over the current generation of alternative energies — and the enormous public subsidies wasted on them — into their proper perspective. Immediately, one sees the political folly of diverting billions in public funds into the 1 percent energy solution. Western nations would be far better served riding on the coat-tails of the energy realities, not driven by rhetoric of the theoretic climate philosophy. The Chinese, a much more pragmatic people, understand this very well and, over recent years, have embarked upon an oil and gas shopping spree of epic proportions. The goal: to secure their national energy future — by locking up much of the world's energy sources.

195

Just how some Western leaders have become bizarrely out of touch and a hostage to liberal and environmental orthodoxy is best exemplified by the almost surreal comments from Barack Obama's administration officials. US energy secretary Steven Chu has suggested that America's energy dilemma could be solved by painting roofs white;[4] Interior Secretary Ken Salazar talked of garnering the equivalent of 3,000 coal-fired commercial power plants out of wind off the US east coast.[5] That would be more than 1500 gigawatts (GW) of electricity. Given the current total power capacity from *all* US energy sources is about 1,000 GW, that talk "raised eyebrows," an amusing understatement from the *Wall Street Journal*.[6]

Meanwhile, US Deputy Assistant Secretary of State for East Asian and Pacific Affairs, David Shear, told the US Armed Services Committee on 13 January 2010, "We are pursuing intensive dialogue with the Chinese on the subject of energy security, in which we raised concerns about Chinese efforts to lock up oil reserves with long-term contracts." Shear was responding to Republican Roscoe Bartlett of Maryland who, rightly in our view, was "worried that the Chinese were aggressively buying up oil all over the world and might not share it with other countries in the future."

Well, what do you know? The Obama administration, whose entire energy posture going back into the presidential campaign has been both ideologically and practically stridently anti-oil, both as an industry and as a form of energy, suddenly was "concerned" about China's oil grab. Well here's news for the White House: If you want to change the game, first you have to get in it. But the Obama administration shows no sign, as yet, either of dealing itself a hand in the great oil and gas acquisition game or of committing to a much more serious strategy to develop the vast wealth of oil and gas within its own borders. *Indeed, not many Americans realize that the US, (if one counts the offshore potential) possesses more oil reserves than the entire Middle East.*[7]

But in a *Newsweek* editorial in April 2009, US Energy Secretary Chu doggedly expressed the administration's persistently Disney-esque energy policies, and the nonsense philosophy behind them: "We must move beyond oil because the science on global warming is clear and compelling: Greenhouse-gas emissions, primarily from fossil fuels, have started to change our climate. We have a responsibility to future generations to reduce those emissions to spare our planet the worst of the possible effects."[8]

Americans should not be surprised by the Chinese moves. China is acutely aware that energy, in short domestic supply, will be the "choke point"[9] in its future development unless the country secures new resources throughout the world. That's why the very capable Chinese oil companies, CNPC, Sinopec and CNOOC, have fanned out in dozens of countries, making hundreds of billions of dollars of oil and gas investments, including in America's backyard, Argentina, Venezuela, and Canada and even the country where America has fought a protracted war, Iraq. Neither does the Chinese quest preclude cutting deals with controversial regimes such as in Sudan or Iran.

In contrast to the public relations straightjacket that western oil companies find themselves in within their societies, the major Chinese oil companies have the full support of the Chinese government and, very importantly, they are admired and praised by the vast majority of Chinese people. In discussions with Chinese intellectuals, government officials, and company executives, the Chinese are often incredulous, all asking essentially the same question: Why is America letting us have a free and uncontested ride in all these energy ventures? In contrast, American "Big Oil," (ExxonMobil, ConocoPhillips and Chevron — the only companies really able to play along and compete with the Chinese majors) not only are not supported or encouraged by the US government but have been routinely vilified by politicians. To the sizeable portion of the American public that's unaware of the role energy plays in the modern world, they are the devil incarnate. It's no different in Europe.

What the world is witnessing is the largest peaceful transfer of power in history. Energy means power, and while the US and Europe are consumed by incoherent and speculative environmental ideologies they will, in the process, be committing economic hara-kiri. Meanwhile, China, riding on energy acquisitions with little competition, is propelling itself into the economic stratosphere. The US and Europe should be concerned, but doing something about it will require an unlikely cultural sea change in both Washington and in Brussels.

A HARD LOOK AT CHINA'S ENERGY AND A COMPARISON WITH THE UNITED STATES

The world energy scene has a number of "also rans," such as ageing and stagnant Europe, but in the very important element of growth it is dominated by the consumption of two countries, the US, which has been the controlling market thus far, and China, which, unquestionably, will dominate in the future.

It is worth comparing the energy mix of the two countries. The US is not much different from the rest of the world. It is using more per capita, but its energy mix is very much like the world mix, with oil accounting for about 40 percent and gas and coal about 23 percent each, for a total of more than 85 percent deriving from fossil fuels. By the year 2035, forecasts still suggest an overwhelming dominance by these fuels.

China is an entirely different matter. Coal dominates with 70 percent of the energy mix, while oil has been growing in some years at an annual rate that is 20 percent larger than the previous and since 2000 almost always by 10 percent. Energy will be China's "choke point," and the search for adequate energy resources will be as important a priority for that nation as for any. And yet the Confucian-influenced Chinese suffer from three serious deficiencies:

First, in imitating their role model, the US, they are prone to fall for the same ideologically-driven silliness in energy currently taking hold there. Desperate to be liked and to be relevant internationally, the Chinese are likely to pay at least lip service to the politically correct mantras of conservation and alternatives such as wind, solar, and "advanced biofuels."

Second, as we have mentioned earlier, conservation has never demonstrated a reduction of total energy use in a developed country.[10] If anything, conservation has done the opposite because becoming more efficient, in a world that has identified energy as an enabler of a better life, has led to new uses of energy. For China, conservation certainly will not lead to a reduction in demand.

Third, China will not become a militaristic power anytime soon, one that would emulate the US in a Gulf War-type of action to safeguard its potential energy sources. A strong-arm presence is not on the horizon. In fact, China is likely to shy away from any sort of confrontational environment, satisfied to go where no one else wants to go, including controversial places such as Sudan, Myanmar, and Iran. If China were the US in this respect, the stand-off in the South China and East China seas over various territorial and thus mineral rights, with neighbors including Vietnam and Japan, would never happen. The country would ignore far weaker nations and forge ahead with oil and gas development. By the same token, Vietnam, the Philippines, Malaysia, and even Japan would never have acted the way they did in "taking on" China had their opponent been the US. If China cannot project its weight in its own backyard, how can it do so elsewhere?

Burdened by real environmental problems, some of which have reached catastrophic levels, China has become very defensive, occasionally making public statements that, if taken seriously, are nothing less than throwing the baby out with the bathwater. "Pollution" thus becomes all-encompassing, covering everything from the real issues of nitrogen dioxide, sulfur dioxide, and particulates to the emissions of carbon dioxide.

Of course, nobody really believes that China will come near becoming a carbon dioxide-constrained economy in its energy use anytime soon. In fact, the danger is that its certain failure to comply with any Kyoto or successor accords may muddle the issues in China and prevent real environmental stewardship in the form of cleaning up water bodies and rivers and, more urgently, improving air quality. China is in real need of this genuine anti-pollution work, and it must act immediately and massively.

Over the last three decades, China's energy consumption has soared. But, as is usually the case with developing countries, that energy use was coupled with low efficiency. This huge increase in energy use, along with abundant and cheap labor, allowed China to become a major exporter of industrial and consumer goods and this stimulated its economic development. Although the Chinese people's lives have improved tremendously, the approach has also been associated with excessive energy utilization, energy shortages, and extreme environmental pollution. China's energy intensity (i.e. energy use per unit of the GDP) has been much higher than that of the US. And while China's energy intensity is improving, cheap energy — subsidized and controlled by the government — has prolonged the country's inefficient use of energy and weakened the nation's development.

Worse yet, since 2000, energy intensity, instead of decreasing, has started to increase, an eminently undesirable event. Although China uses only about 75 percent as much energy as the US (about 75 quadrillion Btu vs. 100 quadrillion Btu in the US) the country's energy intensity — measured in how much energy it takes to generate one dollar of GDP — puts China at a significant disadvantage: 13,800 vs. 8,800 Btu/$ GDP. In other words, China uses about 60 percent more energy per unit of GDP than the US. Also, note that on a per-capita basis, China's consumption is about one-sixth that of the prevailing rate in the US.

Clearly, the Chinese economy has to be sharpened significantly to compete with developed nations, especially as imported energy prices will continue their upward trend and as increasing Chinese labor costs no longer offer major advantages.

After importing more and more energy from foreign sources at much higher prices than the controlled domestic ones, China can no longer afford to subsidize all energy components. Reforming energy pricing, or to be clear, raising energy prices, has become inevitable. In fact, some of the wealthier areas of the country, such as Shanghai, are already seeing higher prices. Of course, raising energy prices has long been the plan, but implementing it has not been easy. During good economic times, the government is afraid of market inflation, and, during the economic downturn, personal and business financial sustainability has been a big concern which is very much tied to social stability.

CHINA'S OIL (AND GAS) SHOPPING SPREE

The signs of China's soaring oil demand are obvious. After phenomenal economic growth in the first seven years of the decade 2001–10, oil demand has grown annually by double digits. A short-lived slowdown lasted for a few months after the dire headlines of the 2008 economic crisis. But, during that time, Chinese economic growth bounced back to more than 8 percent. So did oil demand, which came back with a vengeance. In January and February 2009, Chinese oil imports stood at 3.1 million barrels per day, compared to an average of 3.87 million barrels per day in 2008. But from March to June 2009, oil imports averaged over 4 million barrels per day and in July they jumped to an unprecedented 4.6 million barrels per day, close to a 20 percent increase over 2008 levels.[11]

For China, after the economic crisis exploded in the last quarter of 2008, 2009 was supposed to be a year of economic slowdown and thus, lower energy demand. Certainly, after years of increasing demand in the US, the reigning economic superpower, oil consumption fell by about 5 percent to about 19 million barrels per day.[12] That didn't happen in China. After posting economic growth of 10.7 percent in the fourth quarter and 8.7 percent for the entire 2009, China is now inexorably moving to overtake Japan as the world's second largest economy. With the economic growth, oil consumption also increased, going from 7.83 million barrels per day in 2008 to almost 8 million barrels per day in 2009. The average includes a few months early in the year when things did slow down; the later months saw far heftier increases.

But more significant is that crude oil imports in 2009 reached 4.1 million barrels per day, a record high. China's annual oil production was 1.38 billion barrels and net imports were 1.49 billion barrels. This means that for the first time in the country's history, more than half, or 51.8 percent to be exact, of China's oil needs came from foreign sources. The second significant fact is that China produced domestically 0.5 percent less oil in 2009 than in 2008, even after very extensive and expensive efforts to boost production. For 2010, Chinese officials projected a 10 percent increase in imported oil. At time of writing, they are well on their way to meeting that figure.

Going over the psychological 50 percent threshold made China's "energy security" an inevitable issue among the country's national press, think tanks and the authorities. The deputy director of the National Energy Board, Wu Ning, warned in an article that "now the most acute problem in China is the increased importation of crude oil."[13]

Of course, the energy events of 2009 were unavoidable, considering the country's meteoric path in recent years. Since China became a net oil importer in 1993, the amount of oil from overseas increased from 6 percent to over 50 percent in the total demand, in a mere 16 years. According to the China Social Science Academy, China's oil consumption could reach 10.6 million barrels per day by 2015, and imported oil is likely to reach the US level of 65 percent of total consumption by 2020. It is estimated that China may need as much as 16 percent of the tradable oil in the world market by 2020.[14]

The dilemma for China is how to maintain economic development, even by tolerating environmental problems, while its domestic oil production cannot increase, and it looks like it has peaked already. Thus, some Chinese energy experts have proposed a "ceiling" for Chinese oil imports. But such a ceiling will depend on China's economic and societal development, as well as international situations. Since almost all of China's oil is used for transportation and chemical processing, with the country having just 15 cars per thousand people (compared to almost 500 per thousand people in the US) a ceiling to limit oil use would definitely curb economic development but also affect China's efforts to catch up to the US, a country the Chinese look up to.

Energy security for the Chinese takes a different hue than it does in the US. Although the US relies heavily on imported oil, it is perceived by the Chinese as controlling international oil prices and through geopolitical interventions it can enable China to become master of its own destiny. In contrast, China views itself as a neophyte in energy geopolitics and is uncomfortable at any prospect of geopolitical disturbance where it is a mere bystander, as is the case in Iran and earlier in Iraq. Thus, the strategy for China's oil companies is to acquire more international oil reserves and the government is openly encouraging those moves. Expect massive purchases of foreign oil reserves by the Chinese in the near future, including countries where Chinese presence would have been unthinkable only a few years ago, such as the Americas, North Africa, and Russia.

Such moves may help the Chinese to acquire the oil they crave, but may also arouse a US response, currently seemingly dormant under the Barack Obama administration which, steeped in climate and

Figure 9.1: *Source: Energy Tribune.*

alternative energy issues, seems to have written oil off its national and international agenda. Thus international business newspapers are rife with stories and discussions about blockbuster international oil and gas deals to take advantage of "the relatively low prices of overseas assets," as a senior company executive was quoted by *China Daily* on 12 August 2009. The most obvious deal is the prospective purchase of Repsol's stake in Argentina's YPF for some $17 billion.[15] The buyers: China's largest and third-largest oil companies, CNPC and CNOOC. If the deal happens it will be the largest-ever Chinese oil acquisition. (CNOOC's failed attempt to take over Unocal almost four years ago would have been slightly larger.[16])

The deal is one made in oil heaven. Repsol unloads an economically questionable asset, one that became so because of burdensome political troubles in Argentina. For the Chinese, expanding in South America on a grand scale it is both a psychological milestone and key to diversification outside of their current assets in Asia Pacific, Middle East, and much-criticized projects in Africa, headed by their Sudanese venture.

It is certain that large Chinese oil acquisitions will become common-place. China's latest purchase came in February 2010 when PetroChina paid $1.7 billion to buy a 60 percent stake in a Canadian oil sands operation from Athabasca Oil Sands Corporation. The production from the oil sands investment is expected to be as high as 500,000 barrels per day under full development. And those purchases are further increasing the size of China's biggest oil companies — CNPC, Sinopec and CNOOC — which are now among the largest oil companies in the world. In November 2009, *Petroleum Intelligence Weekly* published

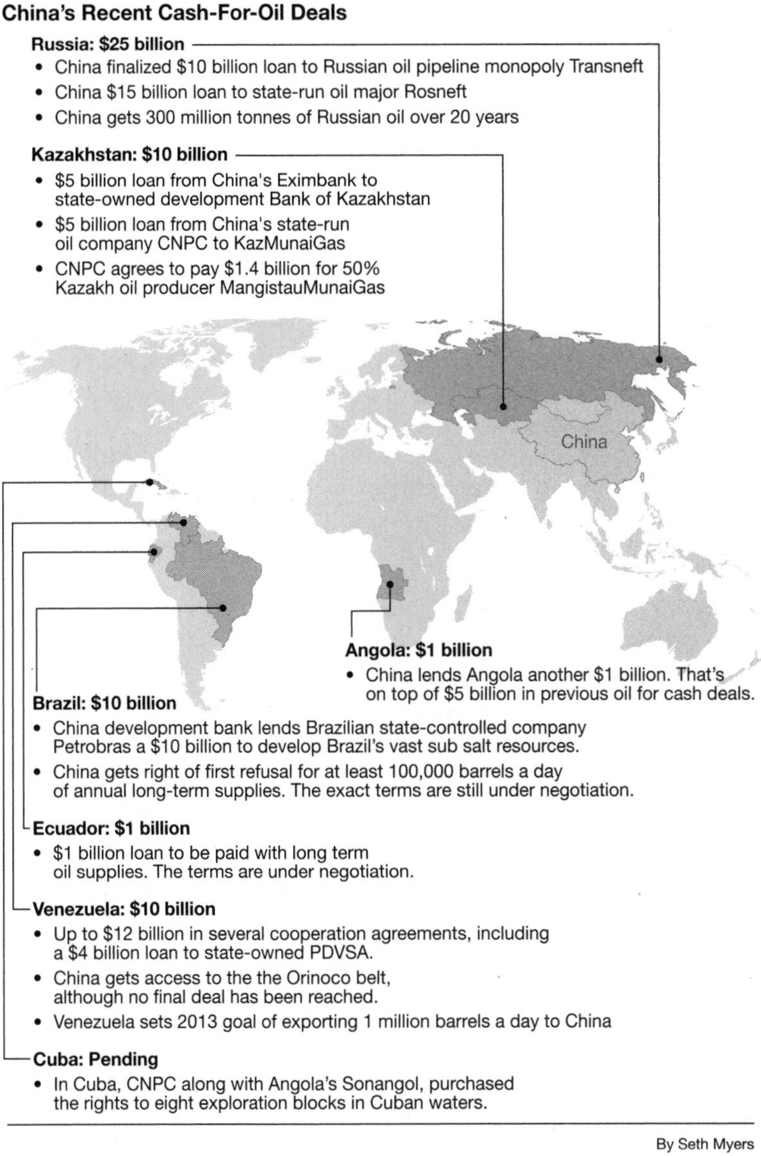

China's Recent Cash-For-Oil Deals

Russia: $25 billion
- China finalized $10 billion loan to Russian oil pipeline monopoly Transneft
- China $15 billion loan to state-run oil major Rosneft
- China gets 300 million tonnes of Russian oil over 20 years

Kazakhstan: $10 billion
- $5 billion loan from China's Eximbank to state-owned development Bank of Kazakhstan
- $5 billion loan from China's state-run oil company CNPC to KazMunaiGas
- CNPC agrees to pay $1.4 billion for 50% Kazakh oil producer MangistauMunaiGas

China

Angola: $1 billion
- China lends Angola another $1 billion. That's on top of $5 billion in previous oil for cash deals.

Brazil: $10 billion
- China development bank lends Brazilian state-controlled company Petrobras a $10 billion to develop Brazil's vast sub salt resources.
- China gets right of first refusal for at least 100,000 barrels a day of annual long-term supplies. The exact terms are still under negotiation.

Ecuador: $1 billion
- $1 billion loan to be paid with long term oil supplies. The terms are under negotiation.

Venezuela: $10 billion
- Up to $12 billion in several cooperation agreements, including a $4 billion loan to state-owned PDVSA.
- China gets access to the the Orinoco belt, although no final deal has been reached.
- Venezuela sets 2013 goal of exporting 1 million barrels a day to China

Cuba: Pending
- In Cuba, CNPC along with Angola's Sonangol, purchased the rights to eight exploration blocks in Cuban waters.

By Seth Myers

Figure 9.2: China's shopping list has been extensive. *Source: Energy Tribune.*

its list of the world's 50 biggest petroleum companies. China's three biggest energy companies were ranked, respectively, as number 5, 25, and 48.

These three Chinese companies have, to early 2010, announced 11 acquisitions with a total value of $16 billion. The biggest deal was Sinopec's purchase of Swiss-based Addax Petroleum for $7.56 billion — by far the biggest acquisition in China's oil and gas trading history.

Some important highlights of Chinese overseas oil and gas purchases include:

- CNOOC and Sinopec's acquisition of three blocks in Angola.
- China Investment Co.'s 11 percent stake of global depositary receipts in Kazakhstan's national oil company and 45 percent stake in the Russian Nobel Oil Group.
- Xinjiang Guanghui Group acquisition of 49 percent stake of Kazakhstan TBM Co. to jointly develop the eastern Kazakh oil and gas blocks in the Zaysanskaya region.
- China Development Bank's $10 billion contract with Brazil for "petroleum and loan exchange" which allows China to get 150,000 barrels per day for 10 years.
- PetroChina's acquisition of 45.5 percent of Singapore Petroleum Co., Ltd.

Through these deals, China has increased its potential oil supply by about 1.5 million barrels per day.

To facilitate oil and gas imports, China is building pipelines. Under construction or already under partial operation are the China–Russia crude oil pipeline, China–Myanmar oil and gas pipelines, and Central Asia gas pipelines. It is clear that the building of the necessary infrastructure, coupled with China's aggressive global acquisition spree, is part of a deliberate effort to increase the country's energy security.

The likely next target will be in Venezuela, where an eager Hugo Chávez is waiting, and on the periphery of Russia, in particular Kazakhstan and Turkmenistan. Almost overnight, the US and the EU will be reduced to mere bystanders while China moves into the geopolitical major leagues. Massive Chinese acquisition of energy assets, while the West is philosophizing on the future of the planet and carbon cap and trade schemes, will lead to a transfer of political and economic power that the modern world has rarely seen. Why the US would be willing to give up competing for what has arguably been (and arguably remains, along with natural gas) the world's most vital commodity and for which there is no credible alternative, is mystifying.

With China's domestic oil demand expected to more than triple over the next two decades, and with China holding around $2 trillion in foreign currency reserves, do not expect China's foreign investment splurge to end anytime soon. Neither is energy investment China's only goal for its power-hungry economy. Indeed, investment in metals acquisitions has been China's leading target in recent years, with almost $43 billion committed in the last five or so years, including a massive $20 billion bid for a slice of Australia's Rio Tinto by China's Aluminum Corporation.

In September 2008, China shocked everyone when it became the largest foreign holder of US Treasury bonds as well as the largest foreign holder of US debt. In January 2010, China's purchases of US businesses were acknowledged to have jumped by a massive 300 percent over the previous year alone, outpacing US purchases of Chinese businesses for the first time. A trend helped by the depletion of American economic assets.[17]

More generally, Chinese overseas investment in recent years is estimated to have exceeded $100 billion in Africa, the Middle East, and elsewhere. But with pre-2005 transactions taken into consideration, it has been energy that has been China's principal target, with over $40 billion committed specifically to the purchase of energy assets of various types.[18]

Perhaps most remarkable of all is that most of the foreign investment deals were negotiated by top Chinese political leaders. On a visit to Latin America in January 2010, Vice-President Xi Ping cut a six billion dollar "loan-for-oil" deal with Venezuela, increasing that country's oil exports to China. Xi also agreed to a similar $10 billion deal with Brazil's Petrobras guaranteeing China a further 160,000 barrels a day at market prices. Most important of all, Premier Wen Jiabao finalized a "loan-for-oil" deal with Russia in Beijing that would see a key oil pipeline extended from Siberia into north-east China. The Western credit crunch and falling profits have undoubtedly combined to induce formerly wary foreign companies and governments to welcome the advances of cash-rich Chinese companies.

But what should alarm Western governments is how enormous Chinese state support is giving Chinese companies such a decisive edge over Western and foreign competitors. As China Petroleum University's Wang Xia points out, "This is a window of opportunity for China's energy diplomacy that we cannot afford to miss. If we wait until economic recovery pushes oil prices up again, it would be much more difficult to secure long-term deals."[19] Nor is China allowing the climate debate that has so much paralyzed Western minds to influence its energy pragmatism.

CHINA DUMPS ON GLOBAL CLIMATE RESEARCH

China's climate science has been in agony. After the "Climategate" revelations in December 2009, Chinese researchers, who for some time accepted "consensus" Western positions, started warning each other publicly to use international climate data cautiously. Two main elements were in force prior to this. The most important was that Chinese, wanting very much to be accepted internationally, went along with climate change claims since it was no skin off their nose. On the one hand they would appear responsible, agreeing with so many governments, and on the other, under no circumstances would they accept any mandatory limits invoking their much smaller "cumulative" emissions over the past.

Climategate and other more recent sordid revelations about Himalayan glaciers, Arctic and Antarctic ice, and rain forests *not* being in jeopardy, were played in China and gave the Chinese a real lever towards the general climate change clamor. Of course, the best way to check the UN IPCC claims about Asia would be to use locally generated data. But in what appears to be emblematic of the IPCC reports and what appear to be unfounded conjectures, Chinese researchers admit that China is very short of raw data measured in-house. Existing actual data are of low quality and low accuracy. Ironically, considering recent revelations, a long-held notion by international scientists is that one cannot trust Chinese raw data when they are not consistent with those of developed nations.

Because of the geographic proximity and China's burgeoning production of CO_2 emissions in an economy highly reliant on cheap coal, the Chinese watched with great interest the unfolding drama when the IPCC admitted on 20 January 2010 that the 2007 report on the Himalayan glaciers melting away by as early as 2035 was downright false and not supported by any real scientific data.

The China Daily on 22 January 2010 did not stop there. It reported other mistakes in the 2007 IPCC report:

1.   The report claimed that the Himalayan glaciers melting speed is faster than that of other glaciers, which is inconsistent with the facts.
2.   The report said that the total glacier area will reduce from the current 500,000 square kilometers to 100,000 square kilometers. In fact, the total actual size of Himalayan glaciers is only 330,000 square kilometers.

Moreover, while the constantly invoked "scientific consensus" has postulated global warming, the Chinese have given ample news time to those researchers who actually claim the opposite is true, i.e. "global cooling" is underway. The group led by well-known Russian astronomer Habibullo Abdussamatov has suggested that solar radiation will reach a low value during 2041–42 and global temperature will decrease about 1–1.5°C over the next 50 years before temperature warms up again. The research of well known Professor Qian Weihong of Beijing University indicates that the current average temperature will decrease continuously until 2030 and then a warming period will ensue until 2060. In other words, normal cyclical climate warming and cooling within historic parameters.

The stunning errors of the IPCC, the global cooling theories and the inability of the Chinese to collect their own data have made them quite bewildered considering the stakes in their economic development. And a record-breaking cold winter in 2009/10 did not help their quandary.

On top of that, back in July 2009, the Chinese had already delivered their rejection of calls by Western leaders for China to show international solidarity on carbon tariffs. Essentially, China's response was: drop dead. On 5 July 2009, just nine days after the US House passed the cap and trade bill (also known as Waxman–Markey), Chinese officials made it clear they were opposed to any carbon taxation scheme. Yao Jian, the spokesman for China's Commerce Ministry, said the bill violates basic principles of the WTO and further maintained that the ruse of environmental protection was being used to protect trade and that it could induce a trade war. "China considers that the carbon emission tax not only violates the basic principle of WTO, it also violates the principles of the Kyoto Protocol about different responsibility between developing and developed countries," Yao said.[20]

In March 2009, US Energy Secretary Steven Chu said that the US was planning to impose a tariff on imported products to avoid unfair competition imposed on the American manufacture industry. There is a clause in the cap and trade bill — officially known as the American Clean Energy and Security Act (H.R. 2454) — that allows the imposition of a "special tax" which stipulates that imported foreign products that do not meet the US emission standard can be heavily penalized. The Chinese are worried that this provision may be copied by European and other countries, and lead to more trade protectionism.

Studies by universities in Beijing and Shanghai have concluded that carbon emission taxes in the US and other countries will gravely hurt China's economy, affecting especially the paper, steel, cement, fertilizer, and glass industries. Their point is clear: developed countries have moved their "dirty" industries to developing countries, and now the CO_2 emissions from those industries are being considered "pollution." The Chinese believe that the developed countries should also pay for part of Chinese emissions since they benefit from China's industries. Moreover, they see a carbon tax more darkly as a new style of developed world economic hegemony over developing countries.

Yao warned that carbon emission legislations will only harass the international trading order. And he said that a carbon tax will not help the world get through the economic crisis, nor will it help the effort on climate change negotiations. "China," he concluded, "is strongly against the carbon emission tax." Let's face it, a country which is largely coal-dependent and is opening a new coal-fired power station every week has no intention of dragging down its burgeoning economy by penalizing its industries with crippling CO_2 taxes.

Speaking at the Center for American Progress in June 2009, Todd Stern, the US administration's chief negotiator at Kyoto a decade before, had made it clear that China's approach to the Copenhagen negotiations was central to the US administration's own. "China," said Stern, "may not be the alpha and omega of these negotiations — but it's close. No deal is possible if we don't find a way forward with China." Even if the rest of the world managed to reduce emissions by 80 percent by 2050 — as Stern said "a thoroughly unrealistic assumption" — China's greenhouse gases alone (under the IPPC's alarmist scheme of things) would deliver a 2.7°C global temperature increase. In the event, Stern's words proved prophetic, at least as far as the prospect for a meaningful international accord at Copenhagen in 2009 was concerned, once China had "bailed."[21]

However, while Western nations appear to prefer philosophical debate to securing their national energy security futures, not quite everyone is letting China have it all its own way.

INDIA AND CHINA FACE OFF IN AFRICA

The nearly insatiable hunger for oil has led the world's most-populous countries to Africa. And while China's efforts to tap Africa's oil resources are well known, India is fast playing catch up.

In December 2009, during an India–Africa summit in New Delhi, which was attended by representatives from 15 African countries, it became clear that India needs to learn from China's success in dealing with Africa. The resource base is certainly attractive. Africa has about 10 percent of the world's oil reserves and the oil tends to be of better quality than the high-sulfur crude found in India. And while India may want to expand its investments in Africa, the Chinese are far ahead, a point made clear in an August 2009 report by the London-based Royal Institute of International Affairs (RIIA) on Asian involvement in Nigerian and Angolan oil industries which said that "China's deeper pockets have certainly put a brake on India's ambitions."[22]

At the India–Africa Summit, it was pointed out that China has also promised billions of dollars in cheap loans to Africa, besides multibillion-dollar deals for infrastructure development and even offered military support in return for resources. Estimates peg loans by China to fund Angola's post-war reconstruction at $20 billion in 2009. In return, China has managed to procure a lot of Angolan oil.

Indian firms have been making some inroads in Africa, however. State-run oil major ONGC Videsh Limited (OVL), India's largest oil exploration firm, has invested in assets in Sudan, Ivory Coast, Libya, Egypt, Nigeria, and Gabon. OVL has invested $2.5 billion in the Sudanese oilfields and is vying for a stake in at least one exploration block in Ghana. Private Indian firms such as Reliance Industries Limited have invested in Sudan and East Africa. Meanwhile, state-owned Indian Oil Corp and privately-held Essar Group have invested in Nigeria and Sudan. Other Indian firms are reportedly negotiating in Chad, Malawi, Niger, Angola, and Mauritania.

Egypt has invited two Indian companies, Alkor, and state entity Gujarat State Petroleum Corporation Limited, to invest in geological surveys as well as in the exploration and production of oil and gas. Upstream companies are having good success in Egypt. Between 1999 and 2007, the country's gas production has more than tripled according to US Energy Information Administration figures. But while Indian firms are finding a receptive audience in Africa, they are still trailing far behind the Chinese. Indo-African trade, which now totals about $30 billion per year, is half the level of China's trade with the continent and Indian investments in Africa are just one-fourth that of China's. Between 2003 and 2008, Chinese direct investment in Africa soared, going from about $500 million to nearly $8 billion. Western observers have also pointed fingers at China for worsening repression and human rights abuses in Africa by supporting the hyper-corrupt regimes in Sudan and Zimbabwe.

However, New Delhi has realized that it cannot let matters drift in Africa. Despite a recent spurt in domestic supplies in oil and gas, demand for hydrocarbons in India far outstrips supply. India's attempts to source gas via international pipelines from Iran, Turkmenistan, and Myanmar have not borne fruit. Thus, it is logical that Indian firms are looking at an aggressive push to tap Africa's natural sources. Officials privately suggest that New Delhi should be open to playing a military assistance role if needed. At the very least they suggest an increase in India's role as part of UN peacekeeping forces.

During the India–Africa Summit, India's federal petroleum minister, Murli Deora, said India is "making a renewed push to open doors for Indian state-run firms in the African oil industry by offering to invest in building new refineries in return for gas and equity in oil fields." Indian firms are now in talks with Nigerian officials to build new refineries to develop the country's downstream sector. And Indian companies are trying to leverage their infrastructure commitments in Sudan to secure drilling rights. Indian firms are developing a 180-kilometer rail link from Khartoum to Al-Masala-Mian. India is actively pursuing acquisition of equity stakes in 22 hydrocarbon blocks in Sudan.

While questions remain about India's ability to effectively compete against China in Africa, Indian firms are signing major deals elsewhere. By the end of 2009, ONGC Videsh Ltd and the Hinduja Group signed accords with Iran to take a 40 percent interest in the $7.5 billion, Phase 12 development of the South Pars gas field. In addition, ONGC recently acquired Britain's Imperial Energy, which has significant assets in Russia. While these deals are important, it remains to be seen how influential India will ultimately be in Africa.

But, like China, India has a fast-growing, power-hungry economy to fuel. Principally, India's economic miracle, like China's, is mostly coal-fuelled. But booming economic growth means greater energy demand. So act it must. Currently, however, new key natural gas reserves discovered off India's coast cannot be exploited until the drawn-out legal wrangle between two brothers, Mukesh and Anil Ambani, over gas rights, is finally resolved. The long running dispute threatens to continue to delay India's push to become the world's third largest economy.

Mukesh and Anil Ambani's fallout has major consequences for India's future. Successful governance requires that private actors not be allowed to undermine the integrity of government policies as it creates uncertainty among other market participants about which rules will govern their investments. The history of the global energy sector proves this conclusively. At the heart of the Ambani dispute is the issue of *which* set of rules will govern the nation's future energy security and thus its economic development. Foreign firms looking to invest in the Indian market and promote its energy development are concerned about the additional risk they would incur if different sets of rules are cut out for special players rather than one set of rules for all.

Indeed, India has had to delay its licensing of a new set of oil and

India's historic and projected coal consumption

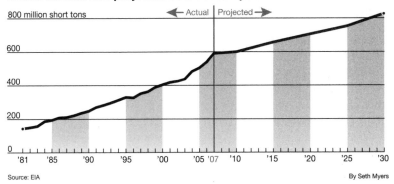

Figure 9.3: India's rising oil consumption.

natural gas leases because foreign firms are worried about whether they should currently enter India's energy markets. Orderly markets demand transparency. Otherwise, businesses may find the investments they make undermined by collusion among other market players.

India is one of the fastest-growing countries on earth. It is the second most populous nation in the world and, by 2030, is expected to be home to the world's third-largest economy. Secure energy development is integral to continue this dynamic growth. Currently, Indians use only about 2.6 barrels of oil equivalent per person a year compared with a world-wide average of 13 barrels; yet India must import approximately 70 percent of the energy resources needed to meet total domestic demand.

The mix of energy resources India uses is also unfavorable compared to the rest of the world. Coal accounts for a highly-antiquated 70 percent of electricity generation, and 50 percent of India's total non-residential energy demand is met by coal. Oil provides for more than 30 percent of its energy needs while natural gas accounts for only 9 percent. By comparison, natural gas meets on average 23 percent of the world's energy demand. In fact, the US meets 25 percent of its total energy demand through the use of natural gas.

The 2008 economic downturn further unsettled India's already delicate energy balance. For example, skyrocketing commodity prices lifted India's oil import bill to nearly $80 billion in 2008.[23] This in turn further increased the government's deficit, the shortfall ballooning to account for larger energy and fertilizer subsidies.

Despite all of this, 400 million Indians remain without what is considered a basic necessity in most developed countries — electricity.

So many Indians live without this necessity due to a lack of power availability and prohibitive cost. A large majority of Indians, therefore, must rely on less efficient and less environmentally-friendly energy sources. Indeed, 87 percent[24] of India's rural population uses biomass to meet their cooking needs.

India's energy development is vital to not only its energy security, but also to international security. The natural gas dispute between Mukesh and Anil Ambani over the Memorandum of Understanding brokered by the brothers' mother in June 2005 has been marring efforts to expand India's clean energy reserves, to the detriment of consumers, businesses and investors alike.[25] Unfortunately, it does not appear that the Ambani dispute is likely to be resolved anytime soon, after a Supreme Court judge recused himself from hearing the case in November 2009 citing a personal conflict of interest.[26]

While Russia's energy imperialism is geared to the recovery of the much grieved over loss of its superpower status, China's global energy shopping spree is geared more to a newfound growing global economic hegemony. In the case of both governments, it is the pursuit of status and international clout, not the betterment of the lives of their peoples that drives national and key energy politics. So much for the world's leading exponents of "people-orientated, people-first" global socialism. In the case of India, as with other large fast-industrializing societies however, like Brazil, national energy policies may well be geared more directly to the benefit and welfare of their populations.

Whatever the motivation behind national energy policies, energy and who has it, who needs it, who controls it, and who is energy-dependent will, in the near future, go a long way to dictating where future international power lies.

Energy-dependent Europe, for instance, with its anti-coal, anti-carbon, pro-renewable lack of energy realism, already displays a declining political clout in world affairs — and it shows. But, in March 2010, a significant development in Sino-Russian energy affairs took place that garnered little media interest but which could well have major geopolitical power implications for both nations, as well as for the new world order. Implications that include, threatening China with a weakened, Europe-like, energy-dependent status.

WILL CHINA SUCCUMB TO RUSSIAN ENERGY DEPENDENCY?

It took four long years of price negotiations, but in early March 2010 an agreement was announced, Russia will supply China close to

2.5 trillion cubic feet (Tcf) of natural gas per year, starting from 2015. There was no mention of the actual price which shows the bargaining intensity between the two sides.

Sino-Russian negotiations for supplying gas to China started in 2006. The original plan was supposed to involve Russian exports of 2.1–2.8 Tcf of gas to China starting in 2011. This much gas would double Chinese natural gas supply which stood at 2.5 Tcf.[27] Because of the undetermined price but also because of Russian domestic problems, exacerbated by the 2008 economic crisis, the negotiations between the two countries had been on and off, and, especially, the pipeline construction had been painfully slow.

China needs gas. In addition to the fact that the contribution from this cleanest of all fossil fuels in the country's energy mix is just 3 percent, a woefully small number compared to international developed country standards of about 25 percent, in 2007, for the first time gas consumption in China was more than gas production. To meet demand, China has been importing natural gas in ever increasing quantities. Even in this climate, gas imports from Russia have proved hard to materialize.

It is not that the problem was neglected by officials, especially the Chinese. The latest show was on 13 October 2009, when Russia and China signed an agreement for Russian natural gas export to China. The trouble is that the agreement was the 14th time that the prime ministers from both countries met and signed agreements expressing intent with nothing concrete resulting. In the October 2009 event, Russia's Gazprom and China's CNPC agreed that the pricing of natural gas would be indexed to Asian crude oil price and that the final gas price would be determined in 2014.

But the Chinese, even after they agreed, had a way out. "If the price Russians ask is too high next year, China may not import the gas, even if the pipeline is finished," according to Li Wei, a Chinese natural gas official.[28] He went on to say that if the international oil price were $60–70, gas price negotiation in 2010 might be easier; but if the oil price were over $100, the negotiation may prove fruitless again.

The favorable oil price was one of the important factors for the "success" of the negotiations in March 2010. But probably a more important reason for the Russians and their inkling towards control, a far stronger motive for them than money, was that the central Asia natural gas pipeline linking Turkmenistan with China's Xinjiang Province went into operation on 14 December 2009. President Hu Jintao was present for the pipeline inauguration, along with the presidents of Turkmenistan, Uzbekistan and Kazakhstan. The 1,801 kilometer pipeline traverses Uzbekistan and Kazakhstan, delivering the natural gas produced by PetroChina in Turkmenistan. Most of the $6.7 billion construction fund was provided by China Development Bank.

Before the pipeline was built, central Asian countries had to sell all their natural gas to Russia, who started selling the gas through pipelines to other countries. The new pipeline provided a vital independence of central Asian from Russian energy infrastructure dominance. The pipeline is also Kazakhstan's first that bypasses Russia. The new pipeline links with China's West–East gas pipeline and delivers gas as far as Hong Kong.

With the 2010 pricing negotiations over, Russian gas is supposed to flow to China in 2015, four years behind the original schedule. This is due to happen through two major pipelines, of which the west pipeline will deliver 1 Tcf per year while the east pipeline is supposed to deliver 1.4 Tcf per year. In the meantime, Gazprom has started exporting to China a much smaller amount in the form of liquefied natural gas.

While issues still need to be resolved, the ramifications of the Sino-Russian agreement should not be underestimated. The fact is that the problems that make Russia an unreliable, badly managed, and corrupt partner, also plague its government-controlled energy sector. Whether Russia actually *has* all the gas production capacity that it claims, to be able to meet its burgeoning international obligations, is unclear. But, considering the European and eastern bloc experience in their energy dealings over recent years, committing to significant future Russian energy dependency is as much as mark of China's increasing energy vulnerability, as it is — for all its current global energy shopping spree — a sign of its current fiscal muscle.

Notes

1 We stress again that current technology means that wind, solar, etc. remain a non-serious contender in the commercial energy stakes. With, as yet, still future technological developments this may change. Meanwhile, pragmatic realism not wishful thinking has, as the Chinese are forcefully demonstrating, must guide national policies.

2 And it does not end with buying up energy infrastructure. China is buying large reserves of the world's metals (e.g. the formerly Anglo-Australian Rio Tinto) and other even major global manufacturing brand names, including Sweden's car manufacturer, Volvo.

3 *Energy: China's Choke Point* (ET Publishing, 2009, page IX) by Michael J. Economides and Xina Xie.

4 "Paint Roofs White to Fight Climate Change, Energy Chief Says," Alex

Morales, Bloomberg.com May 26, 2009. Go to: http://www.bloomberg.com/apps/news?pid=20601072&sid=asoQnPxZIsaM

5 "Gone With the Wind," Dr Robert Peltier, editor-in-chief, Power (Business and Technology for the Global Generation Industry) magazine, June 1, 2009. Go to: http://www.powermag.com/renewables/wind/Gone-with-the-Wind_1928.html

6 "Breezy Talk: Interior Salazar's Offshore Wind Dreams," *Wall Street Journal Blogs*, April 7, 2009.

7 "Study Reveals Huge US Oil-Shale Field," *Seattle Times*, September 1, 2005.

8 *Newsweek* editorial article, April 4, 2010.

9 *Energy: China's Choke Point* (ET Publishing, 2009) by Michael J. Economides and Xina Xie provides a much fuller explanation.

10 See "Conservation v Jevons Paradox" in Chapter 10 for a fuller explanation of this phenomenon.

11 Source: China Customs, August 2009.

12 US Energy Information Administration, see: http://tonto.eia.doe.gov/dnav/pet/hist/LeafHandler.ashx?n=PET&s=MTTUPUS1&f=M

13 "The Planet's Largest, Most Undervalued Mineral Wealth," Energy and Capital online at www.energyandcapital.com January 29, 2010.

14 "China's Oil Imports Continued Their Gallop in 2009," *Maritime Executive*, February 11, 2010.

15 "China Eyes Repsol YPF's Argentine Unit," *Business Week*, August 13, 2009.

16 See: "Why China's Unocal bid Ran Out of Gas," *Business Week*, October 4, 2005.

17 "Chinese Now Buying More US Assets than Americans Buying Chinese," *The Money Game: Business Insider*, January 18, 2010.

18 "Drowning in Cash, Chinese Foreign Investment: Who, What and Why, Part 1 of 3," Derek Scissors PhD, The Heritage Foundation. June 15, 2009.

19 "Energy-China: On Oil Shopping Spree," Antoanata Bezlova, Inter Press Service News Agency, March 2009.

20 "China on Carbon Tariffs: Drop Dead," *Energy Tribune* at www.energytribune.com July 9, 2009.

21 Speech to the American Center for Progress as reported in "China and U.S. Seek a Truce on Greenhouse Gases," *New York Times*, June 7, 2009.

22 "Thirst for African Oil: Asian National Oil Companies in Nigeria and Angola," report published by Chatham House, August 2009. Available online: www.chathamhouse.org.uk/publications

23 "India's Oil Import Bill," Roubini Global Economics online, August 6, 2008.

24 See Chapter 1 of "World Energy Demand and Economic Outlook," US Energy Information Administrations, May 27, 2009.

25 For the full story see: "Navigating the Ambani Dispute: Securing India's Energy Security," by Michael J. Economides, posted at www.energy tribune.com September 9, 2009.

26 "Ambani Dispute Back to Square One as Judge Quits," Pratish Narayanan, Reuters, November 4, 2009.

27 See the "China Profile," US Energy Information Administration, at: http://tonto.eia.doe.gov/country/country_energy_data.cfm?fips=CH

28 "Russian Gas Finally Headed to China?" *Energy Tribune* online at www.energytribune.com March 12, 2010.

10
Energy Wars, Energy Solutions: Getting Real

There are two sorts of forecasters; those who don't know, and those who don't know that they don't know.

J.K. Galbraith

As Western nations continue to prioritize climate discussion above future energy security, there are signs that some of those nations, faced with the very real prospect of regular and widespread power cuts within just a few years[1] are, at least, maneuvering to stake their claims on the last vast hydrocarbon frontier: in deepwater and, especially, off Antarctica and beneath the Arctic.

ENERGY WARS AND THE LAST ENERGY FRONTIER

After the Russians pulled their flag-planting stunt two miles beneath the Arctic ice cap back in August 2007, the reaction from the other four Arctic powers (Canada, the United States, Denmark, and Norway) was predictable and swift. Within days all had declared their right to map and claim — and militarize — huge areas of the Arctic. Not that most of the four have done much to date in support of their stated goal. But no one anticipated what would come next. In October 2007, Britain's *The Guardian* newspaper broke the story that Britain intended to assert its sovereign right over 1 million square kilometers (386,000 square miles) of seabed off British Antarctica.[2] And it is not merely fishing rights that interest Britain.

Within days Argentinian Foreign Minister, Jorge Taina, said his government would stake a claim to "its" part of the continent and the islands around the Falklands. Chile, Australia, and New Zealand, among others, then declared it was also their intention to stake claims.

The British Foreign Office quickly confirmed that data is indeed being gathered and processed for a submission to the UN that could extend British oil, gas, and mineral rights up to 350 miles offshore into the Southern Ocean.

While extraction "is not yet technically feasible" in the deepwater off Antarctica, it is not the only sub-sea claim Britain proposed to make under article 76 of the UN Convention on the Law of the Sea. "There are five claims in total that the UK is hoping to put forward," the UK Foreign Office admitted in a statement in 2007. "They are in the Bay of Biscay, around Ascension Island, off the British Antarctic Territory, around the Falkland Islands, and South Georgia and in the Hatton/Rockall basin, west of Scotland."[3]

Let us just take the insignificant reference, on the face of it, to Britain's claim to "the Hatton/Rockall basin." The basin is in fact part of the Arctic shelf. Rockall, just a tiny crag in the north-east Atlantic, provides the UK with its only claim to an Arctic territory that is estimated to hold one-fifth of the world's untapped oil, and almost a third of its undiscovered gas. While Britain is wasting a vast proportion of its wealth on uneconomic alternative energies, particularly wind farms, it seems the Brits are preparing to play the energy game backing both horses: pioneering renewable energy *and* traditional sources.

But above all, what the bullish nature of the British move reveals is how some states are determined to use just about any political means to justify nationalistic claims to what will become the last new frontier for critical hydrocarbon resources. The question is: how far will states go to protect and actualize these claims in the great mineral share out that lies ahead? The potential for future conflict over mineral and energy rights in deepwater is all too real, as the renewed confrontation in late 2009/early 2010 over the sovereignty of the Falkland Islands in the South Atlantic between Britain and Argentina bears eloquent witness.

While all new territorial claims to Antarctica were frozen under the terms of the 1959 Antarctic Treaty, with mineral exploration banned until 2048 despite strong indications of offshore mineral reserves, the UN Commission on the Limits of the Continental Shelf, with its "use it or lose it" deadline of 13 May 2009, provided a potential way around the UN treaty obligations. And Britain, for one, has carried through on its claims.

On 31 March 2009, Britain lodged a partial submission to the UN Commission on the Limits of the Continental Shelf relating to its Rockall claim in the North Atlantic. And it has already begun discussions with Iceland, Ireland, and Denmark[4] with a view to utilizing Rockall as its base for Arctic penetration. More significantly, on 11 May 2009 — just two days before the UN deadline for claims

Figure 10.1: British Antarctica claims. *Source Energy Tribune.*

expired — the UK lodged its formal submission to the UN Commission on the Limits of the Continental Shelf to the 1 million square kilometers of seabed claimed off British Antarctica.

Writing in *The Scotsman* newspaper,[5] journalist Tanya Thompson provided a bluntly accurate assessment of Britain's claims:

> *Not since the Golden Age of the British Empire has Britain staked its claim to such a vast area of land on the world stage. And while the British Empire may be long gone, the Antarctic has emerged as the latest battleground for rival powers competing on several fronts to secure valuable oil-rich territory.*

Thompson goes on to describe precisely what is at stake:

> *Britain is preparing territorial claims on tens of thousands of square miles of the Atlantic Ocean floor around the Falklands and Rockall Island in the hope of annexing potentially lucrative oil and gas fields. The Falklands claim has the most potential for political fall-out, given that Britain and Argentina fought over the islands 25 years ago, and the value of the oil under the sea in the region is understood to be immense. Seismic tests suggest there could be about 60 billion barrels of oil under the ocean floor.*

In November 2008, ahead of their submission, while granting the Falkland's a new "autonomous" constitution, the UK was careful to retain power "over external affairs, defense, internal security and the administration of justice." Argentina condemned the unilateral British action as a "violation of Argentine sovereignty" filing a counter-claim in April 2009 challenging "the illegitimate British occupation of the southern archipelagos" to which Argentina also lays claim.[6]

Neither is Britain alone in its audacious subsea maneuvering. In the previous chapter we reviewed all that Russia is up to in Arctic waters. With the UN's May deadline looming, Russia chose January 2009 as the time to get in on the South Atlantic act too, sending a parliamentary delegation to Antarctica. Significantly, the party was headed by none other than one Alexander Chilingarov, explorer and Russia's special representative for "international cooperation in the Antarctic and Arctic" — and the man who led the Russian expedition to plant the national flag on the seabed beneath the North Pole in 2007. On this trip, however, Chilingarov contented himself with planting only his nation's South "Pole-jumping" stake: "We are definitely showing the whole world," he said, "that we have serious plans to continue polar research."[7] We don't doubt it.

Australia too has been busy in the region. In April 2009, the UN Commission on the Limits of the Continental Shelf made a landmark, and controversial, decision granting Australia 2.5 million square kilometers in the Antarctic Ocean. As Australia's Resources Minister put it, expanding the country's territory by "five times the size of France" giving them a potential "bonanza in underwater oil and gas reserves." The fact that Australia is the first nation to be granted extensive subsea rights in the area augurs well for other applications, including Britain's. But Rick Rozoff sums up this whole pursuit of "strategic energy and economic interests" as all "part of an accelerating pattern by the major Western powers and their military outposts to gain control over the world's resources, and that at breakneck pace," in his article "Scramble for World Resources: Battle for Antarctica" (to which we are indebted in this section).[8]

What Rozoff maintains is that to pull off success there must be an international quid pro quo at work among some Western powers. Rozoff believes that, "The same campaign by the West, acting in various ad hoc or longstanding coalitions, but especially in the collective military condominium that is the North Atlantic Treaty Organization (NATO), is being conducted in the Arctic Circle,[9] the Persian Gulf,[10] the Caspian Basin,[11] and the African continent, especially in the Gulf of Guinea."[12] To what extent Rozoff's assertion is correct we can only surmise. But we have retained the footnote sources in the above quote on which he relies.

In addition, Rozoff's article quotes Dmitry Yevstafyev of the Moscow Center for Policy Studies sounding a stark warning. Referring to Australia's successful subsea land acquisition and the "Western-engineered secession of Kosovo from Serbia" just two months before, Yevstafyev said, "This precedent is more dangerous than Kozovo's independence. I am surprised that Russian authorities have been silent on the issue. They must declare this is an illegal decision creating a dangerous precedent, and demand that the UN Secretary General explain his reasoning behind the decision." He added that if the expansion of Australia's territory is formalized, "This will open the door to a large-scale re-division of the world, the South Pole precedent could be applied to the North Pole, which will turn the struggle for the Arctic resources into a global war, inevitably involving Russia."[13]

Other "hot spots" around the world are already bubbling away when it comes to disputed territorial waters, and well beyond the New Cold War at the two Poles, too. They include:

- Israel/Palestine: in 2000, the BG Group (then British Gas) discovered a major natural gas field off Gaza that would mean energy billions for a fledgling Palestinian state. Exploitation of the field has, however, been blocked by Israel over fears that Gaza's terrorist-sponsoring Hamas Government would use the income from gas sales to buy arms to use against Israel.[14]
- Israel/Lebanon: in early 2009, Israel discovered a huge natural gas field off Haifa four times larger than field off Gaza (see above). The Lebanese Government is, however, disputing sole Israeli rights claiming the field lies partly in their waters.[15]
- The Spratly Islands in the South China Sea are patrolled by military forces from China, Taiwan, Malaysia, the Philippines, and Vietnam, all of whom have an interest in the prospective oil deposits.
- The Senkaku Islands, an area of less than 2.5 square miles in the East China Sea, have been a constant thorn in the side of Sino-Japanese relations. Waters off the uninhabited islands are believed to contain large oil deposits.
- The islands of Abu Musa and Greater and Lesser Tumb in the oil-rich Gulf have been the focus of a long-running dispute between Iran and the United Arab Emirates.
- Neither should we forget that the first Gulf War was started after Saddam Hussein accused neighbor Kuwait of stealing their oil by "slant drilling" at the Rumaila oilfield on the Iraqi–Kuwaiti border.

While the West's political elites persist in focusing on climate as the major threat to global stability, the reality is that it is the race for *national* energy security — more specifically, the race to "lock in" the planet's unexploited *hydrocarbon* reserves — that carries by the far the greater threat to future global stability.

Nor can we avoid identifying a further obstacle to energy-associated global conflict in the third millennia: the rise of energy-rich Islamist "socialist" regimes.

ISLAMIC SOCIALISM: A (SORDID) TALE OF THREE COUNTRIES

Radical fundamentalism is not an aberration that has suddenly come upon the Islamic world. Instead, it should have been an expected consequence of the sordid state of attempted secular governance in many Muslim countries.

Nothing makes it more obvious than travelling through three large North African countries in early 2010: Egypt, Libya, and Algeria. Their dysfunctionalities are deeply transparent. For decades they have been the real "root causes" of many of the region's ailments: persistent inability to absorb modernity, total misunderstanding of democracy, corruption, and clearly as a defensive crutch by a visibly dispirited population, more Islamic fundamentalism. In a way counter to what the West would expect, more women wear the veil in 2010 than they did 20 years earlier.

The problems in those countries persist irrespective of those regimes' standing with the US and Europe. Ally or foe — and they can change their position readily — they seem unable to evolve into anything that one would consider "progress." And the problems of these countries affect the rest of the world because all of them sit atop some of the largest oil and gas deposits, made all the more important because of their proximity to Europe, and thus, literally, potential power-brokers when it comes to the future of global energy security.

None of them nurtures even a semblance of western-style representative democracy and any free elections would almost certainly bring to power fundamentalist Islamic movements. Islam is, of course, also constantly hijacked by those in power and is used as a justification of their rule or style of governing, as in Libya's "Islamic socialism."

In Libya Muammar Qadhafi has been the country's "leader" for 40 years, as countless huge billboards carry that number all over the country, with him dressed in a variety of costumes, hats, and shades, playing a number of roles in some kind of perverse Hollywood-in-the-desert. Tripoli airport is in a state of permanent disrepair, trash is strewn everywhere, raw sewage is dumped straight into the sea,

Figure 10.2: Enormous images of Qadhafi are everywhere in Libya *Source: Michael Economides.*

government bureaucracy is non-functioning, but from all street lamp poles hang banners proclaiming the great leader's presidency of the African Union.

Like Venezuela's Chávez, Qadhafi would have been an amusing figure had he not been labeled at various times in his tenure as "lunatic" by Egypt's Anwar Sadat, a "supporter of terrorism" by a number of US presidents, and a host of other even less complimentary labels by others. His government was implicated directly in both the Lockerbie Pan-Am bombing in 1988 and the destruction and massive murder on a French passenger plane in flight in 1989. Of course all of this is trumped by the country's known massive oil wealth and even bigger potential, if only the industry can work through a meandering and corrupt system.

Unpredictable and mercurial as ever, Qadhafi started a rehabilitation of sorts a few years ago by first endorsing the move against Saddam Hussein by the US under George W. Bush, then by renouncing Libya's program of nuclear armament, then by taking responsibility for the

Lockerbie bombing (i.e. paying reparations to the victims' families), and then he just about upended everything by later welcoming as a hero back to Libya the cancer-stricken Libyan convicted for the terror.

Hosni Mubarak in Egypt, taking over after Anwar Sadat's assassination in 1981, has run the country for 28 years and only his biological longevity (he is 81 years old in 2010), not any electoral decision, is likely to put an end to his rule. But Cairo, a city with a glorious history of multiple civilizations is probably the worst example of a city mess in the entire world. With at least 25 million people, the beautiful remnants of past glories cannot balance the stench of open sewers, human fetid living conditions, and the constant open-air burning of trash.

The election of Abdelaziz Bouteflika in 1999 marked the end to a horrific decade and brought some new hope for Algeria. But Bouteflika, who won with 74 percent of the vote and was re-elected with 84 percent to a second five-year term in 2004, did not resist the "leadership" disease of the region. Although the Algerian Constitution had a two-term limit for the president, he spearheaded an "amendment" that let him run for a third and, in fact, an infinite number of five-year terms. He was re-elected in 2009.

All three countries have common recent historical backgrounds, and they were created in their present forms by the anti-colonial and anti-imperialist climate of the 1950s and 1960s, colored by the Cold War.

Gamal Abdel Nasser, starting in Egypt in the mid-1950s, pushed the British and their French cohorts out and became one of the shiniest international symbols of the post-colonial nationalist leader. He was even more. He became the face of pan-Arabism, an idealistic vision of an Arab world that would not only act as a counter-balancing presence to European powers, but would also usher in a new era of Middle Eastern and Third World emancipation. Nasser became a key leader in the Non-aligned Movement.

At the height of the Cold War the Soviet Union embraced Nasser with little hesitation, and he accepted the courting eagerly. This led to the construction of the massive Aswan hydroelectric dam, cement factories, other examples of Soviet heavy industry and, of course, military assistance and promises of defending Egypt. The euphoria of liberation and the leader's personality cult made Nasser the lion of Egypt and the Arab people. They, not just Egyptians, wallowed and basked in his limelight.

The Six-Day War of 1967 and the ignominious and swift defeat at Israel's hands had a devastating impact on Egypt and Nasser personally. It has affected Arab psyche to this day, and destroyed the notion that the Soviet Union would defend Nasser and what he represented. It was also the beginning of rampant anti-Americanism in the region. For example, it could not have been the air force of the then two-million populated Israel that totally destroyed the air forces of three far larger Arab neighbors, as a widely circulated story then insisted. It must have been American and British pilots manning jets with Israeli insignia. But Nasser's myth fell apart quickly and he died just three years later, replaced by Anwar Sadat in 1970.

A year earlier, a young colonel by the name Muammar Qadhafi had overthrown the hapless and ineffective Libyan King Idris and the fragile western-oriented establishment and made himself the — eventually undisputed — leader, for 40 years and counting. Qadhafi, like Nasser, played the Cold War card and received military assistance and hardware from the Soviet Union. In 1972 Libya, Egypt, and Syria even formed a short-lived United Arab Republic.

Ahmed Ben Bella in Algeria was also a classic figure of the times. Effective in an era ready to shed colonialism, he became the darling of European and American liberals. He made the French look bad and their military ruthless. After independence, he became Algeria's first elected President in 1962. But in a move that would be repeated over and over again in Algeria and the two other countries, he turned to empty socialist populism, alienating the educated middle class, instituting ill-fated land reforms and shunning any true development.

All three founding men, Nasser, Qadhafi and Ben Bella were secular, charismatic and rode the anti-colonial sentiment, endorsed by Western liberals and finding eager support by the Soviet Union. But none of those leaders bothered to establish any institutions of democracy, independent judiciary, any real people representation, economic liberalization, or the rule of law. All, aided by long cultural affinity for life-long tribal leaders, got intoxicated in their personality cults, first with the pretensions of the anti-colonial struggle. Any opposition was tantamount to treason. How could one oppose such national heroes who, among other accomplishments and virtues, booted out the hated infidel foreigners?

Nasser's 99 percent electoral victories were replaced by Sadat's similar margins until he was assassinated by Islamic militants in 1981. Mubarak took over the mantle and the same margin of electoral victories. Sometime shortly after Sadat took over, Egypt, in a swoop that stunned most of the world, went from stridently anti-American to pro-American and was, accordingly, rewarded with the Camp David accords (to solve the still-to-be-resolved Palestinian-Israel conflict). Since then Egypt has been the recipient of some of the largest cumulative US foreign aid of any country.

Qadhafi never even bothered to pretend the niceties of electoral victories. He was above them. But he was not above crushing the opposition to him though, even in exile. In April 1980 he openly called for the assassination of Libyan dissidents abroad, and dispatched squads to eliminate them.

Algeria went even more astray, becoming one of the most horrific examples of the struggle of post-liberation failures superimposed by cultural conflicts and identity. In 1995, Ben Bella was overthrown by Colonel Houari Boumédienne who was succeeded by another Colonel, Chadli Bendjedid in 1978. The country went into an economic and civil tailspin in the 1980s following the plunge in oil prices and, in the first free elections in 1991, the fundamentalist Islamic Salvation Front (known as FIS by its French acronym) won majority. The army refused to accept the result in a move that is almost certain to be repeated if it ever comes to that point in all three countries.

Shortly thereafter, one of the most brutal chapters in the history of any country unfolded in Algeria. At least 100,000 people were massacred often by unspeakable methods in extent and savagery. Entire villages were destroyed and not just supporters of the government but anybody who was not considered a good or true Muslim. Intellectuals, journalists, even simple teachers became targets. Eventually, man's inhumanity to man reached new lows of randomness and sadism. The Taliban in Afghanistan never fell to that level of brutality. The Algerian army retaliated in kind and by 1999 the country was subdued, though terrorist acts are still a major problem.

The tragedy for all three countries, and there is no other way to describe it other than a bona fide tragedy with little parallel anywhere else, is that all three are endowed with formidable oil and gas resources. Libya is a superpower in oil, Algeria is a superpower in natural gas and Egypt, although, to a lesser degree, has considerable reservoirs of oil and far larger, recently discovered, natural gas deposits. Egypt had a direct line to another rich reservoir, the US Treasury. Yet, none of these societies has come remotely close to the level that they could have benefited from this bonanza, if it was even marginally well managed.

In the economic freedom index published by the Heritage Foundation, the three are pretty low out of about 180 countries that are ranked: Egypt (94), Algeria (105), and Libya (173).[16] It is hard for countries like these to attract investments and even in the oil industry, some of the most reputable players would have difficulty justifying their involvement.

But corruption, graft, and nepotism are even more blatant. In Transparency International's corrupt perception index the three rank as some of the most corrupt countries in the world, with Egypt and

Algeria tied at 111 and Libya languishing even further below, at 130, the same ranking as Nigeria and Uganda.[17]

How much worse can it get if the only discernible method of replacing the leader is through assassination or military coup? Of course that fear tends to create necessary counter-balancing measures, a massive and elaborate "security" apparatus, complete with informants and extra-legal forces, whose only real purpose is the maintenance of the status quo, specifically the life of the leader and his immediate surroundings. One of the fixtures in Tripoli, Cairo, and Algiers are the dark-shade-wearing young men, with no uniform of any kind, roaming the airports and other important venues, while locals nod and whisper to a foreigner's ear, "security."

Unavoidably in Egypt, in the style of hereditary monarchs, Hosni Mubarak's groomed heir is his son Gamal. In Libya, Qadhafi's heir apparent is his son Saif, with the only possible question being whether another of his brothers may challenge him; not that such succession is unheard of in the Arab world. It was only in 2000, after the death of Syria's Hafez al-Assad after 30 years in power, that the country's constitution was amended immediately, reducing the mandatory minimum age of the President from 40 to 34: a move that allowed Hafez' son, Bashir al-Assad, to be elected president.

Two New Year's parties to usher in 2009 and 2010, in, of all places, the US, are telling concerning the impunity that these leaders bestow upon themselves and their kin, far from the idealism of their noble proclamations. Saif Qadhafi threw a private party where Mariah Carey sang for $1 million. Not to be outdone, his brother Hannibal had a party a year later, this time with Beyoncé Knowles singing for a $2 million fee.

And finally, at time of writing, the CEO of Sonatrach, Algeria's national oil company, was arrested and put in jail accused of corruption. One could only imagine the degree of his transgressions. Libya on the other hand has decided to shut out all European citizens from countries that are part of the Schengen visa accord because Qadhafi has declared a jihad on, of all places, Switzerland.[18]

There used to be a time, especially during the Cold War, when remnants of European colonialism could be blamed for all ills afflicting these countries. Justification of all excesses and repression could be blamed on the struggle towards a national identity that had been emasculated and affected by decades of European exploitation. Then, Israel, thousands of miles away, was a convenient *bête noire*. But, 50 years later, countries that could and should be filthy rich from oil and gas exports have zero credibility in blaming others for their problems.

The tale of three countries related here is thus emblematic of the problem of dealing with many energy-rich Arab and Muslim states and regimes. Where foreign energy investment and purchasing could bring dramatic economic and social change to Arab and Muslim populations, quite simply, their systems of governance will *not* allow it to happen. That is why all 23 Arab and Islamic states feature at the foot of lists of the world's worst economic basket cases. But, as Middle East hydrocarbons *will* remain important in the years ahead, the rest of the world is going to have to deal with them. Plainly, as with the Iranian regime's nuclear aspirations, when religious idealism, poor domestic governance, while holding a resource the rest of the world wants, all combine, "fallout" and conflict may never be far away.

As we have said throughout, however, while national energy security will always be a potential causal factor in real wars, there is a whole "other" kind of war going on out there. It is a war for hearts and minds played out against the increasing tendency to politicize science, and thus energy policy. Above all then, we would identify two powerful *obstacles* to progressing realistic science-based energy policies in the third millennium: (radical) environmentalism and (ideological) socialism.

SOCIAL WARS AND THE TWIN ENEMIES OF TRUTH

As we have shown, environmentalism, in its modern manifestation and socialism, has found common cause in the obfuscation of truth and reason when it comes to real science and hard facts. Al Gore is notorious for refusing plenary sessions at the end of his alarmist speeches. Quite simply, he does not like being questioned in his beliefs. For the same reason countless climate alarmists refuse open debate and prefer *ad hominen* attacks against detractors. The mass media, having nailed its colors to the modern alarmist mast, has also joined the anti-intellectual party resulting in the proliferation of a string of populist myths from polar bear extinction to the oil is running out to the belief that carbon dioxide is a pollutant. Patently, none of these things is true. So what has happened to the nature of free speech and public discourse that real debate and reason should have retired to the margins of society, leaving the floor to an increasingly politically-correct, left-leaning and liberal, mass media?

In his excellent short treatise, *The Retreat of Reason*, Anthony Browne describes the politically-correct syndrome that today dominates public discourse. "Moral cowardice has led to intellectual dishonesty permeating and corrupting our public debates," observes Browne. Browne provides context that explains the contempt by swathes of the science research community and mass media when their assertions are questioned, for instance. "The easiest way to overcome the dissonance between what you want to believe and the evidence is not to change what you believe, but to shut out the evidence and silence those who try to highlight it." We echo Browne's powerful sentiment that, "It is an indictment of the politically correct: if they were more confident of their arguments, they wouldn't be so frightened of debate." More pertinent to energy policy, however, is this: "The stifling of public debate, the preference for emotional comfort over reason, and for political correctness over factual correctness, can often make it difficult for policy makers to deal with growing problems."[19]

In his *The Ethics of Controversy*, Sidney Hook put it this way, "The cardinal sin, when we are looking for truth of fact or wisdom of policy is refusal to discuss, or action which blocks discussion."[20] The fact is that representatives of modern environmentalism and political socialism do not welcome serious debate. They have a powerful antipathy toward it, attempting to taint those who question them with a variety of issue-dodging epithets, asserting "hidden motives," that dissident views are "offensive," or that strong denunciation amounts to being "offensive," or language is "hate speech." Instead, they prefer speculation, guesswork and even go so far as to subvert the facts — as the "top" UN IPCC scientists involved with Climategate clearly sought to do — to their ideological agenda.

But let us give a key example of how truth and reality can be distorted by a popular, but ultimately mythical, belief about energy itself — and its conservation. It is important, because it goes to the heart of our theme of understanding the basic energy realities addressed throughout this book.

A popular and often repeated axiom dictates that more efficient energy means, as a nation, we will use less energy, and thus conserve energy, right? *Dead wrong.*

ENERGY CONSERVATION VS. THE JEVONS PARADOX

As we mentioned in Chapter 1, in April 2009 the new US Secretary of Energy, Steven Chu, wrote a *Newsweek* editorial that should have shocked us all. Mostly, because it revealed plainly how high-ranking political energy officials could be so utterly clueless about basic energy realities. First up, Chu failed to offer a single sentence on how the US and the Obama administration would address the "87 percent question" — the need to factor in on-going hydrocarbon dependency — other than by utilizing "advanced biofuels."

What Chu did not seem to know was that biofuels generally have a negative net "energy balance"; more energy is used up to convert the fuel source to another fuel source than is ultimately produced for final consumption — a pointless, wasteful and expensive exercise. Chu's "energy solution" amounted instead to focusing on the US addressing solely the "1 percent solution" (currently unrealistic energy alternatives). Chu said, "We must move beyond oil because the science on global warming is clear and compelling: greenhouse-gas emissions, primarily from fossils fuels, have started to change our climate." Chu asserts "conservation" as "the most direct way to reduce our dependency on foreign oil is to simply use less of it." This from the Energy Secretary, despite the fact *there is no evidence, historical or otherwise that conservation can reduce energy consumption.* In fact, the hard truth is the exact opposite, as one William Stanley Jevons, a nineteenth century English economist, has shown.

What the Jevons Paradox confirmed as an energy truism is that technological progress that increases energy efficiency, tends *to increase*, not decrease, the overall rate of consumption of a particular energy source. Running counter to popular intuition, then and now, it is a paradox well understood in economic circles. The reality is that energy conservation and efficiency leads to an increase in overall total energy demand as growing efficient use in one area tends to lead to society finding new uses, not least as efficiency lowers prices, in other areas. For instance, we may have a more efficient iron in our homes, but we also now have broadband phone hubs that should not be turned off overnight, security alarms that protect our homes from intruders during the day and, often, through the night, digital photo-frames that remain plugged in 24/7, cell phones, e-readers and iPads that all require regular charging, etc. Get the picture? Greater energy demand and consumption is simply a byproduct of our human nature; and our capacity to find more and more uses for new technologies is inevitable.

We should be clear that that this energy paradox is *not* argument *against* energy conservation and greater efficiency. That is not our point — nor was it Jevons'. What we are pointing out is an energy axiom. The intuitive belief that greater conservation and efficiency lowers energy demand denies the energy reality. Politicians and environmentalists can (and often are) entirely ignorant of this basic fact. Thus government policies that impose conservation standards and increase costs (again, hitting the poor hardest) often do so for entirely the wrong reasons. They do so *in the mistaken belief that energy demand and consumption overall will fall as a result.* While energy conservation and greater energy efficiencies are perfectly valid technological pursuits, let us not delude ourselves that they also lead to lower energy demand. They don't.

We have thus far considered the threat of future energy wars and the failure of "green" energy solutions. Finally, it is time to address what ought to be the chief focus of energy solutions and energy strategies for all national governments in the Third Millennia.

REAL ENERGY SOLUTIONS

Once we have grasped the gritty reality, that reduction of energy consumption and demand is simply not going to happen, and that future energy consumption will only rise, it should make us far more cautious about ignoring the energy realities and help us to reprioritizing future energy strategies and policies.

THE CONTINUING PRIMACY OF HYDROCARBONS

First and foremost, governments *must* restore the use of coal and oil, and particularly cleaner-burning natural gas, to the heart of rational energy strategies and policies. And that will mean understanding that the on-going primacy of hydrocarbons in the energy mix, and for future national stability, is a far higher priority than the alleged nebulous threat from continued hydrocarbon use.

But while these myths prevail in the elitist political and media mindset — and remember, they lend themselves to policies that greatly enhance the mindset of those who want greater centralizing (socialist) power — they remain as serious obstacles to the development of realistic national energy policies.

Unless these obstacles are overcome, the current prioritization of alternative energies is likely to continue to "misappropriate" massive taxpayer subsidy, for two main reasons. Firstly, because policies that require centralizing control appeal to socialist governments that know private sector capitalism will not make a serious investment in "loser" non-commercial technologies, in this case renewable energy. This in turn allows centralizing governments to seize greater power for themselves by requiring higher tax revenues to fund their renewable "white elephants," further enhancing the paradigm shift of power away from the private sector marketplace and facilitating greater central control, and a burgeoning "hand-out" state system.

On a broader scale, international supra-government agencies, including the UN, EU, WTO and World Bank, should prioritize policies that allow the oil and gas trade worldwide to go about its business unhindered by over-regulation. And the international energy trade is one area where use of national military could not only enhance the safety of world trade, but could also aid the world in *avoiding* potential future conflicts. This might include, for instance, making international military provision, perhaps at the level of the UN, to prevent the fundamentalist regime in Iran from closing the Straits of Hormuz at whim. A devastating stroke that would instantly cripple the international oil and gas trades, not to mention bring numerous national economies to their knees.

While many socialist European nations have tended to strip themselves of an effective national military, we would assert that the adoption of strong national military, socialist Utopianism apart, has all sorts of stability-inducing benefits. While some Europeans seem to think the post-WWII peace in Europe was sustained during the Cold War with Russia through increasing European "unity," we would say it had far more to do with the presence of the 100,000 American and British troops stationed there.

And when the 2004 tsunami famously devastated Aceh on the Indonesian coast, it was US and Australian warships that were first on the scene and were able to provide a rapid humanitarian response. Who remembers that no significant role was played by the UN or Europe? Equally, after the Haiti earthquake, it was the American military that was mustered to give backbone to the humanitarian response in this former French protectorate. France — singularly responsible for reducing Haiti to its pre-earthquake impoverished condition in the first place — was reduced to offering mere token gestures, having no military, and thus large-scale humanitarian, capability to speak of. Equally, international recognition that energy, as the world's key commodity, will continue to be central to future development and prosperity may, by working to ensure important energy trade routes stay open and unhindered, pro-actively guard *against* potential future conflict, rather than be its chief cause.

The fact that the world's oil and gas reserves tend to be in some of the world's most unsavory places, should act as a spur to exploration and the development of "friendlier" places, not least in North America, and in deepwater. While the concept of energy independence, much-vaunted by politicians, remains yet another mythical pipedream, there is nothing wrong with national government investing in oil and gas drilling operations in their own backyard, including offshore. Where the national emphasis lies in subsidizing alternative energies of course, the governments will be sleepwalking into domestic energy crises of their own making.

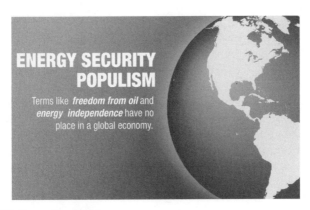

Figure 10.3: *Source: Energy Tribune.*

In Chapter 8 we saw how Russian energy imperialism is already exhibiting itself in respect of oil- and gas-rich Arctic waters. There we stated how, by the strategic, non-aggressive deployment of their own military "facts on the ground," the other four Arctic powers (the US, Canada, Denmark (on behalf of Greenland), and Norway) could help avoid conflict. Earlier in this chapter we saw how the jockeying for position by major powers in the Antarctic may be laying up future problems for the many countries jockeying for mineral rights. At the moment, the focus is on applications submitted to the UN. But the history of the UN in solving international disputes diplomatically — take Darfur, Sudan, and Iran as examples — is, to say the least, abysmal. Does anyone really think that such key disputes are going to be settled by a socialist talking shop with all manner of competing and ideologically-loaded agendas? That military "sabre-rattling" too will not have an influential role? Look at how Britain and Argentina have been facing off over drilling rights around the Falkland Islands. It is only the memory of the bloody 1982 debacle that has caused Argentina to rule out taking military measures this time around. But that won't stop military "sabre-rattling" from being a spur to "diplomatic" resolution.

For all the unnecessary fears it creates, neither can we ignore the "solution" the greatest scientific discovery of the twentieth century offers us.

NUCLEAR POWER: JUST PRESS THE BUTTON

Albert Einstein called it the greatest discovery of the twentieth century. Yet, even today, we fail to grasp the enormous energy contribution the splitting of the atom can make. Fortunately, there are signs that people and politicians around the globe are finally waking up the sheer scale of the contribution nuclear power can make to our future energy mix. Both the US administration and the EU have set themselves on course to develop a new generation of domestic nuclear power plants. Environmentalists, however, remain split over their response, between those who fear the danger of its abuse (by terrorists) or misuse (Chernobyl and Three-Mile Island leaks), and those who recognize its clean fuel, non-CO_2 emitting, reality. As Einstein pointed out, "The discovery of nuclear reactions need not bring about the destruction of mankind any more than the discovery of matches. We only must do everything in our power to safeguard against its abuse."[21]

In a previous chapter we referred to William Tucker's superb essay *Understanding E=MC²*. Having annihilated the case for renewable wind, hydro, solar energy, etc. by showing plainly how the density of each simply does not allow them to be useful on an industrialized scale, Tucker makes a powerful case for the adoption of nuclear energy:

> *By the late 1930s it had become clear that energy in unprecedented quantity could be obtained by splitting the unstable uranium atom.*
>
> *Unfortunately, World War II pre-empted the introduction of nuclear power. This is a historical tragedy. The atom bomb stands in the same relation to nuclear energy as gunpowder stands to fire. While gunpowder has played an important role in history, fire's role has been far more essential. Would we want to give up fire just because it led to guns? Yet the atom bomb continues to cast a shadow over the equally important discovery of nuclear energy.*
>
> *The release of energy from splitting a uranium atom turns out to be 2 million times greater than breaking the carbon-hydrogen bond in coal, oil or wood. Compared to all the forms of energy ever employed by humanity, nuclear power is off the scale. Wind has less than 1/10th the energy density of wood, wood half the density of coal and coal half the density of octane. Altogether they differ by a factor of about 50. Nuclear has 2 million times the energy density of gasoline. It is hard to fathom this in light of our previous experience. Yet our energy future largely depends on grasping the significance of this differential.*
>
> *One elementary source of comparison is to consider what it takes to refuel a coal plant as opposed to a nuclear reactor. A 1000-MW coal plant — our standard candle — is fed by a 110-car "unit train" arriving at the plant every 30 hours — 300 times a year. Each individual coal car weighs 100 tons and produces 20 minutes of electricity. We are currently straining*

the capacity of the railroad system moving all this coal around the country. (In China, it has completely broken down.)

A nuclear reactor, on the other hand, refuels when a fleet of six tractor-trailers arrives at the plant with a load of fuel rods once every eighteen months. The fuel rods are only mildly radioactive and can be handled with gloves. They will sit in the reactor for five years. After those five years, about six ounces of matter will be completely transformed into energy. Yet because of the power of $E = MC^2$, the metamorphosis of six ounces of matter will be enough to power the city of San Francisco for five years.

This is what people find hard to grasp. It is almost beyond our comprehension. How can we run an entire city for five years on six ounces of matter with almost no environmental impact? It all seems so incomprehensible that we make up problems in order to make things seem normal again. A reactor is a bomb waiting to go off. The waste lasts forever, what will we ever do with it? There is something sinister about drawing power from the nucleus of the atom. The technology is beyond human capabilities.

But the technology is not beyond human capabilities. Nor is there anything sinister about nuclear power. It is just beyond anything we ever imagined before the beginning of the 20th century. In the opening years of the 21st century, it is time to start imagining it.[22]

A far more expansive argument, including a major contribution on the safety of modern reactors is set out in Tucker's book *Terrestrial Energy: How Nuclear Power Will Lead the Green Revolution and End America's Energy Odyssey*. It is a book we heartily recommend that anyone fearful of nuclear power should read, with one major caveat.[23]

All of us would be concerned to keep weapons-grade enriched uranium out of the hands of terrorists. That is precisely why the terrorist-sponsoring Iranian regime should not be allowed to develop or possess it, as we argued in Chapter 8. But what of the more prosaic general use to help meet genuine energy demand? More specifically, just how valid are fears about accidents and leaks, and what about the issue of "nuclear waste"?

Nuclear power has, over decades now, more than proven to be extremely safe. Nuclear power provides France with 80 percent of its electricity and at the cheapest rates in Europe. It is a chief contributing factor to France being the second lowest carbon-emitter in Europe too.[24] While Germany and Denmark like to posture about their "non-nuclear" status they omit to tell us that they each import nuclear electricity from France. The fact is that France has never had a serious nuclear accident. Along with many other nations currently building nuclear power plants, the modern nuclear industry is well regulated with reactors being equipped to shut down immediately ANY fault develops. Today accidents are less likely than ever. But whenever nuclear power is mentioned, the incidents at Three-Mile Island and Chernobyl are instantly raised. So let's quickly look at both.

No official deaths were report as a result of the incident at Three-Mile Island. Equally, most studies agree that there was no perceptible rise in cancers within the local communities near the plant. As regrettable as it was, the Three-mile Island incident, caused by human error, happened in the *very early* days of nuclear development. Technology has advanced beyond recognition since those days, with all sorts of fail-safe mechanisms and much better computer technology in place. Okay, so Three-Mile Island was not a big deal, but what about Chernobyl? Well, in truth, given incidents like the Bhopal Chemical Plant disaster — an explosion at a pesticide plant in India in December, 1984 which caused over 2,200 deaths immediately, over 3,700 from gas released, and at least a further 8,000 from gas-related diseases — Chernobyl was small-scale in comparison, contrary to popular myth.

Once again, it is the mass media and green activists who spread all kinds of myths about Chernobyl, myths that lodge in the popular consciousness and become hard to dislodge. In the wake of the incident in April 1986, the BBC and many other mass media were predicting 15,000–30,000 *immediate* deaths. When the long-term effects of radiation exposure were taken into consideration, the media scare machine went into overdrive. CNN predicted up to 3.5 million cancer-related, and associated, deaths. The BBC was more modest predicting up to 50,000. In 2005, however, when the UN published a key report, *Chernobyl: the True Scale of the Accident*, it formally reported *fewer than 50 deaths directly* attributable to the accident.[25] While organizations like Greenpeace like to make up their own figures, often citing around 70,000 associated cancer deaths, the UN report also estimated potentially associated deaths based on 32 years of collated evidence. It found less than 4,000 Chernobyl-associated deaths, ultimately, could be attributable to cancer and related illnesses. Chernobyl *was* a major tragedy, but hardly one of the biblical proportions anti-nuclear protestors like to assert, especially compared to numerous other global disasters. And Chernobyl, remember, is the very *worst* nuclear accident we are able to cite.

In fact, the UN report went further, taking a "swing" at the media fear-mongers who drove anti-nuclear public opinion because of Chernobyl. It went on to assert that the greatest health threat associated with Chernobyl was in fact the "damaging psychological impact due to a lack of accurate information." The effect of numerous authority figures solemnly implanting fears about cancers, deformities, fertility problems, etc. in the public consciousness is a known psychological factor in creating its own public health hazard. No doubt, for years, every cancer and other illness in the region was blamed on Chernobyl.

Appreciating what the Russian operators were actually doing with the Chernobyl reactor prior to the accident, literally, beggars belief. Even back then, the operators totally ignored all basic safety regulations that already applied everywhere else.[26] If Chernobyl is a testimony to anything, it is not just to the dangers of the abuse of atomic power (though it is that as well) it is a testimony to man's foibles, and his ignoring of even the most rudimentary safeguards.

That just leaves the alleged "problem of nuclear waste." Incredibly, while some want to inject massive amounts of carbon dioxide into underground storage caverns, with all the very real dangers that poses,[27] they have major problems with burying relatively small amounts of nuclear waste. But then it depends what you mean by nuclear waste. As William Tucker says in his book *Terrestrial Energy*, there is actually "no such thing as nuclear waste." As Tucker points out, "Almost 100 percent of the material in a spent nuclear fuel rod can be recycled as useful material and is being done so in other parts of the world today. The very small amounts that cannot be economically reprocessed today can be stored safely until it does become financially feasible in the future."[28] It should be "case closed," even for the Greens, but hey, once again, what are facts when we have an ideological agenda?

Decades on, with nuclear safety issues well and truly proven around the world, it is really time to get the oft-repeated myths about the "dangers" into perspective. Set against the facts and the incredible value clean nuclear energy offers, the anti-nuclear movements look increasingly anachronistic. Perversely, many who are left-wing in their politics — allegedly "progressives" — are the ones who chiefly campaign against building nuclear power plants and major clean energy "progress." And, just for good measure, in March 2010, the IEA published figures that blew away the assertion of vocal anti-nuclear wind power lobbyists, by showing how much cheaper nuclear power production actually is in comparison.[29]

There really is no intellectual excuse for not pressing the nuclear power plant button — *and now*, given the amount of time it takes for nuclear plants to come online. All the signs are that this is one facet of the future energy mix that national politicians the world over are at least beginning to realize they can no longer ignore — at least not if they want to keep the "home fires burning."

A VISION FOR ENERGY IN THE THIRD MILLENNIUM

Just as the "de-carbonization" climate alarmist brigade has mustered their forces for all the wrong reasons, we must inform them that: "You are already too late — *capitalistic industry is way ahead of you!*" The truth is that industrialized societies have been moving steadily away from carbon-based economies to hydrogen-based economies *for years*. Once again, instead of being ahead of the curve, modern eco-warriors find themselves well behind it — as is the mass media, which has also failed to grasp the fact.

To begin with, as we have already asserted, natural gas is moving inexorably to become the more realistic dominant "cleaner" hydro-carbon fuel for the immediate future. The reason it is cleaner is simple enough: the balance of hydrogen to carbon in its molecular make-up is greater than in coal and oil.

Like it or not, coal, oil, and gas will continue to be the primary fuels that drive all industrialized, and industrializing, societies for decades to come. But that does not mean we cannot invest in exciting new hydrogen-promoting ventures like hydrogen and battery-less cars, as we are. In fact, as regards the last, battery-less cars, we could

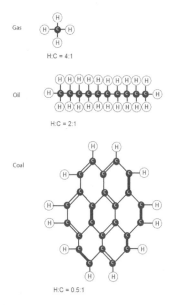

Figure 10.4: Carbon-hydrogen balance means much greater energy return. *Source Energy Tribune.*

even think about electrifying the entire transport system, or at least major parts of it as envisaged in an exciting new study "Transforming America's Transportation Future."[30] Imagine for a moment, cars that no longer need the restrictions imposed by batteries but that run on electricity picked up from the road itself — yet, *without* trailing wires, overhead cables etc.? This, of course, is what we mean by a micro-level real energy solution. So much promise exists for the future of the new hybrid hydrogen-petrol/diesel engines for cars, and, potentially, hydrogen driven cars. But the real danger is in ignoring energy realities by running ahead of ourselves believing the latest development is the answer to all our energy problems. The trouble is, slowly-slowly "catchy monkey." Let's not be pressured into believing the hype that persists in asserting "we must act now!"

What we assert here, is that we must retain far more sensible strategic and national energy policies that reinstate a prime energy focus on coal, oil, and especially natural gas. The hydrocarbon transition to natural gas primacy and to more nuclear power is likely to mature in the next two decades. Along with the inexorable move towards becoming hydrogen economies, we will see a parallel revolution in the miniaturizations of engines, nanotechnologies and a wide spectrum of new, competing, and "cleaner for the environment" fuel cell technology. We find such developments a much more realistic and exciting, capitalist-led, proposition as a vision for our energy-driven futures. A future where, not only is the environment a major winner, but where the poorest in society need not be the hardest hit, as energy prices rise inexorably to pay for the latest erroneous government-instigated "green" thinking "nonsense on stilts."

We would also suggest that many re-consider their funding of the highly politicized agenda of the anti-science, anti-intellectual, socialist siren voices of Greenpeace, Friends of the Earth and the World Wildlife Fund when it comes to funding their climate activism. Let's face it, these groups are never going to support *any* new energy project, no highway, no power plant, no harbor, no airport — and no new oil and gas exploration. In the words of one Marxist (Groucho), their position is always going to be: "Whatever it is, *I'm against it!*" It is time to start seeing these organizations for what they really have become: socially legitimized romanticists, who believe in a former Utopian way of life that, in truth, never existed.

For the time being, the Middle East will remain vital to help meet world oil and gas energy demand. Western governments, however, might take a leaf out of China's book and, instead of playing the populist card that persists in vilifying evil "Big Oil," help to facilitate new oil and gas exploration, especially in friendlier places.

Where new technology is concerned, and the need to adapt to new needs and real threats, we might start trusting the free market and man's inherent ingenuity in pursuing new technological developments. In their seminal book *The Bottomless Well: The Twilight of Fuel, the Virtue of Waste, and We Will Never Run Out of Energy*,[31] Peter Huber and Mark Mills assert two key truths. One is stated in the sub-title: that we will never, because of the plentiful planetary resources, run out of energy. As they say, "Energy supplies are — for all practical purposes — infinite." The other is this: the genius of man to come up with real solutions to life's problems. Necessity, when all is said and done, has always been the mother of invention. History proves it. It will always prove thus.

As we have seen, however, derailing ideological propaganda can be a recurring theme whenever the pursuit of empirical truth is involved. And we need to be wary of its deleterious influence when it comes to scientific endeavor; by holding observable, verifiable facts, reason, and logic more important than the latest prophetic insight and speculation, no matter how thinly-disguised in pseudo-scientific political garb it may be. H.L. Mencken wisely observed, "The whole aim of practical politics is to keep the populace in mind — and hence clamorous to be led to safety — by menacing it with an endless series of hobgoblins, all of them imaginary."[32] And we need to be perennially alert that the latest (among countless) TV and newspaper-led "global threat" is backed by nothing more than the desperate need of a dying media to attract viewers and sell newspapers.

On that note, we propose to leave the final word to a writer and scientist who we have often quoted in these pages — and to whose memory this book is dedicated. A man who latterly grew increasingly concerned over the growing politicization of science for ideological ends, to the detriment of empirical facts and the search for objective truth.

In his paper, *Science Policy in the 21st Century*, Michael Crichton observed, "I think probably everybody understands that legislators ought to specify outcomes and not procedures. Yet time and again, they decide they want to be in the car business, or some other business. What then is the role of central planning in a technological society? I would argue that, increasingly, there will be no role; and that the very concept of central planning and control is an anachronism of the industrial age of the 19th century. It will vanish completely in the 21st century."[33]

Let us hope so, Michael, let us hope so.

Notes

1 The UK in particular is at serious risk of regular power cuts within 5–10 years as a result of the Government's procrastination over pushing the "nuclear button" to replace its fast-ageing power plants. See "Britain Facing Blackouts For First Time Since 1970s," *Daily Telegraph*, August 31, 2009.

2 "Britain to Claim More Than 1 M Sq Km of Antarctica," *The Guardian*, October 17, 2007.

3 Ibid.

4 The latter in its capacity as holding sovereignty over the Faroe Islands.

5 As reported in "Scramble for World Resources: Battle for Antarctica," by Rick Rozoff, Global Research, May 16, 2009 for the quotes from *The Scotsman*. The authors are also indebted to Rick Rozoff's article for the details relating to the British submissions to the UN Commission on the Limits of the Continental Shelf in 2009 in this immediate section.

6 Associated Press, November 7, 2008.

7 RIA (Russian Information Agency) Novosti, January 15, 2009.

8 Report, "Scramble for World Resources: Battle for Antartica," Rick Rozoff, Global Research, May 16, 2009.

9 "NATO's, Pentagon's New Strategic Battleground: The Arctic," Stop NATO, February 2, 2009.

10 "NATO in the Persian Gulf: From Third World War to Istanbul Cooperation Initiative," Global Research, February 7, 2009.

11 "NATO Bases from the Balkans to the Chinese Border," Global Research, March 4, 2009.

12 "Global Energy War: Washington's New Kissinger's African Plans," Stop NATO, January 22, 2009.

13 Russian Information Agency Novosti, April 24, 2008.

14 "Hamas Supremacy denying Palestinians Energy Billions," Peter C. Glover, *Energy Tribune.com*, June 25, 2009.

15 "Israel's Natural Gas Bonanza," Peter C. Glover, *Energy Tribune.com*, June 5, 2009.

16 Heritage Foundation's Economic Index of Economic Freedom, 2010 (as stated online at June 16, 2010).

17 Transparency International, Corruption Perception Table 2009 at http://transparency.org/policy_research/surveys_indices/cpi/2009/cpi_2009_table

18 "Switzerland Unruffled by Qaddafi's Call for 'Jihad' in Wake of Its Ban on New Minarets," *New York Times*, February 26, 2010.

19 Extracts all taken from Anthony Browne, The Retreat of Reason (The Institute for the Study of Civil Society, 2006).

20 "The Ethics of Controversy," Sidney Hook, included in *Philosophy and Public Debate* (Southern Illinois University Press, 1980).

21 http://albert-einsteinquotes.blogspot.com/

22 "Understanding E=MC²," Energy Tribune, October 21, 2009. For the complete article go to: www.energytribune.com/articles.cfm?aid=2469

23 *Terrestrial Energy: How Nuclear Power Will Lead the Green Revolution and End America's Energy Odyssey* by William Tucker (Bartleby), 2008. Tucker, as the sub-title to the book hints, has been taken in by the global warming alarmist argument. From the outset, Tucker writes, "There is wide agreement on the basic facts of global warming." (p. 13). As we saw in chapters 5 and 6, that is anything but true. Tucker even indulges in the usual slurs climate alarmists reserve for climate scientists who disagree, referring to "Richard Lindzen, the maverick meteorologist" (p. 15), for instance. Richard Lindzen is widely recognized as one of the world's *leading* climatologists. Or at least he was, until he had the temerity to disagree with the science "consensus."

24 Behind Sweden.

25 And most of those were of ill-equipped Russian rescue workers sent in the disaster's aftermath. For the entire report go to: http://un.by/en/chernobyl/prs/05–09–05–01.html

26 William Tucker's *Terrestrial Energy: How Nuclear Power Will Lead the Green Revolution and End America's Energy Odyssey* (Bartleby) 2008, carries the whole story. It is well worth reading.

27 A study in late 2009 by Professors Michael and Christian Ehlig-Economides found that geological (underground) carbon storage is not a viable scientific proposition, as it is simply not physically possible to inject vast quantities of CO_2 into underground aquifers without fracturing the surrounding rock. In addition, incidents like that at Lake Nyos, Cameroon, in 1986, where the water in a lake in a volcanic crater holding CO_2 beneath by pressure, "flipped," shooting sequestered CO_2 250 feet into the air. When it came down it asphyxiated 1,700 people and thousands of cattle.

28 William Tucker's *Terrestrial Energy: How Nuclear Power Will Lead the Green Revolution and End America's Energy Odyssey* (Bartleby) 2008, p. 344.

29 "IEA: Nuclear Power is Cheap, Wind Energy is Expensive," Robert Bryce, *Energy Tribune*, March 25, 2010. Go to: www.energytribune.com/articles.cfm?aid=3621

30 "Automated Electric Transportation: Transporting America's Transportation Future," a co-publication between a number of US state universities, research laboratories and public and private energy companies.

31 *The Bottomless Well: The Twilight of Fuel, The Virtue of Waste, And Why We Will Never Run Out of Energy* (Baker Books, 2005), p. 181.

32 Working Minds (website): Quotations from H.L. Mencken (1880–1956). See http://www.working-minds.com/HLMquotes.htm

33 Michael Crichton, "Science Policy in the 21st Century," speech to AEI-Brookings Institution, Washington DC, January 25, 2005.

PostScript . . . from the authors

There is an unfortunate trend in our increasingly anti-intellectual, sound-bite age. It is the tendency to avoid the "inconvenience" of public debate and engaging with articulated argument by name-calling, as with the pejorative "deniers," or, by plain old-fashioned *ad hominen* attack.

Chief among the barbs when it comes to energy and climate issues, is the assertion that the author, writer, or speaker must simply be "a shill for" or "in the pay of" Big Oil *et al*. For some it seems that disagreement with their view can only be a reflection of a hidden (probably paid) agenda.

Our only comment to any such absurdity is this: "If only . . ."

After-Word

Since completing the manuscript the authors have published articles highly relevant to the themes of this book, two of which are re-produced here. Both appear as they were published by Energy Tribune.com and by multiple publications in May 2010 (though without their hyperlinks to source materials).

COULD THERE BE A BRIGHT SIDE TO THE DEEPWATER HORIZON DISASTER?
BY MICHAEL J. ECONOMIDES

Although the US petroleum industry is understandably in a state of panic after the recent spill in the Gulf of Mexico and some, both friend and foe, have even resorted to outrageous speculation that the accident would mean "the end of offshore oil," there is an optimistic take to the events.

Properly handled by the industry and credible experts, it may educate the American public — who, during the past few years, have become bigger and bigger victims of ideologically driven misinformation — on the realities of energy production.

The April 20 blowout of a BP well that was drilled by Transocean's state-of-the-art Deepwater Horizon rig brought to the surface pent-up emotions, ideologies and, of course, the unassailable fact of the excruciating technical challenges that come with drilling in 5,000-foot waters. Even more important are the reminders that always must go along with the quest for oil and gas and, just recently in West Virginia, coal: There is no such thing as risk-free production of energy sources that are inherently volatile and explosive. What makes them such valuable and irreplaceable forms of energy also makes them dangerous.

In the ensuing political and environmental clamor, one tragic result that seems to be constantly forgotten by the press and pundits is that 11 people lost their lives in the accident. Then the "blame game" took on BP as the obvious target. After all, they had been involved with a number of previous disasters — from the Texas City refinery fire that killed 15 people in 2005 to the near sinking of their huge Thunder

Horse platform in the Gulf of Mexico to the temporary shutdown of the Alaska pipeline. These incidents may signal a BP laxity but they may also be simply coincidences or bad luck, and nobody yet really knows what happened on April 20. But BP has become, for both the enemies of the oil industry and even for some of its friends, the poster boy of disaster and perhaps carelessness.

To be certain, the oil industry did not need this catastrophe and the cleanup will be long, arduous, and expensive. It happened at a time of acrimonious debate over the future of oil and all fossil fuels. For some people, including key members of the Obama administration and certainly many of his supporters, global climate change and other real or imagined dangers can be blamed squarely on oil. For the Left, the Gulf of Mexico disaster was a self-fulfilling prophecy, and from some of their statements one can glean an almost bizarre and macabre satisfaction. For them, the bigger the disaster the more it justifies their inherent position that oil is bad. To them it makes no difference how unrealistic or expensive alternative energy sources may be. Wind and solar, which to almost all knowledgeable people cannot even remotely replace a tiny portion of oil and gas anytime soon, if ever, are preferable to the prospect of a blowout and leaking well.

The predictable threat of shutting down all offshore drilling came next, and some environmentalists have called for a permanent ban on all offshore oil. Considering that the US already imports two-thirds of its 20 million barrels per day of oil use and that about half of US domestic oil production comes from offshore fields, such a policy would have a devastating impact on US oil supply. Imports would have to fill the gap. (Of course, for radical environmentalists the US should stop using any oil, period, no matter what the dire consequences may be.)

Despite the ideological overtones, a well blowout is in many ways similar to an airline accident. It can be due to pilot/operator error but it can also be because of basic physical problems, such as an unconsolidated formation, like the one in the Gulf of Mexico where the cement sheath may collapse, providing a huge conduit for a blowout. Such potential (and I am not saying that this is what happened but it is all too possible) has little to do with human actions, although safeguards are built exactly for those eventualities. A critical piece of the ongoing investigation is why the blowout preventer failed. It is possible that an entire sequence of problems and their chain reaction may never be known perfectly.

There is another analogy between this event and an airline accident. They are both quite rare. And similar to the fact that people do not stop flying after an accident, so too this disaster should not divert people and the government into ridiculous positions. But the Obama administration is not exactly a friend of oil or the industry, and this may be just the event they need to tell everybody "I told you so."

And of course there is always the scam of biofuels. It is no coincidence that just a week later, on April 28, Obama was saying "I believe in the potential of (ethanol) to contribute to our clean energy future, but also to our rural economies."

But there may be a ray of hope and a semblance of sanity, thanks to the American public. Just two weeks before the accident, a Gallup poll for the first time showed that 50 percent of Americans want to develop US energy resources even if doing so will lead to environmental "suffering" of some kind. (That marks a 16-point increase from just three years ago.) Assuming that the leak is capped in a reasonably short period of time, the accident may actually work to the industry's favor.

BP's bad luck or even negligence notwithstanding, the offshore industry's track record in environmental stewardship is actually exemplary. Solving the problem and cleaning up the mess will send a resounding message of the industry's "can do" attitude. It would also serve to point out how rare these instances are in an industry that serves such a vital function in the US economy.

BRITAIN'S POWER CONUNDRUM
BY PETER C. GLOVER

David Cameron, Britain's new prime minister, may have succeeded in bridging his country's political power gap, but another looms that could very quickly short-circuit the Tory leader's grip on national power, unless his coalition government gets real — and quickly — over energy and environment.

For one thing, the sale of two-thirds of the nation's power utilities to European competitors has effectively led to Brits subsidizing their EU neighbors' energy costs; for another, just as the next election season rolls around in five years time, he is likely to find his autocue a little difficult to read as the nation's lights start going out.

POWER GAME

Big Oil is the usual whipping boy for the public when it comes to energy. But British energy consumers might feel the time is ripe to turn up the heat on Big Power.

While UK energy prices spiralled upwards by 16.7 percent in 2009, the average increase across the rest of the European Union was a mere 3.8 percent. All of this while global energy costs generally fell by around 40 percent. It is a price differential that could not fail to bite into British industrial competitiveness. And in May it did exactly that, putting an end to a 100-year association between the American owners of Celanese Acetate and its British subsidiary — a company that once employed 20,000 people — now due to close at the end of the year. The Celanese Corporation will concentrate production in Belgium, the United States, and Mexico, where energy costs are much cheaper.

Bob Walters, General Manager of the Derby-based British company, was compelled to admit that the British arm's operating costs "remain the highest in Celanese Acetate." A spokesman for the company told the local media that, "A lot of work was carried out to reduce costs but there was no way to make any inroads into reducing our fundamental energy costs, which are much higher in the UK than overseas." He confirmed, "The biggest differential in costs between ourselves and other sites in the group is the price of energy."

George Cowcher, Chief Executive of the Derbyshire and Nottinghamshire Chamber of Commerce, was equally unequivocal, "Our energy prices are substantially higher than in France, Germany and Belgium. Global companies operating here will put information about their sites into a spreadsheet and if the UK operation is the most expensive it will be the one that goes." Cowcher adds, "The concern is that other multinationals will do the same."

Conway Standing, Managing Director of the commercial energy broker, Utility Exchange Online, concurs. "Most of Britain's energy companies are owned by German, Spanish and French companies which have kept any increases lower in their own countries but allowed the prices in the UK to remain high." He adds, "Research shows that, since last summer, wholesale energy costs have fallen by 40 percent but most of the big energy suppliers have failed to pass that on."

Early in 2009 suspicions that Britain's mostly foreign-owned power utilities were allowing UK energy prices to rise, while keeping prices in their home countries low, appeared confirmed when the OECD Consumer Price Index report showed that the German, French, and Spanish owners of four of the UK's Big Six appeared to be doing exactly that. The Index revealed UK energy inflation running at a high of 12.1 percent in the previous year, though it actually fell by 0.6 percent in Germany, 6.5 percent in France, and 7.2 percent in Spain. While the two British owned power utilities British Gas, owned by Centrica, and Scottish & Southern Energy (based in Perth, Scotland) eventually did announce a 10 percent cut in prices, none of the other four followed suit. E.ON and NPower are based in Dusseldorf, Germany, EDF is French and Paris-based, and Scottish Power is owned by Iberdola, the huge Spanish utility company. In the year 2008–09 Britain saw the highest price rises in Western Europe.

But Britain's energy problems don't end there.

"Smart grids" is the new buzz phrase in the geopolitics of European energy. In a report published in February 2010 by the EU's Strategic Energy Technology Plan Information System (SETIS), led by the Joint Research Centre (JRC), smarter power grids are central to plans if Europe is to become a low-carbon-energy economy. The report even describes the importance of electricity transmission grids as "the back-bone of the EU's economy." With an EU target of reducing CO_2 emissions levels by 20% from 1992 levels, that would require a return of 20 percent of power from renewable energy sources. That, in turn, translates to 30 to 35% of electricity power consumption from renewables, all by 2020.

Integral to a strategy of constructing a series of "mutually supportive" power grids across Europe, are plans for an offshore grid in the North Sea able to integrate power from the offshore wind farms. The UK, with the natural advantage of being the windiest country in Europe, is duly forging ahead taking the lead in Europe's offshore wind-farm development. At the beginning of 2009, Britain's Crown Estate asked for bids, as part of its Round 3 proposals, for up to nine wind farm sites around its coastline. The bid process was concluded at the end of 2009. By late April 2010, when German energy giant RWE announced that its renewables arm, RWE Innogy, had signed on to build up to 4,000 MW of wind power for two of the sites, the blueprint for construction was consolidated. When finally completed the whole project is expected to produce a total installed capacity of 25,000 megawatts.

Even so, the North Sea Offshore Grid consortia were reported in late March 2010 as concluding that the North and Baltic Sea grid would take up to 15 years to be fully operational. But given the enormous technical difficulties and other issues that lie ahead for the development of such a major enterprise in deepwater, it is a goal that may prove optimistic in terms of helping the UK's looming energy woes.

In addition, in April, the Confederation of British Industry (CBI) warned that a new European Directive could well force the closure of up to 14 of the UK's ageing power plants. The recent decision by MEPs, amending provisions to the Draft Industrial Emissions Directive, will force power plants, says the CBI, to embark on an expensive upgrade program to help them comply with air pollution targets — or have to close by 2016. With a succession of UK governments shelving the responsibility to green-light construction of a urgently needed new generation of nuclear reactors, gas-fired plants and generators, the timing could not be worse. John Cridland, Deputy Director General of the CBI, said, "Given these plants are old and due to close in the 2020s, letting them run their course would allow for a smooth transition to new low-carbon energy sources and avoid creating a serious energy gap." A final vote on the Directive is due shortly.

The bottom line is a stark one for the UK caught between a rock and a hard place. The new EU Carbon Directive will be expensive and most of the new power plants being discussed will take more than a decade to come online. Second, a significant contribution from renewables may be up and running and able to make a contribution, but that too is over a decade away. With North Sea oil declining and with no real oil and gas deals in place and with bids to the UN for access to deepwater in the Arctic and Antarctic Oceans, even with drilling for gas off the Falkland Islands currently under way, no real production return is expected, again, for a decade or so.

And that's the essential point: The spectre of regular power cuts, within just a few years, is all too real. Last October, Britain's regulator, Ofgem, published its Project Discovery report which predicted black-outs across Britain by as early as 2014 given the obstacles to bridging the energy gap. Alternative assessments are not much more optimistic.

At the same time, UK consumers find themselves paying far higher energy prices than their European neighbours — effectively, crudely forced, by foreign-owned power utilities, to subsidize their European neighbours.

In short it is hard to see how Britain will be able to ignore the pragmatic energy reality that hydrocarbon fuels will remain the staple of the country's major energy mix for the next decade. In that case, the nature of the rock and a hard place — Cameron's real power conundrum — is likely to come down to a straight choice: carbon target cuts *or* power cuts.

Bibliography

Andreasen, M. (2009), *Brussels Laid Bare: How the EU Treated Its Chief Accountant When She Refused To Go Along with Its Fraud and Waste*, St Edward's Press.

Browne, A. (2006), *The Retreat of Reason, Political Correctness and the Corruption of Public Debate in Modern Britain*, Civitas.

Clarke, D. (2007), *The Battle for the Barrels: Peak Oil Myths & World Oil Futures*, Profile Books.

Economides, M. and Oligney, R. (2000), *The Color of Oil: The History, the Money and the Politics of the World's Biggest Business*, Round Oak Publishing.

Economides, M. and Xie, X. (2009), *Energy: China's Choke Point*, ET Publishing.

Ellul, J. (1973), *Propaganda: The Formation of Men's Attitudes*, Vintage (reprinted).

Hayek, F.A. (1944), *The Road to Serfdom*, Routledge Classic.

Huber, P.W. and Mills, M.P. (2005), *The Bottomless Well: The Twilight of Fuel, The Virtue of Waste, and Why We Will Never Run Out of Energy*, Basic Books.

Lewis, C.S. (1980), *The Last Battle: The Chronicles of Narnia*, Lions (reprinted).

Micklethwait, J. and Wooldridge, A. (2005), *The Right Nation: Why America is Different*. Penguin.

Nova, J. (2009), *Climate Money: The Climate Industry, $79 Billion So Far — Trillions to Come*, paper published by Science and Public Policy Institute, July 21.

Scruton, R. (2006), *A Political Philosophy: Arguments for Conservatism*, Continuum.

Svensmark, H. and Calder, N. (2007), *The Chilling Stars: A New Theory of Climate Change*, Icon Books.

Thatcher, M. (2002), *Statecraft: Strategies for a Changing World*, Harper Collins.

Tucker, W. (2008), *Terrestrial Energy: How Nuclear Power Will Lead the Green Revolution and End America's Energy Odyssey*, Bartleby.

Index